So There I was...
Tales from the Flight Line

by

Blaine J McMillan

©Copyright 2019 Blaine J. McMillan CD1 BCrim
All rights reserved. No part of this book may be reproduced in any form or by any means, electronic, mechanical, photocopying, recording or otherwise without prior permission of the author.
ISBN 978-0-9916825-1-5
Publisher prefix ISBN 978-0-9916825

Edited by Simon Cumming, MBA
Reviewed and ethically filtered by Irene Dworschak, BA

Front Cover – July 2002, Canadian Armed Forces Hercules 130338 tipped onto its left hand wing due to an uncontrolled fuel migration that occurred overnight at CFS Alert.

Disclaimer

This is a work of non-fiction. The information contained in this book is meant to expose the reader to the experiences of a member of the Canadian Armed Forces. Where possible those experiences were correlated by others who were in attendance at the time of the occurrence or have been documented with verified references. The author has tried to recreate events from his memories of them. In order to maintain their anonymity the author has, in some instances, changed the names of individuals. The conversations in the book all come from the author's recollections, though they are not written to represent word-for-word transcripts. Rather, the author has retold them in a way that evokes the feeling and meaning of what was said and in all instances, the essence of the dialogue is accurate.

Dedication

This book is dedicated to all service members, both women and men, who have been employed in a military aviation environment.

"Maintainers work independently and as part of a team all at the same time. Our work is not purely physical, in fact most of it is mental. The outsider sees someone just walking along with a flashlight but we know what's going on. A practiced eye backed up with loads of experience and knowledge of the aircraft systems are being synthesized to ensure that she is safe for flight. And we may be working alone at any given moment and yet there is a whole team, past and present, backing up the maintainer in order to provide a weapons system that meets the needs of the nation. Maintainers are the unseen and unsung warriors that put those contrails in the stratosphere."

David T. Chamberlin CMSgt USAF ANG Crew Chief 1980-2018

I would like to thank all of my friends, former co-workers and former Crew Chiefs who have put up with my persistent pestering for those minute obtuse details that I could no longer recall. I would also like to thank my wife, Irene, for putting up with my latest catharsis. Only two (or three) more to go!

Preface

Take two ex-military guys who have never worked together, provide an opportunity of a chance meeting in an airport waiting room or a bar and before you know it they will be trading stories of their daring exploits. They could be from opposite ends of the country, different branches of the service or from different generations and still the process would remain the same. First, they'll ask where they've been stationed and if they had served with so and so. Next, they'll compare the working conditions experienced during their careers and inevitably the tales will gather momentum and begin to move forward with the immortal phrase **"So, there I was..."** Stories beginning with this phrase are often told to enlighten those within earshot of an adventure or an exploit. The amount of truth in the tale may be an inverse proportion to the volume of alcohol consumed. But rest assured, as outlandish as the story may sound deep down, beneath all of layers of suspected bullshit there will be a nugget of truth.

I hope that you will enjoy my tales of **"So, there I was…"**

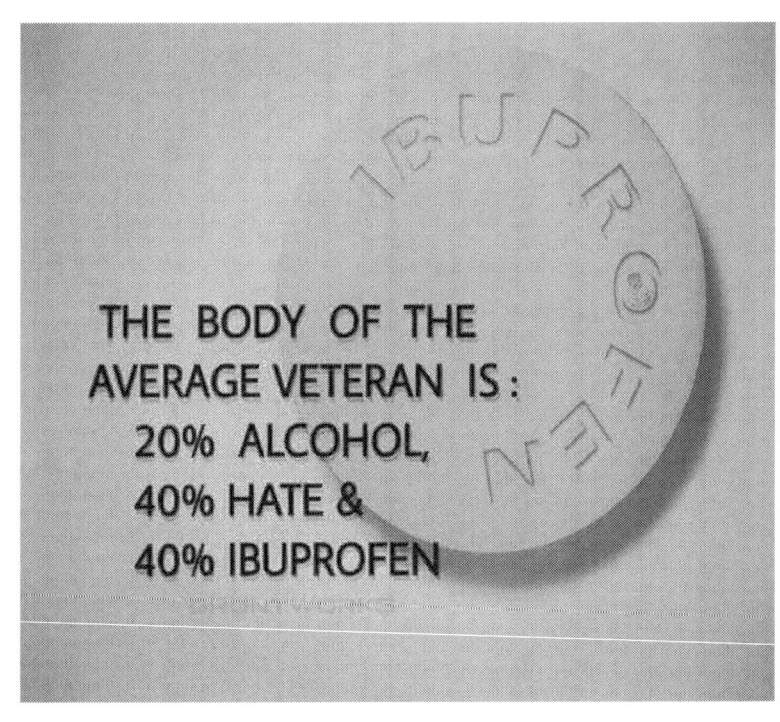

Contents

Title Page ….	…. 1
Dedication …	…. 3
Preface ….	…. 5
Contents ….	…. 7
Basic Training ….	…. 9
Trades Training ….	…. 37
Westward Bound …..	…. 53
Moving Down the Line ….	….101
By the Centre ….	…. 143
Crossing the Hall ….	…. 199
Just for Shits & Giggles ….	…. 253
The Current State of Affairs …As I See It ….	…. 273
A Final Word… Or Two ….	…. 315
Glossary ….	…. 331
Appendix ….	…. 335
References ….	….341
About the Author ….	….349

Basic Training

So there I was... Stumbling down the stairs of a Greyhound bus, half awake and confused by the unfamiliar surroundings on a rainy night in the autumn of 1981. All I could see was the very angry man in a uniform who was standing at the front of the bus and screaming at us to get into a straight line.

"Get off my bus and get in line! You stupid dick heads. I said a straight fucking line! Do you need someone to hold your bloody hand, my sweetheart?"

Welcome to the Recruit Training School at Canadian Forces Base Cornwallis, Cornwallis, Nova Scotia. Course 8142, Mad Dog 4 Platoon.

I was one of one hundred and forty some individuals who had decided to embark on a new life path. Together, we would sweat, bleed, laugh and cry our way through the next eleven weeks of hell and in the end fewer than one hundred of us would graduate from this serial. And, despite the debilitating lack of sleep, the constant screaming and the persistent mind games coming from our NCO's (non-commissioned officers) there would be moments of pure enjoyment.

For the first week every last one of us was named "Alice." Not by our instructors. No, they had more interesting, more derogatory and much more demeaning names for us. Garbage. Maggot. Piece of shit. The lowest form of life on Earth that would have to grow up just to be a piece of shit. Those were the monikers applied by the NCO's and usually with an expletive attached to it. No, "Alice" was the term given to us by all of those who had been in Recruit School long enough to have their head shaved by the Base barbers. "Alice" would be your new name until you too went through the shearing process. The short hair cut is the first step in removing your individuality as well as reducing the propagation of head lice.

Your first haircut in CFRS Cornwallis was free and regardless of how well coiffed your locks were and its length on the day you arrived, the hair on your head would be reduced to stubble in about five minutes or less - not including cleaning your nape and around your ears - with a straight razor. So, no flinching! If you do the math: 140 people x 5 minutes per person ÷ 60 minutes ÷ 3 barbers results in roughly four hours for the entire platoon to get their haircut. To that you can add the time it took for the barbers to occasionally sweep the floor plus marching to the mess hall and back for lunch. Going for lunch was no picnic either because half the platoon was clean cut and the other half were still a bunch of Alices. One poor bastard was half way through his haircut when the barber said, "That's it, go for lunch!" As a result, Andy Nemeth, with his long feathered southern Ontario rock-and-roll hairstyle went to eat with half of his head shaved and the other half hanging down past his shoulder. Barbers can be such assholes!

To ensure that military recruits receive their daily dietary requirements, all meals were to be eaten in the dining facility and it was strictly against the rules to take any food out of the mess hall. Not a cracker, an apple or even a grape. Of course, these conditions did not prevent people from skipping the occasional meal, especially breakfast, in order to finish preparing their equipment for the morning inspection.

A problem arose when Recruit Meal Skipper asked his buddy, Joe Bloggins, to bring him back a couple of hefty PB & J sandwiches. Naturally, Joe wants to help his fellow course member so, while having a sumptuous breakfast of scrambled eggs and stale toast, he puts together a couple or three gifts for his hungry friends back in the barracks. Now, here comes Recruit Bloggins trying to hide the bulges in his coat pockets as he walks out of the mess hall.

"Halt!"

On hearing the command Private Bloggins comes to a quick and immediate stop. He stands at attention. His heels are together. His arms held stiffly by his sides.

"How was your breakfast, Recruit?"

"Very nutritious Master Corporal!"

"Recruit Bloggins, did you have enough to eat?"

"Yes, Master Corporal."

"You do know that it's against the rules to take food from the mess hall?"

"Yes, Master Corporal."

"What's in your coat pockets?"

"Nothing, Master Corporal."

"Recruit, do you think that I'm fucking blind! Don't you lie to me! What's in your goddamned pockets?"

The jig was up. Having no choice but to confess to his crime, Private Bloggins blurts out, "Sandwiches, Master Corporal!"

"Well, Recruit Bloggins, you wouldn't be taking these sandwiches to your buddies in the barracks would you? You know that taking food out of the mess hall for other people is against the rules?"

"No, Master Corporal!" lied Pte Bloggins.

"No, what?"

"The sandwiches are not for anyone in the barracks Master Corporal!" replied Bloggins.

"Well, if they are not for someone else that would mean that these are your sandwiches. And, if they are your sandwiches, that would mean that you're still hungry. START EATING, RECRUIT!"

And so, while a number of recruits from other platoons continued to stream in and out of the mess hall, poor Recruit Bloggins stood before the NCO and began to consume all of the sandwiches he had made for his buddies back in the barracks. Another lesson learned… the hard way.

Unlike some other countries, the Canadian military is comprised entirely of volunteer members. As you can well imagine, not everyone who enlists is suitable for employment in Canada's military and therefore they must be culled from the herd. Even if an individual has passed all the required initial prerequisites, the first opportunity to punt out any slackers is given to the platoon NCO's. There could be any number of reasons for ejecting a recruit from CFRS Cornwallis – some of them real and some of them not so real. For example, if a recruit fails to achieve and maintain the proficiency standards set out before him then he may be re-coursed.[1] Or, if a recruit fails to live up to the Code of Service Discipline he will most definitely be released.[2] Naturally, a service member always has the right to request a release from his military contract at any time and suffer any subsequent financial penalties, such as a reduced annuity.

The job of the NCO is to guide and train the recruits in his charge. A squad NCO will ask, order, cajole, mentor and, if necessary, even lead an individual by the hand. In order to get his point across to the masses he will often make an example of any recruit within sight and it doesn't matter who it is. For the targeted recruit it was imperative to simply PLAY THE GAME. In other words, regardless of the task you're asked to perform you must do as you are told and do it to the best of your ability. You may not

---

[1] Re-coursing is the time honoured process of sending an individual back several weeks to repeat some of the training. If the trainee is successful in completing the performance objectives he/she will continue on. If not, a re-muster or release of service may be in the offing.

[2] The Code of Service Discipline is the basis of the Canadian Forces military justice system. It is designed to assist military commanders in maintaining discipline, efficiency, and morale within the Canadian Forces.

like what you have to do but you do it anyways without bitching. Bitching will only make things worse. Trust me, you don't want worse.

The Canadian military did not (and does not) want a bunch of mindless robots who would march blindly into battle nor did it want free thinkers. Mindless robots are just so much cannon fodder and free thinkers too often question why orders have be followed. So, if they didn't want either, what did they want? Obviously, it would have to be a balance made up of each component and during recruit training the balance beam leaned quite heavily to the robot side. Sometimes an educational incentive was required before a recruit would realize that it was better to just shut the hell up and do whatever was asked of him. Naturally, yours truly had some difficulty in understanding this concept.

During Week One of Basic Training we had been instructed to simply brush shine our boots. This allows the oils from the polish to permeate through the leather while we broke in our footwear by marching all over this hidden gem on the Nova Scotia coastline. I had what was termed as *pre-service training*; that is to say I had spent four years in army cadets learning various military subjects including dress and deportment, weapons handling, field craft, orienteering and lots of foot drill. All of that *pre-service training* should have been a benefit to me and it would have, if only I had played the game and kept my face shut. But oh no. I thought I knew better than my Master Corporal. It all came to light during a routine morning inspection.

"Private McMillan!"

"Yes, Master Corporal!"

"Is that a brush shine that I see on your dress shoes?"

"Yes Master Corporal!" I lied. I had been secretly spit shining my shoes for a couple of days.

"Bullshit! I know a spit shine when I see one. Did I tell you to spit shine your foot wear? Well, did I?"

"No, Master Corporal!"

"Obviously, you need to learn to do as you're told."

And with that, he snatched up one of the dress shoes resting on the top of my barracks box. Holding it by the centre of the sole he proceeded to drive the toe of the shoe onto the corner of my barracks box which was followed by raking the heel along the fins of the steam heat radiator before sending it flying under my bunk. Even though I couldn't see the damage I knew the late night toiling on my shoes had been destroyed in a few seconds of sadistic violence and it would take twice or even three times the work to bring them back up to scratch.

"Right then! Listen up everybody. After today, I want to see a spit shine on your foot wear. And you, McMillan…!"

"Yes, Master Corporal!"

"You'll do as you are damn well told and don't you ever lie to me again!"

"Yes, Master Corporal!"

Lesson learned.

In Week Three of Recruit Training everyone got sick. Not from food poisoning, even though there were individuals who did have some dietary issues. And not from a reaction to the multitude of vaccines injected into us in Week One, even though there were some who did have an adverse reaction to the concoctions brewed by the pharmaceutical chemists in the bowels of the National Defence Medical Centre (NDMC). During Week Three everyone came down with a cold, which was not surprising. If you take one hundred and forty-odd people from across the country each of them, to some extent, will be resistant to their regional strain of the common cold. But dump all these individuals into a group where they eat, sleep, bath and perform all other bodily functions in close proximity to others and they will be exposed to various strains of the common cold for which they have no defences. Everyone coughed, ran a fever and had the shakes. All you wanted to do was sleep and/or die. There were times in Week Three when I had fallen asleep in the laundry room while polishing my boots only to wake up beside my bed with my boots polished. Regardless of your ills you still had to perform. It didn't matter if you were sick because your uniform, your locker and your bunk space had to be maintained to an exacting standard regardless of your personal condition. If you went to the hospital you ran the risk of being recoursed because the medical staff could quite easily declare that you were too sick to continue and hold you back until you felt well enough.

It was also in Week Three of Basic Recruit Training that the platoon began to be reduced in numbers as the instructors started weeding people out, especially those individuals who did not embrace the military way of life. This was carried out with the masterful use of head games and the morning inspections soon became a daily psychological test. On Monday our NCO ripped everyone a new asshole for not having the underwear in their locker folded to the correct military dimensions of 3 x 3 inches. Tuesday was the day we were all picked up for the condition of our footwear. On Wednesday we were informed that the barracks floor and common living areas were the perfect example of the most disgusting shithole known to mankind. And on and on and on.

It didn't matter how hard we worked on our personal kit it was never shiny enough, clean enough or pressed flat enough. Every day the contents of our lockers would be tossed about the barracks and you couldn't see what kind of destruction the inspecting NCO was inflicting because we stood with our bunk spaces behind us. But, the guys on the other side of the room could see everything that was going on!

Across the floor from my bunk space lived a recruit by the name of Jameson, a tall, thin, likeable fellow from Vancouver. Unbeknownst to him on this day the Wrath of God in the form of MCpl McLean was about to descend upon him. With Jameson standing at attention and facing the centre of the room McLean began to inspect his bunk space.

"Recruit Jameson, did you dust your locker?"

"Yes, Master Corporal!" answered Jameson.

"Don't you fricking lie to me recruit!"

From my vantage point facing Jameson's bunk space, I watched as MCpl McLean produced a white glove from his pocket, attach it to the end of his pace stick and then proceeded to thrust it deep into the farthest reaches of Jameson's locker. The result wasn't pretty.

"If you dusted your locker then what in the name of the Lord Jesus Christ do you call this?"

With the smudged tip of the inspection glove now held directly in his focal view Jameson replied, "Dust, Master Corporal!"

"Goddamn right it's dust! Let's see if I can help shake it out for ya."

Our side of the barracks all watched as MCpl McLean reached up and grabbed the upper frame of Jameson's locker. With a mighty tug the open locker rocked forward spilling its contents all over Jameson's bunk.

"Jameson!"

"YES, Master Corporal!"

"Get the shit in your locker squared away. Pronto!"

With furtive glances, the guys on my side of the barracks watched as Jameson first heaved his locker back into an upright position and then hurriedly began to replace each pair of unworn rolled socks, the precisely folded virgin underwear and several knife edge creased shirts back into their pre-dumped locations while McLean crapped all over the poor Jameson, going on and on about how much of a screw up the poor guy was. McLean bitched about Jameson's lack of focus and even his potentially inadequate masculinity.

"Done yet?"

"Yes, Master Corporal!"

"What the hell do you call this? Jameson, why is your bunk not made to regulation?"

"It was Master Corporal, but then you dumped my locker?"

"And why did I dump your locker?"

"Because it was dusty, Master Corporal."

"Say it again Jameson. Nice and loud, so everyone can hear!"

"BECAUSE IT WAS DUSTY, MASTER CORPORAL!"

"Precisely! What you need is a little incentive to motivate your attitude. Jameson, open that window. Recruit McMillan, step over here and grab this end of Jameson's mattress. Jameson, pick up the far end"

"Yes, Master Corporal."

As ordered, I stepped smartly across the aisle, picked up the near end of the mattress and on the next word of command I assisted Jameson in pushing his mattress, complete with sheets, blanket and pillow, out of the second story barracks window. It tumbled freely to the rain soaked ground far below.

"I don't care how you do it Jameson, but you had better have your bed squared away by the time lunch rolls around or you'll really be in the shit!"

Turning to face the entire room Mcpl McLean, in his best parade square voice, issued the following words of command, "SQUAD! AHHH-TEN-SHUN! FORM UP OUT ON THE ROAD!"

We quickly scrambled to secure our lockers before departing the barracks and every squad member was wondering the same thing:

How in the hell was Jameson going to find the opportunity to get his mattress and bedding back into his bunk space by lunch time? It would be a daunting task. Attendance was taken at the start of every class so there would be no ducking out. Missing a class without permission would be considered to be AWOL and that was a chargeable offence. What would McLean do to him if he didn't have it made? And this was only the start of the third week of recruit training. Things could only go downhill from here.

After attending three different classes in the morning the platoon was marched to the mess hall. None of us wanted to eat but we had to. What we really wanted was to see if Jameson had been able to magically get his bed back upstairs. After a quick bite of some high carb empty calorie nutrition the squad raced back to the shack to find that Jameson's entire mattress was back on his bunk. It was clean, dry and made to the precise military standards complete with razor sharp 45° hospital corners. To this day it is still a mystery to me as to how his bedding returned home. It didn't really matter anyways. In the eyes of the instructors Jameson was a marked man and by the end of the Week Four he had been recoursed to another platoon.

It was Monday noon of Week Six. We had just finished lunch and returned to the barracks for a quick nap. It might be only twenty minutes of rack time but by God it was our twenty minutes! However, there was a fly in the ointment. The Platoon Sergeant was waiting outside the barracks until all the members of Three Squad had returned from lunch. It didn't take long.

"Three Squad! Leave your boots on and get to your damn bunk spaces! Now!"

We didn't know what the hell was going on and it didn't really matter. When the Platoon Sergeant spoke it was as if the voice of God Himself was commanding you. We raced up the stairs and, obeying the words of command, we kept our boots on to walk across the high gloss waxed floor to our assigned bunk spaces.

"SQUAD! AHHH-TEN-SHUN! Now pay attention!"

The Platoon Sergeant didn't have to worry about that. His very presence on the squad's floor had everybody's undivided attention.

"Some of you had liberty this past weekend and were allowed to go off Base. But some of you think this privilege allows you to take advantage of my good nature by bringing in contraband and hiding it in the barracks. I want everyone to look this way."

Even though we were standing at attention we turned our heads in unison so we could see the end of the barracks. Directly in front of the door to the smoke room was a number of glass bottles. They appeared to be empty 26ers and mickey's. Some of them were broken. Some of them were still intact.

"What I want to know is who brought these bottles into the barracks and hid them up in the ceiling? Nobody? Well, we can stand here all bloody day and all bloody night until someone owns up to it! And, whoever that person is…whoever thinks they can abuse the trust of their fellow squad members and place their careers in jeopardy…That SONUVABITCH IS GONE! THAT SLIMEY

INCONSIDERATE INDIVIDUAL WILL BE RELEASED! Now, who is it?

Seconds ticked into minutes. Nobody moved. Nobody did anything. There were still thirty five members in Three Squad. Maybe a dozen or so had been allowed to go off Base for the day on Saturday. No one had brought alcohol back onto the Base. It would have been impossible to do so for two reasons. First, recruits returning to the Base were inspected by the military police which included all bags and packages. Second, if someone had smuggled alcohol into the barracks it would not have been a secret for long.

"I'm waiting for someone to admit their guilt. Now PROVE!" bellowed the Platoon Sergeant.

To "prove" an individual simply bent his right arm at the elbow so the lower portion of the arm was now parallel to the ground. In this position the person in command only had to look down the line and see the arm sticking out.

"That's it McMillan! You piece of shit. You are OUT OF HERE!"

With my right arm bent at 90° the Platoon Sergeant was able to spot me halfway down the barracks floor.

"I'm sorry Sergeant. But, you cannot kick me, or anyone else, out of Three Squad."

On hearing the challenge to his authority, the Platoon Sergeant stalked menacingly down the floor to my bunk space.

"And why can't I punt your ass out of here? You admitted that you did it!"

"Sergeant, I admit that someone did bring those bottles into the barracks. But, I do not think that it was a member of this squad or this platoon. Sergeant, when we arrived the military police took our fingerprints. Now, some of those bottles are not broken. Have the MP's print the bottles. If mine or any member of Three Squad has touched those bottles our prints will be on them and those individuals deserve to be kicked out. But, Sergeant you are not going to kick someone out of the military without the evidence."

The Platoon Sergeant simply stared at me. He was in shock. Maybe even dumbfounded. No recruit in their right mind would ever challenge an NCO. Especially, a sergeant. In Cornwallis a sergeant was God! However, whatever I said must have struck a chord with him.

"Three Squad! Fallout on the road! Double time! You're late for class. And, McMillan! You'll clean this floor before you have supper this evening."

"Yes, Sergeant!"

Our physical fitness training took place every day in one form or another. On our very first day in the gymnasium the entire platoon was lined up in evenly spaced rows across the floor. The head PERI (Physical Education Recreation Instructor) was a Master Corporal. I don't know what his last name was and I don't think he even told us. It wouldn't have mattered because none of us were going to be on his Christmas card list anyway.

"On the word 'GO', I want you to walk down, touch the far wall and then fall back into position," he ordered.

"GO!"

Zoom! Off we went. Sprint down. Slap the wall. Sprint back. And line up. Done!

"Everyone get down and give me twenty five push-ups," the PERI bellowed.

"One, two, three....twenty-four, twenty-five. Stand Up!"

"I said WALK down and touch the wall! GO!"

As ordered we walked, sauntered really, down the length of the gym floor. Touched the wall and ever so casually traipsed back into formation. Done!

Addressing the platoon, the head PERI informed us, "That will be the last time you will ever walk on this gym floor!"

So, every day we hit the gym. Or the pool. Or both. And when we did both it was always a nice long workout in the gym first, followed by a strenuous dip in the pool. Never the other way around. This wasn't so much of an issue except for the one or two individuals that *insisted* that they be perfectly dry before exiting the building. Meanwhile the rest of the platoon - who had heeded the words of our NCO's to "Hurry Up and get the HELL OUTSIDE! FORM UP IN THREE RANKS YOU SORRY SACKS OF CRAP!" - were all standing outside shivering in the cold with our damp clothes freezing to our bodies.

Did we complain that we were cold? No. To do so would result in having to do more push ups just to keep warm. And as for the two individuals who demanded to be completely dry? Let's just say that retribution in the form of a bucket of cold water in the middle of the night taught them both a lesson.

During Week Seven recruits would have to run a seven mile course. Naturally, the day before the seven-miler we ran a five mile course just for fun. For both runs we wore t-shirts, combat pants, wool socks and combat boots and this was in the last week in November.

Not every day in CFRS Cornwallis was filled with twisted head games and continual physical exertion. Despite all the strict "Yes Sir! No Sir! Three Bags Full Sir" bullshit there were times when we could actually relax. Maybe even order in some take-out food from the local burger joint called The Hollow Spot. When we were allowed to most of the platoon went to the Green and Gold Mess, to blow off a little steam at the end of the week. Supposedly, recruits were limited to having only four beers in an evening. If this was the case cooler heads would have certainly prevailed.

Late Friday night at the end of Week Eight a group of drunken recruits, returning from the Mess, burst onto the squad room floor. In the very centre of the mob were two platoon members, one from Ontario and the other from Cape Breton. They were desperately trying to punch the living hell out each other while six other guys tried their best to pull the two combatants apart. Suddenly, in the middle of this melee, in walks Recruit Dupuis, the designated Course Senior - aka the Course Knob. He was the eyes and ears of the regular staff during the off-duty hours. In other words, he's the rat. Recruit Dupuis was a bell shaped individual with a large overbite, from some place in southern Ontario, who was planning on becoming a medic. Like a lot of us, he was in his early twenties but unlike a lot of us he was very religious and very naive.

"You should let them fight. It's God's Will."

Hearing this, Jeff Nickerson, who detested Dupuis as much as anybody in the platoon, spun the Course Senior into the nearest wall. While loudly proclaiming, "I'll show you God's Will", Jeff drew back his fist and let it fly right at Dupuis's face ... and...

BOOM! BOOM!

Jeff's clenched fist completely passed through both sides of the wall as it missed the Course Knob's face. Immediately everything on the squad floor ground to a halt. The two combatants ceased their fisticuffs and Dupuis, fearing for his safety, scuttled away crab-like for the platoon office to file his report.

"Holy shit Jeff! What are you going to do now?"

"I don't know. I'll figure it out in the morning."

On this particular night the angels must have been working overtime. When he extracted his arm Jeff discovered that his clenched fist had missed hitting a stud by mere inches. Even more amazing was that the only thing damaged was the sheetrock on both sides of a dividing wall.

First thing Saturday morning, Jeff headed for the Canex to search for building supplies. On his return to the squad he began trying cover up the holes using newsprint and sloppy polyfilla. News of Jeff's handiwork had spread pretty quickly throughout the platoon as individuals from the other squads began to arrive for a look see. All this extra attention only added to Jeff's frustration and it wasn't long before MCpl McLean walked onto the squad floor.

"Squad!" McLean shouted. "Get to your bunk spaces. NOW!"

Like frightened mice we all scrambled to attention in front of our bunks as McLean purposely strode down the centre of the floor. He stopped to survey the damaged walls.

"Who in the hell did this? PROVE!"

Jeff's right arm was now in the prove position.

"Get to my office! The remainder, STAND AAAAAHT EASE!"

McLean marched quickly down the barracks floor following Jeff through the smoke room at the end of the squad floor and into his office.

We remained standing "At Ease" in front of our bunks for an extended period of time. Head and eyes looking forwards, Shoulders rolled back. Our hands were clasped behind our backs, feet placed a shoulder width apart. All of us wondering how long it would take before Jeff was kicked out for malicious damage to government property.

"Squad! Squad, Aaah Ten Shun!"

MCpl McLean was pacing down the squad floor with Jeff in tow. Jeff stepped into his bunk space and came sharply to attention as McLean stood in front of the damaged walls.

"Everyone look this way. Just as a reminder, there will be no smoking on the squad floor. If you want to have a smoke you must be in the smoke room or outside in the smoke pit before you light up."

To make his point abundantly clear, MCpl McLean took two large adhesive "No Smoking" stickers and placed them precisely over each fist sized hole. Once this was done, he turned on his heels and walked out of the barracks without saying another word.

To my knowledge Jeff was never punished for the holes he had put in the wall. But I do know that over the next several nights Dupuis was on the receiving end of a resounding blanket party courtesy of the members of Three Squad. For the uninitiated, a blanket party is a function whereby a blanket is thrown over an individual while he is sleeping. It is held firmly in place by several individuals covering the head and upper body while several other individuals take turns punching the extremities. Body shots and headshots are not allowed as the object is to exact retribution and not physical damage. A "blanket party" could be held for any number of reasons. For example, if an individual was consistently dropping his weapon during training thus causing the entire unit to suffer through additional training, then a blanket party would most certainly be in order.

Recruit Phil Lekowski nearly ended up on the receiving end of a blanket party as well. At the start of Week Seven he had surprised MCpl McLean by having all the shirts in his locker ironed in such a manner that the outward facing sleeves were interlocked together at a precise 45° angle. Oh sure. It looked really sharp but when he saw it MCpl McLean ordered the entire squad to have it copied for Tuesday morning's inspection. The next morning the Platoon Warrant was invited to inspect Three Squad and when he saw all the shirts effectively right dressed he ordered the rest of the platoon to do the same for the upcoming Company Commander's inspection on Thursday. There were now ninety some individuals who were not too pleased with the extra work that Phil had created and as such the Warrant Officer decried that he was not to be touched.

    Week Nine found Mad Dog Four Platoon outdoors. We were now living out in the woods at the Granville Training Area carrying out basic field exercises. We were to be tested on orienteering, weapons handling and basic camp protocols like carrying out sentry duties, fire picket, the construction of a sleeping shelter, using an immersion heater to produce hot water and how to use a Coleman stove for cooking. Having had pre-service training, all of this outdoor stuff was second nature for me. But for some, especially those who had never left the comfort of their parents' home in the big city, the thought of sleeping in a lean-to on an air mattress for a week in December was absolutely absurd. The prime focus of our week in the Nova Scotian woods was to qualify on the Canadian standard battlefield rifle – the FN-C1A1. This semi-automatic weapon was chambered for 7.62 x 51mm (.308 Winchester) ammunition and it weighed eleven pounds with a fully loaded twenty round box magazine making it a bit of a beast to carry around. But, unlike the current standard issue C7A1 rifle, which is chambered for a much smaller round (5.56 x 45 mm), being equipped with the FN meant that if an enemy was hiding behind a tree, you would just shoot through the tree.

The Fabrique Nationale (FN) C1A1

Our reason to be out in the woods may have been to qualify on the FN but that did not stop our instructors from having a bit of fun. For those who had left their weapon unattended the punishment included a couple of hundred push-ups followed by taking MCpl Buddy for a quarter mile run down the hill to the guard post and back. MCpl Buddy was a five and a half foot long 4x4 post. On opposite sides of the post were crudely drawn arms emblazoned with Master Corporal chevrons. On the front of the post was a smiling face and on the backside was a frowning face. And you had better learn which was which.

"Recruit MacDonald! YOU SLACK AND IDLE WOG! Where is your rifle?"

"Over there Master Corporal."

"Go get your weapon MacDonald and report back to me!"

MacDonald retrieved his weapon from where he had left it unattended and went to see MCpl House.

"Recruit MacDonald, this is MCpl Buddy. MCpl Buddy hasn't had his exercise for the day and he needs to go for a run. I want you to sling your weapon, pick up MCpl Buddy and take him for a jog down to the sentry post at the bottom of the hill. When you return I want you to present yourself and MCpl Buddy to me. Got that? Now go!"

MacDonald slung his rifle across his back and picked up the cumbersome 4x4 post before heading off at a fair clip down the hill. When he got to the bottom of the hill MacDonald did a loop around the flag pole and started back up the road. He knew that all eyes were on him and he knew that he didn't want to look bad before his squad members so he picked up his pace as he neared the range buildings.

Standing at attention, with his weapon still slung and the 4x4 post gripped beside him on his right hand side, Recruit MacDonald called out, "MCpl House, MCpl Buddy has returned from his run!"

"Recruit Macdonald, do you think that MCpl Buddy enjoyed his run?"

"Yes, Master Corporal!"

"I don't think he did. You had better take him for another lap."

MacDonald wondered what the hell was going on but he dared not question the order. So, like a good little lamb he picked up the post and headed off down the hill. When he got back he went through the same procedure of presenting MCpl Buddy and received the same answer. Back down the hill for a third lap. It was on the way back up the hill for the third time when MacDonald had an epiphany. He noticed the faces drawn on the post and realized that when he had presented MCpl Buddy the smiling face was turned towards himself meaning the frowning face was facing MCpl House. This time he wouldn't make a mistake.

"MCpl House, MCpl Buddy has returned from his run!"

"Did he enjoy his run, Recruit MacDonald?"

Knowing that he had the post facing the correct way, MacDonald hollered, "Yes MCpl House! MCpl Buddy enjoyed this last run the most."

Seeing that MacDonald had figured it out, House replied, "Very good, Recruit. To your duties, diss …missed!"

You would think that it wouldn't take long before everyone in the platoon would know which way to present MCpl Buddy after being taken on his run. Not a chance. Information like that is best kept to oneself, lest sharing it was cause to complete some other mindless make-work task and so some unobservant individuals would loop past the flag pole four or five times before catching on. Shortly after spending the week out in the woods of Granville the head games suddenly stopped.

By Christmas 1981 we had completed nine weeks of training. Everyone - all the recruits that is - would be transported home by planes, trains or automobiles. After the holidays, there would be very little left for us to do except study for some minor exams and begin the final preparations for our graduation parade along the subsequent party. But for now, the members of Three Squad were just hanging out waiting for their flight serials to be called when in walked MCpl McLean. Immediately, the first person to see him called the room to attention by yelling out, "ROOM!"

"To your bunk spaces," barked McLean. And we quickly scrambled to where we belonged.

"Mr. Hollingsworth! I see empty spaces Mr. Hollingsworth! As the Squad Knob, do you know where all your people are?"

"No, Master Corporal. I mean, some people are at the Canex and some are at the Dry Canteen but I don't know where they all are."

"Well, you had better find out. I want everyone in their bunk spaces in twenty minutes or else you're in the shit, Private Hollingsworth!"

Ron sent runners out across the Base to fetch all of the wayward squad members. They were to check the Canex and the dry canteen and in less than twenty minutes everyone was standing "At Ease" in their respective bunk spaces.

"Three Squad is present and accounted for Master Corporal!"

"Three Squad! AHHH-TEN-SHUN! Mr. Hollingsworth come with me."

McLean turned on his heels and disappeared into the smoke room at the end of the barracks with Ron in tow. The minutes ticked by and we were still standing at "Attention" when Ron came back onto the squad floor.

"Three Squad! One step, FORWARD...MARCH!"

We all took one pace closer to towards the center of the room.

"Three Squad! Advance Right…Turn!"

"IN SINGLE FILE, QUICK ...MARCH!"

We marched around the squad floor until we had filed into the smoke room where MCpl McLean had us all find a seat. This was really bizarre behaviour. None of us knew what was happening, but we did as we were told just the same. Once we were seated McLean disappeared into his office only to reappear moments later with two two-fours of Schooner beer. Placing the cases on the table before us he uttered the immortal words, "Merry Fucking Christmas!"

The four dozen Schooner brand beer was just the right amount as the squad had been reduced from a cumbersome forty-two at the start of the course to a precise twenty-three. And, with the Master Corporal making up number twenty-four everyone was able to enjoy two beers each. In talking to the other members of the platoon, only Three Squad received such a fine pre-holiday gift.

On the day of our graduation everybody was pumped up. Our uniforms were pressed beyond belief. Our boots shone to a reflected depth of eight inches or more[3]. We were lean. We were mean. And soon, we would no longer be recruits. We were proud of what we had accomplished and I think our instructors were too. We were all set to march to the main drill hall when we were told by the Platoon Warrant that there would be a delay in the program.

It would seem that the roads had not been cleared of the two feet of snow that had fallen over the night. When they were finally cleared the only bare portions were from our barracks to the drill hall. All the other roads on Base remained buried for several more days. The junior platoons that were to accompany us were still snowed in and as a result only Mad Dog Four Platoon was on parade.

By the end of our eleven weeks of basic training it was time to say goodbye to Mad Dog Four Platoon, to CFRS Cornwallis and to

---

[3] If you held a ruler vertically up against a pair of parade boots you could clearly read eight inches of the ruler.

Nova Scotia in general. It was time to say goodbye to the long hours cleaning, polishing, mopping, ironing, dusting, studying, marching and running. Was it any wonder the favourite song of recruits who finished Basic Training was "Farewell to Nova Scotia!" Now was the time for the graduates of Course 8142 to look ahead to the future and to the new training that would continue in places like CFB Kingston, Garrison Petawawa and CFSAOE Borden.

The Instructors of Course 8142 taken at the Granville Small Arms Range. MCpl McLean is in the top left. The Platoon Sergeant is missing from the photo as he was on leave at the time.

Trades Training

After an exhausting late night flight from Halifax to Toronto and an even more uncomfortable bus ride on Ontario's desolate winter highways, six members of Mad Dog Four Platoon arrived at CFB Borden sometime after midnight. Along with a hundred more incoming students, we were processed through the Base Administration unit. Once our name, rank and Social Insurance Number were confirmed and cross-referenced by some poor admin clerk who was unlucky enough to draw this all night duty position, we were told to get back on the bus. It was some unknown duty sergeant who escorted us into the barracks block. Building A-149 would be our new home for the next six months.

"Here's your room. The sheets and blankets are in the locker. Make your beds and get some sleep. You don't have to be tidy except on your weekly inspection day."

There were four bed spaces in the room. One bed was already occupied but our new roomie was absent. I dumped my luggage next to a bed and rummaged through the locker to find the standard military bedding consisting of a real goose feather pillow and a pillow case, a pair of white sheets with the obligatory "Property of DND" stenciled on one end, a thin blue counterpane (akin to a bedspread) and finally one wool blanket, again with "Property of DND" stenciled on it, to keep off the persistent chill residing inside the barracks. This wasn't the time for proper hospital corners. It was time to get some shut eye.

Life at CFB Borden soon took on a routine. It wasn't the same routine that had been so enjoyably experienced during Basic Training. No, this was different. Quite often we were on our own personal time. Left to our devices as it were. No one was telling us when to go for meals or when to go to bed. A close inspection of our uniform and barracks room was carried out once a week. It seemed as if all the things that were the focus of our very existence in Recruit Training no longer existed. The world was our oyster. Our only job was to concentrate on our studies and regardless of any previous trades experience we may have had we were now taught by the numbers. For example, in Common Mechanical Training (CMT) we were introduced to the three main types of screwdrivers available in Canada, of which only two were used in the military. It soon became obvious that there were some individuals on our course who could not identify the Common, the Phillips or the Robertson screwdriver.[4] Then there was the whole "Righty Tighty, Lefty Loosey" thing that some people just could not understand.

---

[4] Despite being a great Canadian invention, the Robertson screwdriver, with its square tip, was not used on any aircraft in the Canadian inventory or on any aircraft that I know of even to this day.

Another former restriction no longer monitored by the instructor cadre was our consumption of alcohol. In CFB Borden there were four drinking establishments or Messes that served students in their need for indulgence and self-destruction. The Algonquin (The "A") Club, the Ojibwa (The "O") Club, the Curling Club and Snoopy's. The first two were designated for the students and the instructors were not allowed in unless they were acting in a Base Duty capacity. This provided a place where the students could let their hair down, so to speak, away from the prying eyes of the instructors. The Curling Club was open to both students and staff. The fourth club, known affectionately as Snoopy's, was for service members who had been promoted to the rank of corporal. This provided a place where "senior" students, such as those attending a speciality course, could quietly have a drink without having to contend with the constant buzzing whine emanating from the younger crowd. No longer were we allotted only a couple of beers in the evening. The taps were now wide open and the amount a person drank was limited only by how much cash you had in your wallet. Mind you, the responsibility was squarely on your head.

Getting drunk and attracting the unwanted attention of the Military Police could easily result in you performing the hatless dance at an Orders Parade. The words of command for such an occasion would be - "March the guilty bastard in!"

And the only two questions you would be asked were, "How do you plead? Guilty or... guilty?" If this scenario was played out too many times the military would simply cut its losses and release the member from his contract.

So there I was... Formed up with about 800 or more other students in preparation to march off to the Canadian Forces School of Aerospace and Ordinance Engineering (CFSAOE) in what we called the Great Green Bus. It was then that we noted that our classmate, Pete Campagna, was not with us. It was difficult to miss Pete. He stood six and a half feet tall giving him the status of being the Permanent Right Marker for every parade that he had participated in. We searched all around but Pete was nowhere to be found. Maybe he went to the Base Hospital on sick parade? Oh well, he's a big boy now and can look after himself.

We were in the midst of the oxygen phase of our trades course. This phase is one of the largest and most demanding portions of the safety systems trade course. Safety Systems, also known as Aviation Life Support Equipment, includes all of the emergency equipment that would be required by the aircrew and/or passengers to increase their odds of survival in the event of a catastrophic accident. The survival equipment on a military aircraft includes fire suppression systems (both fixed and portable), oxygen breathing systems (gaseous, liquid and portable), parachutes, emergency egress (ejection) systems, personal survival equipment such as helmets and oxygen masks, survival kits of all sizes and flotation systems (both personal and life rafts).

As you can well imagine the safety systems trade is a huge responsibility. On an aircraft the engines can stop turning and a wing could fall off but fail to pack a pilot's parachute correctly or neglect to maintain his ejection seat or improperly install an emergency life raft and somebody's life will be in jeopardy. For these reasons I always took great pride in my work and I always felt that the trade was overlooked for its importance. But, more about that later.

We were all sitting in the oxygen classroom. It was nearly 10 a.m. We had just came back from a scheduled coffee break and had started to review our notes for an upcoming test when there was a knock on the door. The whole class looked towards the doorway and there stood Pete, firmly at attention but with a slight wobble in his stance. He looked pale and sweaty and his uniform resembled a Class A bag of shit. It was quite obvious to everyone that he was still impaired.

"Master Corporal Beauregard! Request permission to enter the class."

"Private Campagna! Why are you late for class?"

"Yesterday was my birthday Master Corporal and I may have celebrated a little too much last night."

"Well, I suppose congratulations are in order for your honesty. You will report to the instructor's office immediately. Wait for me outside the office. I will be there shortly."

Of all the instructors we had in CFSAOE, MCpl Beauregard was the worst. If he even suspected a student of stepping out of bounds he would hang the person by his thumbs, so to speak. MCpl Beauregard was so straight laced that he didn't smoke, didn't drink and it was rumoured that he and his wife didn't even have sex because he probably thought it was too messy. To top it all off, he detested anyone who even dared to indulge in any form of vice. In other words, Pete was screwed!

The trial took place several days later. The accused, the hatless Private Pete Campagna, was flanked by two escorts, Private Jody McArthur and Private Rodney Sands. As escorts to the accused their job was twofold. Historically, they were there to restrain the accused as punishment was handed down but realistically they were there to witness the proceedings and report back to the rest of the troops. Under the "no bullshit" direction of the school's chief disciplinarian, Warrant Officer JW McKendry, all three were MARCHED into the Major's office in double quick time, which is supposed to be at the impossible blistering speed of 240 paces per minute, brought to a sharp HALT and then ordered to execute a crisp ADVANCE RIGHT TURN.

Private Pete Campagna was charged, under Section 119 of the National Defense Act, with the crime of CONDUCT UNBECOMING OF A SERVICE MEMBER. The witness for the prosecution was MCpl Beauregard and as there was no witness for the defense, not that it would have mattered anyway, Private Campagna was found guilty as charged, a fine was levied and would be summarily deducted from his pay at a later date.

Being in the military, you never know when a gift or a reward will be bestowed upon you. In truth you never expected anything and you never asked for anything but sometimes someone higher up the food chain might say, "Take an extra twenty minutes at lunch or let's have an extra-long coffee break." The important thing is to say "Thank You!" However, working above and beyond or routinely doing extra jobs without any acknowledgement will surely sour a working relationship to the point where people will no longer step up to stay late or to just help out because their GAFF[5] has gone out the window.

"I need a couple of volunteers for a special tasking on Sunday. Who would like to help out?" asked MCpl Wayne Adams.

Having been led down the Primrose Path several times before, nobody in the class raised their hand. We could only imagine what sort of "special tasking" one of our instructors had in mind. It would probably be some menial job like moving all of the desks out of a classroom just so we could wash and wax the floor or polish all of the brass handrails in the stairways for some upcoming inspection. And on a Sunday? Sundays were for recovering from Saturday night, for doing laundry, tidying your uniform and maybe studying for the inevitable 'surprise' quiz on Monday. So, forget it.

"Whoever volunteers to assist me on Sunday will come to my house after the job has been completed for a barbequed steak dinner complete with all the fixins. That would include my wife's Caesar salad, a baked potato and beer."

Still no takers.

MCpl Adams was getting desperate for some assistance.

---

[5] GAFF – **G**ive **A** **F**uck **F**actor

"And, you won't have to come to class until 10:00 hrs on Monday."

And, there's the hook!

My roommate and I looked at each other and figured what the hell. A steak dinner and extra time off. Whatever the job was it would certainly be worth it.

On Sunday at 09:30 hrs we met MCpl Adams at the CFSAOE building. He had two large trolley carts loaded with an assortment of survival equipment that we were to take to one of the training hangars. Our task was to set up a display for a group of air cadets and answer any questions that they might have. That was it! From 10:00 hrs until 15:00 hrs we answered questions to the best of our ability about the life support equipment and when the dog and pony show was over we packed everything up before taking it back to the school. By 16:00 hrs we were out of uniform and on our way to MCpl Adams' home in the nearby town of Barrie. True to his word, we dined on juicy one inch thick T-bone steaks complete with baked potatoes, a side salad and plenty of beer to wash it all down. It was sometime near midnight when his wife dropped us off back at the barracks. The good Master Corporal had ridden shotgun because he was in no condition to drive. The next morning we slept in until 07:00 hrs and lounged in our room after breakfast before marching ourselves to school for 10:00 hrs. Sometimes life is sweet.

Several months later we were in the Flotation Phase of the course. During this portion of the course we learned how to

inspect and pack all different kinds of survival kits. Aircrew and passenger kits, basic kits,
first aid kits and emergency life rafts. We were there to learn. The instructors task was to teach subject and to play with our heads.

Our instructors were forever dreaming up ways to ensure we used caution and diligence in our studies. During the Sewing Phase we would cautiously enter the classroom, each of us looking to see if there was a single solitary screw or some other innocuous component placed prominently on the 3 x 3 inch piece of white cloth beside our sewing machine. If there was an item sitting on the cloth the student would have to strip down, inspect and reassemble a Pfaff medium duty sewing machine before it could be used. Sometimes on inspection, it would be discovered that the loose part was not from your sewing machine at all. It was just something the instructors had placed on the white cloth so you would have to tear apart your machine. We quickly got into the habit of inspecting our sewing machines even when there was nothing on the cloth because the timing mechanism may have been altered or the thread incorrectly directed through the machine or the power cord might simply be unplugged from the wall.

Use of the correct terminology was also stressed. "It's an ejection seat not an ejector seat!" Or, "the aircraft is outfitted with an oxygen system not an air system!" To assist us in using the correct terminology the instructors began to keep a running tally of how many times each student spoke an incorrect term. Each mistake would cost the student a drink, a beer or a shot, that would be paid out to the instructor at the course graduation party.

I was the Course Senior during our Flotation Phase. I had not earned the position. The job was assigned on a rotational basis to each member of the course. For a period of two or three weeks the Course Senior, aka the Course Knob, was responsible for all the members of the course, ensuring their attendance at school and at any mandatory after hours functions as well. The "Knob" was also the person responsible for the actions of his classmates whenever the instructor left the room.

So, there we were... In the midst of repacking the ten person life rafts. Each raft consists of two inflation tubes stacked one on top of the other forming the walls of the raft and four arched tubes that join together in the center above the raft. During an actual emergency the raft is inflated with the use of a CO_2 gas cylinder that is mounted in a support sleeve on the outside of the raft wall. To initiate the inflation cycle a cord, called a painter line, is clipped to the side of a downed and sinking aircraft and the raft is thrown overboard. Once the painter line is fully extended the cylinder head cable releases the CO_2 gas which in turn inflates the raft. This process will take place regardless of the location either on a sinking plane or on the shop floor. If the painter line is pulled the cylinder head will fire and the raft will inflate.

I think you know where this is headed.

It was a Friday afternoon. Beauregard had recently been promoted from Master Corporal to the rank of Sergeant which made him an even bigger prick than before. However, he did grant us one gift whereby we would get out of class early as soon as we finished packing up our rafts. We should have realized that it was a false promise. Nobody in the history of all military courses held at CFB Borden ever got out of class early, especially on a Friday and especially from the newly promoted Sgt Beauregard's class. But this dangling carrot would only be the impetus for what transpired over the next few minutes.

"Alright class. As soon as the rafts are packed and the tools have been placed back on the tool board we'll see about getting you out early today. Course Senior, I am going to the staff room. I'll be back in a few minutes. Make sure that there is no funny business!"

"Yes, Sergeant," I replied. Beauregard was always concerned that there was far too much funny business going on. And the last thing anybody would want is funny business on a Friday afternoon.

The course was divided into three teams. Rodney, Jody and I were working on one raft. Dearman, Andy and Pete were tackling another while Rob and the girls - Connie, Diane and Debbie - worked on the last ten-person raft. With the notion of getting out of class even a few minutes early planted firmly in our minds, we all pulled together with true `esprit de corps. The sea survival kits were placed inside the rafts. Suction hoses were attached and the compressors were started - thereby evacuating air out through the relief valves - while one person per team prepped the two halves of the packing valise by loosening off the lacing cords.

It didn't take long before my group was nearing completion. The survival kit was tied in. The raft had been completely sucked down and the CO_2 cylinder was attached. We had folded the raft and were fitting it into the two halves of the protective valise. It was at this point that Rodney, in a very clear and loud voice, announced, "I'll put the wrench back on the tool board!"

With the wrench in his hand, Rodney crossed the floor of the class towards the tool board.

BANG! WHOOOOOOSH!

An explosive rush the compressed gas flowed from the cylinder through the Y-valve and into the still half-filled inflation tubes. That's right! In an attempt to speed up the packing of their raft Andy's group had attached the cylinder to their raft before it had been completely deflated. In addition to this major faux pas this group had also neglected to secure the painter line to the cylinder sleeve which would have prevented a mishap from initiating the inflation cycle. The causes did not matter but the effects did as the raft got bigger and BIGGER until a seam finally burst releasing a billowing cloud of French chalk into the air.

"Holy shit, Rodney! What the hell did you do?"

"Hey! All I was doing was putting the wrench back on the tool board."

"Well, I'll have to report this."

Leaving the classroom, I started to think of how I was going to break the news to Sgt Beauregard. As my boots clicked down along the polished corridor, I realized that there was no way of reporting what happened other than by telling the truth. And what was the truth? We were all deflating our rafts. One team had not followed the safety procedures by attaching the cylinder to a partially inflated raft with an unsecured painter line. The line was accidentally (?) pulled, initiating an over-inflation and the subsequent destruction of a training raft. The story sounded good to me but would the instructors buy it?

Arriving at the entrance to the office I came smartly to attention and knocked on the door frame.

MCpl Smith, our future Escape Systems instructor, was seated just inside the door. "What do you want?" he snarled.

"Is Sergeant Beauregard here? I have something to report."

"Hey, Beau! It's one of your kids!"

Sgt Beauregard quickly appeared from inside the rabbit warren of office desks and coloured cubicle dividers.

"Well, Course Senior? What do you have to report?"

"Sergeant Beauregard. I would like to report that we have blown up a raft!"

Without any hesitation MCpl Smith jumped at the chance to score a free drink, "Aha! McMillan, that'll cost you a Cherry Snapper (a shot of Cherry Whiskey). What you meant to say was you INFLATED a raft?"

"No, Master Corporal! I'm quite sure that this raft has been blown up."

Sgt Beauregard immediately stomped through the doorway

towards the classroom with me trailing close behind. He was muttering to himself something about, "Goddamn little kids. Can't leave them alone for two bloody seconds!"

When we returned to the classroom the air was still filled with the fine talc powder from inside the raft. Those students whose rafts were still in one piece had completed packing them and were now sitting patiently at their desks awaiting Sgt Beauregard's approval for an early dismissal. Good luck with that idea. Needless to say, we spent the rest of the afternoon cleaning the classroom over and over again as the French chalk continued to settle on everything. Dusting and wiping. Then sweeping and finally mopping. Late in the afternoon we were released from our duties only because the mess hall was soon to be closed and we could not be held from having a meal.

Several months later our graduation from CFSAOE went as well as expected. It was a casual sit down affair complete with coffee and cookies. We had lost a couple of people off the course. Debbie, who had been romantically involved with a Weapons Land technician, got pregnant and left the course early. Another was Rob, who despite our attempts to help him study, had failed several exams and the re-writes. Luckily, he was allowed to re-muster to the Administration trade.

Our posting assignments had already been handed out. I was now headed to 409 All Weather (AW) Fighter Squadron based at CFB Comox on Vancouver Island. Diane Dunham was posted to Comox as well but she was going to the Base Aircraft

Maintenance (Bameo) section. My roommate, Jody, was headed to Summerside, PEI. Goodbye, good luck and good riddance. After eleven weeks of Basic Training and six months of Trades Training I had enough of him and he was quite tired of me. Andy started with a posting to Trenton and wound up in Cold Lake, Alberta years later. Connie Smeltzer went to Cold Lake directly from our trades training and spent most of her time in the Drag Chute shop or in the Mess, which may be the reason why she may not have completed her initial five year contract. Three course members were off to CFB Edmonton and two of those were headed to the Canadian Forces Parachute Maintenance Depot (CFPMD). MWO Sova had rooked Campagna and Dearman into taking the posting to CFPMD citing there was more money in it as they would receive an extra $150.00 a month for being a qualified parachutist. Big deal! While at PMD, Campagna had a bad jump and broke both his legs. After the accident Pete left the PMD and went back to being a regular Safety Systems technician. The extra $150 per month to jump out of a perfectly serviceable aircraft seemed hardly worth it,

 Warrant Officer J.W. McKendry, the school's chief disciplinarian was in attendance as well. He stood there in the parachute classroom with a very contented look on his face as I am sure that he was happy to see us leave. WO McKendry was also being posted to 409 Squadron this summer but he didn't know that I had knew of his posting.

 "You know, Warrant," I began. "When I get to Comox I'm

going to let my hair grow, I'm not shining my boots and I'm going to get an earring. And all because you won't be there to give me a hard time."

Figuring that he had me over a barrel, WO McKendry played it real cool. He simply continued to puff away on his pipe, "We'll see McMillan. We'll see."

Westward Bound

Where do I go?
Where do I sleep?
And, of course…
where is the mess hall?
Back in 1982, when a service person was posted to a new base he or she would be assigned a sponsor. This was especially true if the incoming personnel was fresh out of basic training or from a trades school. The sponsor was usually an individual selected by the gaining unit who would welcome the incoming person and assist with any needs or wants. While enroute from Borden to Comox I had taken leave (holidays) to visit my parents and I had, as is required, informed my unit of the change of my arrival date. As I stepped off the plane in Comox it was quite obvious that none of this information had been passed along because no one was there to greet me. Not to worry. A helpful US Air Force (USAF) sergeant, who was also on my flight into Comox, gave me a ride to the Transient Quarters building.

The first few weeks in Comox quickly became a blur as I was initiated into the rhythm of the squadron. It too had a life of its own. From the man on the top rung, the Commanding Officer (CO) to the person on the bottom rung, yours truly, 409 (All

Weather) Fighter Squadron was a living, breathing entity. It was no different from any other Canadian military unit in that era. We took pride in our work. Pride in our unit. Pride in our mission. And, pride in our being. The Squadron was a family, with the CO at the head who asked only that, regardless of our task, we worked hard and we played hard. This phrase was a fact of life and as a result squadron functions were always well attended.

Shortly after being posted to CFB Comox, I realized that I had had quite enough of this living on base stuff. There was not enough space in the room and too much noise in the barracks. Then there were the weekly room inspections. All bullshit. It was time to move out. So, a friend and I found an apartment about 2 km from the base. It was far enough away from the noise of the flight line but still close enough to walk to work if your car died (or walk home if you had too many beers at the Mess). Now that I had my own apartment, my parents decided to ship me some of my personal effects such as my bed, desk, stereo, bookcase and anything else they could empty out of my old room. A local company was hired to pick it up there, deliver it here and the best part was that it was all claimable. However, there was an issue with the canoe.

"Private McMillan, the Canadian Armed Forces will not pay for the shipping of a canoe, bye," said the sergeant from the Claims Section. He was from Newfoundland and had a bit of an accent.

"Excuse me, Sgt Smith. But, what canoe?" I replied.

"It sez right here on da waybill dat you had a canoe shipped from your parent's house. And the military will not be paying for dat!"

"Can I see the waybill, please?"

"Look at it. It sez right dere, C. A. N. O. E !"

"Uh, Sergeant Smith. That's the address where my parents live."

"Whaddya mean?"

"They live on 72nd Street in Salmon Arm, BC. Well, 72nd Street is an area of Salmon Arm that used to be a separate town called Canoe. It's now a suburb like Shearwater is to Halifax or Burlington is to Toronto. Clearly, the moving company didn't know where 72nd Street was and when they asked my mom they simply wrote the word 'Canoe' on the waybill."

"I'm telling ya Private that there is no such place as Canoe, BC and I am

---

McDonnell CF-101B Voodoo

Crew – two (pilot and air weapons navigator)
Length – 67 ft 5 in
Height – 18 ft
Wingspan – 39 ft 8 in
Max Speed – Mach 1.72 at 35,000 ft.
Weight - 28,495 lbs (dry)
         - 45,665 lbs (wet)
         - 52,400 lbs (max)
Range – 1,520 mi
Ceiling – 58,400 ft
Armament
- 2 x AIM 4D Falcon IR missiles
- 2 x AIR-2A Genie nuclear rockets

not letting this claim go through!"

"Just give me a minute. I'll be right back."

I left the office and returned a minute later with a road map of British Columbia. I opened the map to the portion showing the North Okanagan and dropped it on his desk with my index finger pointing to the dot along the Shuswap Lake.

"Look there Sergeant Smith! Canoe, BC! I suppose you don't think there's such a place in Newfoundland as 'Dildo' or 'Come-By-Chance' either?"

"No bye, those are real places. I'se been there. But, because Canoe is on the map I'll have to approve your claim."

"Thank you, Sergeant Smith."

In 1962, 409 Squadron was outfitted with the CF-101B Voodoo replacing the CF-100 Canuck interceptors. Our role was to be the first line of defence against any hostile aircraft entering Canadian air space. There were two other Voodoo intercept squadrons in Canada. CFB Bagotville, Quebec was the home of 425 Squadron and 416 Squadron was based in CFB Chatham, New Brunswick. It may sound silly now, but in 1982 the Cold War between the NATO alliance and the WARSAW pact was still very much alive.

Each of our intercept aircraft could be armed with two Hughes AIM-4D Falcon air to air missiles as well as a pair of Boeing MB-1/AIR-2 nuclear missiles. As part of Canada's commitment to NORAD the squadron maintained two aircraft, armed with Falcon missiles, in a state of high readiness which had to be airborne within five minutes of an alert being called. It was always exciting to hear the "**BOOM! BOOM!**" of the afterburners igniting. Each of the two Pratt & Whitney J57-P-55 turbojets produced 16,900 pounds of thrust. In other words, they were a very efficient method of turning raw JP-4 aviation fuel into unadulterated noise. Sometimes late at night you could hear the Q-birds, the armed aircraft positioned in the Quick Response Area or QRA, thundering down the runway as they were launched on a vectoring intercept with an unidentified aircraft encroaching on NORAD's airspace.

My shop, or section, was responsible for maintaining the aircraft emergency egress system (ejection seats), the liquid oxygen breathing system and the deceleration or drag chute system. The remainder of the aircrew personal survival equipment - including the survival seat pack, the pilot's parachute, helmet and Mae West life preserver - was inspected and maintained by the Base Safety Systems section. As a young private, my only job was to learn whatever I could from all the technicians who had more T.I. (time in) than myself. In other words, everybody. Actually, I had three jobs. As previously mentioned, I had to learn as much as I could but I also had to do as I was told and try not to get into trouble. With only some minor difficulties I did my best at all three. I was like a sponge trying to absorb every scrap of knowledge and trick of the trade that was passed on to me.

Sergeant John Dutchyn, Master Corporals Gil Bullock, Bill Ellison, Harry Robertson and Ian Neilson and all the corporals in the shop had a lot of valuable information. If I could only learn one tenth of their amassed experience I would be leaps and bounds over anyone who shunned the opportunity. I felt that this concept was so important that I would continue to promote it later in my career when I had junior technicians working for me.

One of my first tasks was the inspection and maintenance of the deceleration (drag) chutes that were used to slow the Voodoos on landing. There were fifteen aircraft in the squadron. The two Q-birds often flew twice and sometimes three times a day. That meant six spent chutes. The main flight line was comprised of A and B Flights with six aircraft each.[6] Mind you, not every plane went flying every day. Some of them were in for maintenance and sometimes the aircrew were unavailable to fly. Out of a dozen available aircraft, at least eight would fly twice a day. That's another sixteen chutes. Add to that all the visiting transient aircraft that also used drag chutes. CF-104 Starfighters, CF-116 (F-5) Freedom Fighters, the US Air National Guard F-106 Delta Dart and the numerous variants of the US Navy and Marine F-4 Phantoms. Interestingly enough, since the Voodoo and the Phantom were both built by McDonnell Douglas, by some quirk of fate the design of the drag chute had not changed. The only significant difference between the two of them occurred during the installation process as the drag chute in the F-4 was placed in an

---

[6] I know, two planes in the QRA and six in each flight only added up to fourteen. The fifteenth Voodoo, A/C 101057 had been damaged in an accident and was permanently grounded. It is now mounted as the gate guardian at CFB Comox painted in the Hawk One paint scheme.

inverted position from that of the CF-101. The deployed drag chutes were released from the aircraft on the runway at the high speed cut-off and later collected by safety systems technician assigned to the flight line servicing crew.

Work in the Drag chute section was a never ending cycle. Not only did the spent chutes have to be repacked but old chutes, worn beyond their limits, would have to be reduced to scrap and replacements built up with new components. According to the Canadian Forces Technical Orders (CFTOs) the service life of a Voodoo's main drag chute was twenty-five deployments but, depending on the availability of replacement parts, these chutes were often extended to twice that. Mondays were the worst because nobody packed any of the spent chutes during the weekend. Sometimes there would be a dozen or more, piled on the floor next to the packing table. If they were wet, as they often were in Comox, they would be hung up to dry in the parachute well, a thirty-foot tall humidity controlled and ventilated shaft.

As a young nugget private I spent a great deal of time doing nothing but building and packing chutes. Sometimes, when the flying was exceptionally heavy, the chutes would be piled nearly waist high on the shop floor. All of them had to be inspected and repacked. Working day in and day out on just one task was called paying your dues and if you were good at it, and you kept your nose clean, you might even get to touch an aircraft in about six months. One person from my Basic Trades Course in Borden who didn't quite understand this concept spent almost a year packing spent drag chutes for the three squadrons of CF-104 Starfighters at CFB Cold Lake before she was allowed to train in another section.

A couple of months after I had arrived I was up on an aero stand washing down the ass end of a Voodoo. As part of the Primary Inspection every trade had a portion of the aircraft assigned to them: fitters did the underside of the aircraft and riggers did the top side. The safety systems trade was responsible for cleaning the rear end of the empennage that included the drag chute bucket. This area was prone to being particularly filthy as it was directly above the flow of the engine exhaust. To clean the surface of the aircraft we used varsol and some cloth rags. No mask. No gloves. No environmental protection. No hazmat. Just an open bucket and some rags. Wipe it on and wipe it off.

"McMillan!"

I thought to myself, "I know that voice". Looking down from my perch a dozen feet off the ground I saw WO McKendry standing on the hangar floor. "Yes, Warrant" I replied.

"I want to see you in my office right now."

"As soon as I am done my job, Sir." At which point, I began to wash the aircraft down for a second time. Out of the corner of my eye I could see McKendry standing below, looking up at me and the longer he stood there the slower I got. Finally, he gave up and walked away. "See me when you're done, McMillan!"

Ten minutes later I finished the job and, after putting everything away, I went to his office in Servicing. "You wanted to see me, Sir?"

Exerting his command, WO McKendry bellowed, "Get a haircut, McMillan!"

"Yes, Sir."

WO McKendry was pure old school. He preferred to refer to his technicians as "airmen." As the head of flight servicing he ruled with an iron fist and common sense. Nobody dared to screw up because you would have to suffer his wrath but at the same time nobody from outside the unit would dare mess with "his people" because he was so protective of us. Once, during a major NORAD exercise, McKendry looked into the crew room and saw that almost everyone was lounging about half asleep.

"Everyone outside in three ranks!" he shouted.

Both servicing crews and the USAF weapons techs filed outside into the drizzling rain wondering what in the hell was going on. But, there was no sense in arguing. You just did as you were told.

"Three ranks! Double arms distance! Move it!"

McKendry looked us over a couple of times and once we were positioned to his satisfaction he gave us the following words of command. "Take your right hand and touch your left foot! Now take your left hand and touch your right foot!" After ten or fifteen minutes of doing regimented toe touchies we were now wide awake before being ordered back inside where it was dry.

There was an ebb and flow in the shop. Some days the drag chutes waiting to be packed were piled high and some days we would almost fight over who got to pack them because we were so bored. But there were always chutes to pack and everyone took their turn. Unless of course you had an excuse. Corporal Turcotte always had an excuse.

Corporal Byron Turcotte was a tall lanky guy who had remustered from the PPCLI[7]. He did not drink. He did not smoke. He loved the ladies. And, he loved playing sports. The one thing that Byron didn't like was work and he always had a reason for not doing it. Baseball tournaments and hockey practice were his perennial seasonal favourites peppered with hanging out at Air Force Beach. Once, during a weekend servicing shift, Cpl Turcotte took the drag chute truck down to the beach where the Military Police found him playing beach volleyball when he should have been carrying out his servicing checks on the alert aircraft. Naturally, all of this athletic activity occasionally lead to an injury of some sort. Byron's current injury was described as an over extension of his right arm for which he was medically placed on light duties. Under the orders of the Base Surgeon, Cpl Turcotte was not to engage in lifting objects over five pounds or carrying bulky items and he was not be moving his right arm in a swinging motion. Therefore, twice a week he would travel by inter-base transport to CFB Esquimalt to undergo physiotherapy and until further notice he was excused from carrying out any flight line servicing functions, participating in parade formations and just

---

[7] The PPCLI, Princess Patricia's Canadian Light Infantry, is one of Canada's infantry regiments.

about any damn thing where he might just have to swing his arm which included packing drag chutes.

This really pissed me off because while the bunch of us would be sweating our asses off stuffing twenty-five pounds of shit into a ten pound bag good old Byron would be sitting back drinking a coffee or reading a magazine. He played the medical orders to the max and wouldn't lift a finger to help anyone out. But the one thing that Byron forgot was that those very same orders excluded him from participating in sport activities too.

So, there I was…Carrying out the task of the Base Duty Private. During my five hour shift I was to ensure that personnel utilizing the Base Gymnasium were doing so with appropriate authorized footwear (NO STREET SHOES ALLOWED), that any sports equipment issued was recovered by the end of my shift and that any damage to the facility or physical altercations were to be reported to the proper authorities. A pretty simple job really. You hand out basketballs and tell people to clean their shoes before hitting the floor. Other than that, you sit in the office bored to tears.

I looked up from my book and what did I see? Cpl Byron Turcotte playing badminton for all he was worth. Smashing down the shuttlecock to win point after point.

At first I really didn't want him to see me but I knew that it was inevitable as I would have to conduct a patrol of the facility. Sure enough, as soon as I left the office Turcotte spotted me walking through the gymnasium and when I returned he was waiting for me.

"If you say anything about this at work I'll kick your ass!" he threatened.

I have never responded well to threats. It kind of gets my back up, if you know what I mean.

"Well Corporal, I think if you are well enough to play badminton then you should be well enough to pack some drag chutes. And, as for kicking my ass... that would constitute an assault charge."

The following morning I took my turn packing chutes along with Cpl Rick Kroeker and MCpl Ellison. Cpl Turcotte sat at the small table reading one of MCpl Neilson's many Time magazines. As I finished off another chute, I caught his eye and motioned towards the packing table. In reply, almost imperceptibly, Byron closed his fist and shook his head.

Well, I had nothing to lose but fear and common sense.

"Sergeant Dutchyn, can I speak to you in your office?"

"Sure, c'mon in."

And, as God is my witness, when I walked into that office Cpl Turcotte stood up from the table, stretched out his arms and proclaimed to everyone in the shop that he was feeling pretty good that day and maybe he should try to pack a drag chute or two.

"What did you want to ask me, Blaine?"

"Is it true that we're getting every Friday afternoon off work?"

"I don't think so Private! Now get back to work and stop wasting my time!"

"Yes, Sergeant!"

Eventually, I was moved from the drag chute shop out onto the active flight line. Back in the early 1980's the flight line at CFB Comox, what with four active squadrons and all kinds of visiting aircraft, was a very busy place. As previously mentioned, my squadron had fifteen CF-101B Voodoos. The CP-140 Auroras at 407 Squadron were constantly patrolling for Soviet submarines in the waters off of the Pacific coast. Over at 442 Search and Rescue Squadron, the CC-115 Buffalos and CH-113 Labrador helicopters were always active while VU-33 Squadron kept their venerable CP-121 Trackers and CT-133 Silverstars in the air assisting the other units and Federal Fisheries. Depending on the flight schedule the activity on the flight line was pretty much non-stop.

A typical day in 409 Squadron began with the two Q-birds lifting off for a patrol at 0800 hrs. This would be followed by a launch of five or six aircraft from the main flight line at 0900 hrs. Sometimes there would be a second morning flight departing at 1030 hrs. In the afternoon the aircraft from the main flight line would launch at about 1300 hrs with the Q-birds carrying out a second patrol at about 1400 hrs. On top of that there may also be night flights.

With an internal fuel capacity of about 7800 litres or 13,000 pounds, the flight duration of a CF-101 Voodoo was about an hour and in that time it could cover 2,500 kilometres. Prior to any flight the various aircraft trades technicians would perform a *Before Flight* inspection, commonly referred to as a B check. On its return, an aircraft would undergo an A check or *After Flight* inspection. If the aircraft was going up for another flight within two hours of landing, a combination of the *After Flight* and *Before Flight* inspections, known as A/B check, would be done. Regardless of which kind of servicing inspection was required whenever a Voodoo landed the drag chute would routinely be deployed and a freshly packed chute would have to be installed. That's where I came in. As a newly minted safety systems technician I had the most enjoyable task of replacing spent drag chutes with new ones and then retrieving the spent ones from the drop zone at the high speed cut off. In Comox the job was often wet and dirty but it was anything but dull. When one of our Voodoos returned from a flight I would position the servicing truck under the tail of the aircraft and climb up the ladder at the rear of the truck. On the right hand side of the empennage was an access panel held fast with a dozen or more dzus fasteners. With the aid of a large common screwdriver, I could pop off the panel in seconds and drop it onto the platform atop the truck. It was a simple matter of jamming the shackle into the locking jaws and, after giving the riser a quick tug to ensure that it was secured, I would then slide the chute into the fiberglass bucket mounted inside the tip of the tail. Finishing the installation required a co-ordinated slam of the drag chute door, the access panel needed to be remounted in place and finally the "remove before flight" flag was yanked out to "arm" the drag chute. Total time required under optimal conditions…ten minutes. Total time required in a driving west coast rainstorm…three minutes…tops!

Other than stuffing drag chutes into the ass end of an aircraft, the most noticeable job carried out on the flight line by a safety systems technician was replenishing the liquid oxygen system.

In order to survive at altitudes above 10,000 feet, human beings must be provided with an oxygen (O_2) breathing system. Early military aircraft were fitted with a low pressure gaseous O_2 system. It was comprised of numerous storage cylinders and hundreds of feet of plumbing. Later, new innovations led to planes being fitted with a high pressure gaseous O_2 system, which weighed less overall and was much more efficient. The Voodoos and most of today's modern fighter aircraft have a liquid oxygen or lox system. Once again, by reducing the weight of the components and increasing the efficiency, the lox system was a vast improvement over a high pressure gaseous system. Liquid oxygen is a cryogenic liquefied gas with a boiling point of minus 183° Celcius. Lox has many industrial purposes from gold mining to rocket fuel but when used by aircrew for assisted breathing one particular property comes to the forefront. Liquid oxygen expands at a rate of 860 times its volume at the same pressure meaning a very small amount of lox can provide a lot of 100% pure gaseous oxygen. Despite what you may have seen in the movies it is impossible to breathe liquid oxygen. But, after travelling through a series of differential pressure check valves, plumbing and heat exchangers, the lox will have expanded in a controlled manner to a gaseous state and is at a breathable temperature. Canadian Forces fighter aircraft, depending on the aircraft type and the number of users, were fitted with either a five or a ten litre liquid oxygen converter. The venerable C-130 Hercules also has a lox converter and having a large number of aircrew stations, it utilizes a twenty-five litre converter.

On Mondays, Wednesdays and Fridays, come rain or shine, the squadron's safety systems technicians working the morning shift would be at 7 Hangar by 05:45 hrs with loxing operations starting around 06:00 hrs. We would begin with the planes parked in the QRA and then proceed to the aircraft parked on the main flight line. Our squadron's planes were always serviced first before moving on to any visiting fighter aircraft which could be a CF-104, a CF-116 or some American F-4 Phantoms. Some days we wouldn't finish replenishing all of the planes until 08:30 hrs and will have gone through two full carts or 100 US gallons of liquid oxygen.

Working in flight servicing became a passion for me. Every day was a different day. Sure, the aircraft were continually being launched on a routine schedule but the numbers of planes sent aloft and the various types of visiting aircraft were far from routine. And so were the maintenance issues, or snags as they were called.

Problems on the aircraft were divided into two categories, majors and minors. An entry in the Aircraft Unserviceability Report (CF 349) is a major entry and the aircraft cannot be flown until the problem is rectified or downgraded to a minor entry. An entry in Aircraft Minor Defect Record (CF 336) is also classified as a major entry until a technician, who is both qualified and authorized, signs the centre column. By doing so the technician is certifying that the defect has been inspected and the aircraft is safe to be flown. At this point, the problem is considered to be a minor entry which would be fixed at a later date. In other words, an aircraft could still fly with a minor snag that was not rectified as long as a technician certified it first.

One of the most persistent problems on any flight line are birds. Not only are they a hazard when the aircraft are flying but they are also a huge problem when the aircraft are on the ground. In Canada, the principal bird nesting season is from May to September. During this time period any aircraft parked out on the tarmac is a prime target for birds who will build a complete nest in any small opening on an aircraft. Bird nests can and will jam flight controls, close off air intakes and damage wiring. It is the job of the ground crew to inspect the aircraft as often as every four hours to remove the nests and anything that may be in them. Naturally, another option is to remove the birds.

Some bird species that reside in a hangar are quite beneficial. Swallows, for example, consume vast quantities of annoying insects and they roost not in the aircraft but high in the rafters of the hangar. Owls and other raptors are also acceptable in a hangar because they prey on vermin and small birds. No, the species of bird that was most troublesome in 7 Hangar were European Starlings.[8] These little buggers could build a complete nest in less than an hour and as soon as it was removed they would be right back at it. After gathering grass and sticks from the infield, they quickly fly into any opening and begin to weave a nest. As soon as a technician removes the nest the expecting parents start building one all over again in a never ending see-saw battle. The squadron's technicians were fed up with having to deal with the starlings and they wanted something done about them. At one time there was a product called ticky tack. It was like a double sided tape that would be placed on the rafters of the hangar. One side of it was really gummy and if a bird landed on it the bird was held fast until it perished from starvation. It was extremely effective, but unfortunately it did not discriminate between good birds and bad birds so the use of ticky tack was discontinued. The use of poisoned seed was also refused for the same reason. The squadron was at a loss as to how it could reduce the burgeoning bird population. That was, until the Crew Chiefs from Snags and Servicing came up with an idea.

---

[8] The common or "European" starling is an invasive species deliberately introduced into North America in the late 1890's by the American Acclimatization Society in New York City's Central Park. By 1950, they had reached the Pacific coast of North America. In the winter its flocks can number as many as 20,000 individuals.

"On Saturday morning, all those individuals who own a pellet rifle and who wish to participate in the First Annual 409 Sqn Bird Hunt will report to the Snags Desk at 08:00 hrs. Coffee and ammunition will be supplied."

And, so it began. First thing on Saturday morning the weekend duty crew towed all aircraft out of the hangar and left the doors open while the 'hunters' had a coffee. The hangar doors were closed and the shooting started. Twenty minutes later the hangar doors were opened while everyone took a break. After a quick smoke break, the doors were closed and the shooting re-commenced. For the next three hours this pattern was repeated over and over again until finally at noon a ceasefire was called. After lunch everyone grabbed a broom and began to sweep the hangar floor. The bodies of the fallen were bagged and taken to the dumpster. How many starlings were killed? If memory serves me correctly the average 'hunter' had taken down about 40+ starlings with a high count of over 80. It was a lot of birds. In the end, there were a lot fewer starlings in the aerodrome and a lot fewer bird nests were found in the aircraft for years to come.

Yes, life in 409 Squadron servicing was an interesting place to work. So imagine my surprise when one fine Friday afternoon in the summer of 1983 I found myself working in servicing with a skeleton crew. The rest of the squadron was participating in a beer call, which was a mandatory part of squadron life back then. A beer call was a means for the members of a unit, be it a section or an entire squadron, to gather socially to enjoy each other's company, tell tall tales and drink beer. All of which was quite acceptable. Not attending a squadron beer call was almost treasonous.

So there I was…On a sunny Friday afternoon. With none of our aircraft flying there wasn't really much to do except wait for my shift to end. At the time Sgt "Spider" Crawford was manning the servicing desk.

"Watch the phone Private. I have to go to the bathroom."

Sure enough, within a minute of his departure the phone rang.

"409 Squadron servicing. Private McMillan speaking. How may I help you?"

"Yeah. Get a hold of Larry. Tell him that me and the boys are coming down for some beers."

"Uh...Larry, sir?"

"Yes! Larry Lott, your Commanding Officer! Tell him that we'll be there in about 45 minutes."

"Sir, where are you calling from?"

"Cold Lake."

"And, you're going to be here in 45 minutes?"

"That's right."

"Get stuffed!" I replied, just before hanging up the phone.

It sounded quite preposterous to me that someone could be calling from the servicing shack in Cold Lake, Alberta and say that he was going to be landing at Comox, British Columbia in less than an hour. It's almost 1200 km. between the two bases.

On his return from the washroom Sgt Crawford asked, "Did anyone phone?"

"Yes, Sergeant Crawford. Someone from Cold Lake called and told me that he and the boys would be here in forty-five minutes to have a beer with the CO."

I was waiting for Sgt Crawford's snort of derision but it didn't happen. Instead, he calmly picked up the phone and called the squadron's operation centre.

"Hello, Ops? This is Sgt Crawford at the servicing desk. Do we have any inbound aircraft? Okay. How many? Eight. Thanks Ops."

And then, turning to me he said, "Well Private. You had better be prepared to receive eight 104's. They will be landing in about forty minutes."

Eight CF-104s! I hadn't counted on that. The CF-104D Starfighter was like a manned missile that moved through the sky at over Mach 2. It could easily cover the distance between Cold Lake and Comox in less than an hour and when they arrived I would have to install the fresh drag chutes. The storage bins on the drag chute truck carried a number of spare chutes. Sixteen for Voodoos or F-4 Phantoms, four for CF-116 Freedom Fighters and four for the CF-104 Starfighters. It was obvious that I would need more. And, in a hurry.

True to his word, in less than an hour from the initial call, eight 104s landed in Comox. They deployed their drag chutes and taxied onto our flight line. After installing a new chute in each

Starfighter, and retrieving the spent ones, I headed into the servicing shack. Waiting at the desk was the Commanding Officer of 417 Squadron.

"Where in the hell is Pte McMillan?"

It was a very short expletive filled conversation. Pretty much one sided, too. The Lieutenant-Colonel did all of the talking and I did all of the listening.

Lesson learned.

Wednesday, August 31, 1983

I was working night shift on the flight line. In the early evening the Q-birds had carried out a routine night patrol and had returned to base at about 2100 hrs. Once they had been turned around and the flight servicing checks completed my shift was over. Unlike the other air trades, safety systems technicians did not hold a standby position in the QRA. Instead, whoever was slated for the night shift duty carried a pager that sounded off like a klaxon when the alert aircraft were launched. The duty technician would rush into work, jump into the drag chute truck and head to the QRA. If the aircraft had already returned, serviceable chutes would be installed as part of the A and B checks. The spent chutes would be collected at the high speed cut-off before the technician went home. Back at the section the spent chutes were then suspended in the parachute well and the truck re-loaded with its full complement of chutes.

Once the drag chute truck had been restocked I headed for home. It was a short drive to my apartment, about a mile from the

Base, so I was usually home in time to catch the nightly news with Lloyd Robertson. To my utter shock the lead story on tonight's newscast was the downing of Korean Airlines Flight 007 by the Soviet military forces.[9]

The first news report was sketchy at best. It seems that an airliner had strayed off course and into Soviet airspace over the Kamchatka peninsula. Initially, the Boeing 747 was thought to be a US Air Force RC-135 aircraft that had been flying an infinity lazy-8 pattern off the coast monitoring Soviet radio transmissions and collecting other military data. The Soviets knew the RC-135 was patrolling their eastern coast but as it had remained outside their territorial limit there was absolutely nothing they could do about it. When Flight KAL-007 strayed across the border the Soviets, believing it was the American reconnaissance aircraft, sent two SU-15 fighters (NATO code named Flagon) on an intercept course and also a Mig-23 fighter/interceptor (NATO code name Flogger). The lead SU-15 fighter pilot, Major Osipovich, tried several times to make contact with the intruder and when all attempts failed the Soviet ground controllers commanded the air defence pilots to shoot down the invader. What follows, in part, is the Soviet portion of a coordinated transcript intercepted by a listening post at Wakkanai, Japan and was released publicly on 07 September 1983 to the United Nations Security Council.[10] In 1993, a transcript of communications of

---

[9] Flight KAL 007 was a 747-230B with 29 crew and 240 passengers. It was enroute to Seoul Korea from New York via Anchorage, Alaska.

Soviet Air Defence Command Centres on Sakhalin Island was released after a change in government in the USSR. The cockpit voice recorder (CVR), which was secretly withheld for ten years, was released at the same time.[11]

Time UTC   **Comment**

1551 hrs   KAL 007 entered Soviet airspace over the Kamchatka Peninsula.

1745 hrs   KAL 007 re-entered international airspace over the Sea of Okhotsk.

1749 hrs   Capt. Solodkov: "Two pilots have just been sent up, command at the command post, we do not know what is happening just now, it's heading for our island (Sakhalin), to Terpienie (Bay) somehow, this looks very suspicious to me, I don't think the enemy is stupid, can it be one of ours?

---

[10] On 7 September 1983, Japan and the United States jointly released a transcript of Soviet communications, intercepted by the listening post at Wakkanai, Japan to an emergency session of the United Nations Security Council. These intercepts captured only one side of the Soviet transmissions - those of the high-flying fighter aircraft. The International Civil Aviation Organization (ICAO) co-ordinated the times of Soviet transmissions with the time-stamped communications intercepted by Japan, as well as air traffic control recordings, to create a complete picture of events. Some Air Combat Controller fighter vectoring, fuel readouts and inter-command post "chatter" is not included in the transcript for clarity..

[11] Korean Airlines Flight 007 Transcripts, Wikisource, https://en.wikisource.org, 06 June 2016.

First documented order for shoot down

1753 hrs   General Anatoli Kornukov, commander of Sokol Airbase on Sakhalin to the command post of General Valeri Kamenski, Commander of Air Defence Forces for the Far East Military District,"…simply destroy (it) even if it is over neutral waters? Are the orders to destroy it over neutral waters? Oh, well."

Ground controllers are given orders on how to direct the jets to intercept

1800 hrs Kornukov: Bring him up bring Osipovich in to the prescribed distance. You do not engage him to the target from the aft hemisphere, you do not engage him right on the tail, keep the angle of approach.

Kozlov [Fighter Control, Sokol airbase]: "Roger, executing."

Kornukov: "Don't forget, it [the target] has cannons in the rear there"

Kozlov: "Roger, executing."

Kornukov: "But faster, for the fighter, rather, the target is entering the zone above the one-hundred-kilometers waters [identification zone]."

Kozlov: "Wilco"

Ring! Ring!
"Hello?"
"Blaine?"

"Hi Robbie. What's up?"

"Get into work right away and bring an away-bag!"

"What's going on? And, what's an away-bag?"

"Have you seen the news? The squadron has been placed on alert. So, get your ass into work and bring a bag with whatever you need for a couple of days' cause we may be going away."

Following my boss's orders, I grabbed a bunch of socks, underwear, a pair of pants, a couple of t-shirts, a jacket and my shaving gear, crammed it all into a bag and sped off to work. By the time I returned work the flight line was already a buzz. The squadron's technicians were now pouring into 7 Hangar where the aircraft were undergoing B checks before being towed out. MCpl Robertson and I were tasked to top off all the aircraft with liquid oxygen. As we headed down the apron to the cryogenics building to retrieve a lox cart the other members of the section were gathering together the deployment gear. Tools, some spare drag chutes and the portable packing press were packaged up for loading onto a transport aircraft. Within an hour of the initial call the CF-101 Voodoos of 409 Squadron were nearly ready. The B checks had been completed, protective plugs and covers were removed and lox had been topped off. As we took the lox cart back to the building we watched as the armourers trained out the weapons. There were two or three towing mules with a number of trailers behind each of them and on each trailer were two missile coffins each containing a single Hughes AIM-4D Falcon missile. And then we waited for the word to go. All of the start crews, having been assigned to a specific aircraft, sat in the servicing shack while the aircrew were upstairs in the squadron briefing room and the load crews babysat their packages out on the tarmac.

In a discussion with my former commanding officer, Colonel (retired) Larry Lott, I was informed that NORAD had indeed placed 409 Squadron, and presumably all the other NORAD intercept squadrons, on a high state of readiness but the weapons had not been loaded onto the aircraft. Eventually, cooler heads prevailed and the squadron was ordered to stand down.

With 409 Squadron soon to be closing, somebody higher up the food chain decided that all outstanding supply requests had to be fulfilled before the end of the fiscal 1983 year. For the federal government and its agencies that would be 31 March 1984. Without warning, the main supply group in 7 Hangar began calling the various sections in the squadron for items to be picked up. All manner of equipment or parts were being delivered including things that had been ordered for an aircraft that had been in maintenance four or five years earlier. I was sent down to pick up a drag chute release cable. Shouldn't be a problem. Except, it was a clad cable, which meant that it was a cable inside of a metal tube and it was almost the length of the aircraft. The next day I had to pick up some mottled brown naugahyde (leatherette) that somebody had ordered three years earlier. The amount ordered was 100 feet (f). But, the unit of issue is in metres (m). So, instead of converting 100 feet into 30 metres, some enterprising supply technician (aka a Bin Rat) simply changed unit of issue (f) to (m) and as a result we ended up with three bolts of naugahyde, 33 metres in length each. What the hell were we supposed to do with three times the amount we had requested when the unit was closing in less than six months? You couldn't take it back. Cloth and other similar materials were identified as Class C or consumable stock. Supply didn't want it, that's for sure. That's when the horse trading started.

Somebody must have let it slip that we had some "extra stuff." Sure enough, someone came sniffing around. MCpl "Oggie" Ogden walked in to the shop with a request.

"Hey, Ian. I was looking for some kind of material to recover the seats of my eighteen foot boat. You have anything that might be usable?"

"It just so happens that we do," MCpl Neilson replied. "Blaine, show him the stuff that came in yesterday."

I walked past the drag chute packing table and pointed out the three bolts of material. "How does this look to you, Master Corporal?"

"Looks great!"

"How much do you need, Oggie?" Ian asked.

"Well, my 18 foot runabout has those fold down seats that are built facing back to back. I need enough to tuck under at both ends, I think about ten feet for each seat. So, twenty feet should just about do it."

MCpl Neilson and I placed a brand new bolt of mottled brown naugahyde at one end of the drag chute table, ran out three full lengths of the packing table and cut it off.

"That looks like twenty feet to me," Ian said.

After folding the material into a double walled garbage bag MCpl Ogden asked if we would be interested in some one hundred foot long heavy duty grounded extension cords with a multiple female end. It seems that supply issued one for every order that had been previously cancelled. He had ten extras that he was giving away.

By the spring of 1984 the number of personnel in the squadron was being reduced. All of the sections were losing people. Heavy aircraft maintenance was now closed. The drag chute shop was down to five or six people. A sergeant, a master corporal or two, a couple of corporals and me. It was during this time when we had a high ranking VIP come for a visit. The Spanish monarch, King Juan Carlos, had come to view the Canadian military's new F-18 Hornets that were being flogged by the American military industrial complex.

I don't know the political reasons why the King of Spain couldn't have done this in the United States but I think there may have been other financial reasons behind the visit. The perpetually struggling Canadian aircraft manufacturing industry also had products that they were desperately trying to market and with King Juan Carlos being a pilot it would be an excellent opportunity to highlight their own aircraft.

The official state visit kicked off in Ottawa on March 12, 1984. The visit to CFB Comox was to be the following Saturday, March 17, 1984. Everything was to be low key. No press. No parade. Just the king, his security detail as well as a complete Canadian government dog & pony show entourage. His Royal Highness would arrive on a De Havilland Dash-8 and would depart on a Canadair Challenger. Two CF-188 Hornets, looking sleek and mean, had arrived the day before. I was told that the Spanish monarch had wanted to go flying but both of the fighters from CFB Cold Lake were single seat aircraft. One was to be on static display and the other on flying status. We carefully wiped down every exposed part of the static display plane - lest His Royal Highness rub up against a greasy landing gear - and positioned a couple of maintenance platforms 'just so' to provide a perfect view of the cockpit.[12]

To observe the air demonstration in all its ear-splitting glory, the Royal Entourage mounted the viewing deck on the second floor of 7 Hangar. Sheltered under the gray-green nylon gazebo they watched as the pilot looped, rolled and generally punched high speed holes in the clear blue sky. This is when things got really interesting.

---

[12] As reported in The Prince George Citizen, (March 19, 1984) "At the armed forces base in Comox, the 46 year-old king who had originally hoped to fly an F-18 military aircraft was unable to because his itinerary didn't allow for briefing time on the aircraft. However, he was delighted with a green summer flying jacket emblazoned with the word "king" in gold lettering that was presented to him."

On this particular day, a good friend of mine, Private Jim Morrison, (not of *The Doors*) was working as the duty Met technician. The Meteorological section was located on the second floor at the north-east corner of 7 Hangar, which just happens to be at the same level as the viewing deck. Jim was totally unaware of the goings on when he stepped out from the office to do his weather observation. Standing on either side of the access door was a member of the King's security detail. In a flash, Pte Morrison was spun round and pinned to the wall by one man-mountain as the second one swept back his trench coat to pull a machine pistol from a belt clip.

Thrusting the gun against Jim's chest, he demanded, "What are you doing here?"

"I'm just a Met tech doing my observation," Jim stammered nervously.

"Can you do it from the ground?"

"Yes."

"Good. Do it then!"

Released from a potentially deadly situation Jim made a hasty retreat back into his section, locked the door and placed a "Do Not Use" sign over the window. In the meantime, much to the delight of the onlookers the Hornet was still zooming all around the aerodrome. Those of us down on the ground in 409 Sqn servicing really appreciated the first-hand look at Canada's newest plane as well. On landing, the sleek gray fighter/bomber taxied in and stopped on the center helipad directly in front of 7 Hangar. Then, deliberately, the pilot folded the right hand wing tip to the stowed position and then unfolded it back to the flight position. The pilot had just saluted King Juan Carlos of Spain! I don't know if this feature was germane to his decision but in 1986 the Spanish Air Force began to receive the first of 72 F/A-18 aircraft to replace their aging fleet of F-4C Phantoms, F-5 Freedom Fighters and Mirage IIIs. The king must not have been impressed with the other aircraft as Spain did not purchase the DeHavilland Dash-8 nor the Canadair Challenger.

After work and over a round of beer, Jim and I compared notes on the day.

"The King of Spain was in to see the Hornets."

"I know," retorted Jim. "His guards almost shot me!"

"Okay, you win!"

A month after the royal visit, 409 Squadron hosted a final Voodoo aircraft exercise between the members of 425 Squadron and ourselves. The two squadrons were pitted against each other in a friendly rivalry to seek out enemy aircraft hiding along the lengthy British Columbia coastline. The target aircraft fleet was comprised of CT-133 Silverstars and an EF-101B Voodoo from North Bay, Ontario. Commonly referred to as the "Electric Voodoo", aircraft CF-101067 had been outfitted with an electronic jamming suite taken from a USAF Martin EB-57E Canberra bomber and was used to hone the abilities of Canada's interceptor aircrew. The target aircraft would take off prior to the chase planes and head for one of the many fjords along the province's coastline to hide in. The chase planes, paired off from both squadrons, would then go hunting for them. Kills were registered on the NADAR tape that was later reviewed for crew and fire control performance.

The exercise went on for most of the week with the flying taking place around the clock. In order to feed the hungry masses a secondary kitchen located on the middle floor of 7 Hangar was pressed into use. Food, consisting of over-fried pork chops, cold boiled potatoes and luke warm mixed vegetables, was brought over from the main mess hall in hay boxes. My mother always said that beggars can't be choosers and if nothing else, it filled your stomach. It was during a late meal session that I overheard an interesting conversation. Sitting across from me were two aircrew members, Captain "Speedy" Fast, a CT-133 pilot, and Captain Bernie Hughes, a 409 Squadron Navigator/Weapons Systems operator. Being only a Private, I kept my head down and focused on my plate of cold offerings.

"I'm telling you Speedy, the safety systems trade is good for hardly anything. Oxygen and drag chutes, that's it. The rest of their trade can be absorbed by another."

"I don't think so, Bernie," replied Speedy.

I was in total shock at hearing this little snippet. Here was an aircrew member whose very survival depended on members of my trade doing their job. Sure, the engines could fail or a wing could fall off, but if any portion of his survival system was maintained incorrectly - from his flying helmet to his emergency life raft, the ejection seat or his parachute - then he was a dead man. There was nothing that I could say. Nor would I, for I was just a private, the lowest rung on the ladder. But I did want to know what to do if this situation ever arose again and for that I needed to ask someone who had more experience than I, namely my master corporal.

Now, despite being a self-centred pragmatist, MCpl Ian Neilson was my current immediate supervisor and so I took my case to him. I explained what had happened just a short time ago and asked what I should do if the situation ever arose again.

"It's quite simple," he replied. "If he ever comes to you to say, 'Thanks for being there' you tell him to go to hell."

Several months later the squadron was nearing the end of its existence. The venerable Voodoos were on their way out and were being replaced by the CF-188 Hornets. All of the CF-101 squadrons across the country were soon to be closing with 409 Squadron being the first to go. But until then the QRA would still be manned around the clock and regular sorties flown. There was much flying to do and the aircrew were bound and determined to rack up their flying hours simply by punching holes in the sky.

One afternoon I had just finished topping up a couple of transient US Navy F-4 Phantoms with liquid oxygen. They had been parked far down the flight line by the access to the QRA. After filling the lox converters I was returning the lox cart to the oxygen building when the two Q birds taxied out to the hold line. I watched as they sat there. Brakes on, engines running up, waiting for the word from the tower to go at which point they would ignite the afterburners, slip the brakes and rocket down the runway. It was always an impressive sight. But, something was wrong with this picture. The exhaust from the second aircraft, aircraft 101007, was thick and black like the exhaust from an F-4 Phantom. I immediately looked for help and saw Cpl Sandy Caravan walking on the flight line. I drove over to her and pointed to the Q birds.

"Holy shit! He's on fire! Call the tower!"

When Sandy started running across the infield I switched to the tower frequency.

"Tower, drag chutes."

"Go ahead 'chutes."

"There's a ground emergency on one of the Q-birds. It looks as if he could be on fire!"

"Can you identify which aircraft?"

"Tower, it's 007!"

"Thanks 'chutes!"

By the time I had relayed the info to the tower, Cpl Caravan had crossed the grass and was standing alongside the active runway. Motioning to the aircrew in aircraft 007, she began giving the ground signal for an engine fire by pointing to the affected engine with one hand and looping the other around in a big lazy eight.

Seeing her waving at him, the weapons operator in the back seat waved back.

"Hi!"

Sandy shook her head, "No!" And continued giving the big lazy eight signal, "Your engine is on fire!"

The tower must have reached them on the radio because suddenly I heard "Boom! Boom!" The lead plane lit its afterburners and screamed off down the runway while the pilot of aircraft 101007 chopped the fuel flow to both of the engines and raised the canopy. Both he and the navigator were in such a hurry to depart the aircraft that they un-strapped their seat harnesses and jumped from the cockpit more than ten feet off the ground. You could hardly blame them. With a potential fire on an armed aircraft waiting for a crew ladder was definitely not an option.

With the ground emergency secured aircraft 101007 was towed from the active runway. First it was taken back to the QRA to have the two Falcon missiles offloaded and then moved down the line to 7 Hangar where a full engine inspection could be carried out. The preliminary inspection revealed that raw JP-4 fuel had been flowing unchecked into the afterburner section of the engine to the point where it was running freely onto the ground. The uncontrolled fuel was being super-heated by the engine exhaust and that is why it looked like the dirty exhaust of an F-4 Phantom. After the engine was removed an in-depth inspection by the fitters (engine technicians) revealed two problems. The first snag was an unserviceable fuel control unit (FCU) for the afterburner. These devices control the fuel supplied to the combustion chamber of a jet turbine engine including the afterburners. They may be hydro-mechanically or electronically controlled. Simply put, the FCU is a valve that opens and closes as the pilot increases or decreases the throttle settings allowing more or less fuel to flow into the combustion chamber. When the pilot selects the afterburner setting the FCU opens to allow extra fuel to enter the afterburner and shuts off the fuel flow when it is deselected. In the case of aircraft 101007, the FCU on the afterburner FCU was stuck in the "OPEN" position before the afterburner setting had been selected and was allowing the raw fuel to flow through the afterburner section of the engine. Additionally, several of the pig-tails - the twisted fuel lines within the afterburner - were cracked which increased the flow of excess JP-4. In a conversation with a number of aero-engine techs, they stated that if the ignitors had been engaged the extra fuel pouring out of the afterburner section would have exploded destroying the entire armed aircraft.

While the squadron's fitters repaired the engine, my section determined that since the plane was going to be grounded for several weeks, we would have the time to change the time expired (tx'd) explosives used in the ejection system. Because the aircraft could still be flying for some time, just not with 409 Squadron, the tx'd charges would have to be changed by the end of the month. Due to safety concerns no other trades were allowed to work on the aircraft while we were changing the charges. But, it didn't take long. In just a few hours, we had changed out both front and rear seat catapults, all the initiators on both front and rear seats, the internal and external canopy initiator and the canopy extractor.

With the paperwork completed, aircraft 101007 was once again available for the other trades to work on.

By the time the fitters had finished repairing the engine it had been completely stripped down and rebuilt. The engine, which was mounted on a movable stand, was towed to the run-up building where it was connected to a set of external controls and a fuel tank before being put through a full set of test parameters. Any required adjustments were made and it was run again. Once this series of tests was completed the engine was remounted into aircraft 101007, the aircraft was then towed out to the run-up pad and chained to the ground. Next, a full engine ground run including the use of both afterburners was carried out. On completion, A/C 101007 was declared serviceable for flight. All was good.

So there I was…On the 22nd of June 1984, crossing the hangar floor to the flight servicing section to get a coffee. There were a large number of people, both ground crew and aircrew, working on raising a large winter white camouflage net as a false ceiling above the hangar floor. With the squadron shutting down, a massive reunion/close out party was planned for the end of June. Food, wine lists, entertainment and guest lists were created and the tasks were distributed throughout the unit. As I passed through the work party I overheard Captain Bernie Hughes talking to another air weapons officer.

"Your ride is ready to go!"

"I can't go. I have to get this damn camo net hung up!"

"Well, if you can't go then I'll take your ride."

"Go ahead."

Wandering into servicing I talked to couple of techs who were going to the party. I could tell that they were pretty excited about it. Unfortunately, I had drawn the short straw and had to cover the flight line servicing over the weekend. With a cup of coffee in hand, I headed toward our shop at the other end of the breezeway pausing just long enough to watch one of our Voodoos thunder off to punch more holes in the sky.

I had only walked forty feet down the breezeway when a two-bell crash alarm sounded followed by a voice from the control tower on the PA system.

"ATTENTION ALL PERSONNEL! THIS IS THE CONTROL TOWER! WE HAVE AN AIRBORNE EMERGENCY ON A CF-101 WITH TWO SOULS ON BOARD!"

At the sound of this announcement I turned and headed back toward the servicing shack. This was the plane that I had just watched taking off but I had not gone a dozen paces when a one bell alarm sounded followed by another message came over the PA system.

"ATTENTION ALL PERSONNEL! THIS IS THE CONTROL TOWER! THERE HAS BEEN A CRASH OF A CF-101!"

All normal activity on the aerodrome ground to a sudden halt as the entire Base waited for some word, some indication of the fate of the two aircrew. In the meantime, all aircraft in the circuit were ordered to land. All outbound flights, including civilian aircraft, were halted and told to taxi back to their starting positions. Ground emergency vehicles and personnel rolled out onto the tarmac and waited for further orders. There was no way of knowing what had caused the crash nor if the aircrew had ejected safely. Down the flight line the standby Labrador helicopter from 442 Search and Rescue (SAR) Squadron lifted off and headed south east. The standby SAR Buffalo was also starting up, its crew preparing to look for the two missing fighter aircrew.

By now Base Flight Safety knew which aircraft had crashed - CF 101007 - and had the names of the aircrew on board - Captain Tom Chester (pilot) and Captain Bernie Hughes (navigator/weapons systems operator). For each of the aircrew they needed to collect the CF-363 Aircraft Support Equipment Maintenance Record Set for the DH 41-2 helmet, the A-13A oxygen mask assembly, the aircrew mae west, the survival seat pack which contained, among other things, a radio and a single place life raft. They also needed the CF-363 for the B-5 parachutes. The CF-363 is commonly referred to as a log book as they are used to "log" or document all of the maintenance carried out on the aviation life support equipment (ALSE) including all of the inspections, parts replacements, modifications, special inspections and who carried out the work. The documentation of the work performed is critical. If it was determined that a piece of personal survival equipment failed to operate correctly and a resulting injury or death was attributed to improper maintenance the technician who had certified the equipment would be facing severe disciplinary actions.

The Base Flight Safety officer and his team headed for the Base Safety Systems section on the top floor of 7 Hangar to gather all the CF-363s.

"We need the log books for the seat packs in Voodoo 007 and for all the personal equipment for Captain Tom Chester and Captain Bernie Hughes!"

The shop supervisor, Warrant Officer Denis Hebert, quickly directed his personnel to retrieve the log books and in short order the maintenance books for the helmets and the life preservers were handed over to the flight safety team.

"Where are the rest of the books?"

"Sir, the log books for the seat packs are in the survival kits room and the books for the parachutes are downstairs in the chute shop. I'll take you there."

"Thanks, Corporal."

Crossing the hall, the flight safety team followed the corporal into the Kits Section and were provided with the log books for the survival seat packs including the books for the PRQ-501 radios and the single man rafts.

"Where's the parachute shop, Corporal?"

"It's one floor down, sir."

"Thanks. Let's go!"

On their arrival into the parachute section the Base Flight Safety officer asked MCpl Al Brodie for the parachute log books for Chester and Hughes.

Looking up at the locator rack, MCpl Brodie deftly pulled the CF-363 for Captain Chester's parachute and then looked for the next one. To simplify things, the log books in the locator rack were filed according to the squadron and then by alphabetical order according to the pilot's last name. The aircrew from both 409 and VU-33 Squadron wore emergency parachutes all the time. The CP-140 Auroras from 407 Squadron carried an emergency parachute for each aircrew position so they were listed according to the aircraft number they were installed on and then all of the spare parachutes were organized by their serial number.

"Sir, it would appear that Captain Hughes' parachute is currently on inspection."

"Well then, what the hell was he wearing?"

"He must have signed out a spare from the main shop, sir."

When an individual is assigned a parachute it must be fitted to the user. On opening, especially at high speeds, an improperly fitted parachute can cause physical damage to the user. Therefore, man-carrying parachutes are not to be loaned to another individual and if the user's chute is on inspection he or she must be fitted with a spare parachute from the Safety Systems section. Fitting a parachute to the user is a simple procedure that usually takes no more than ten minutes. The individual puts on the parachute, does up the harness and sits down on a chair. By loosening or tightening the webbing through the buckles the harness is adjusted to the user. The webbing is then hand tacked into position. In the winter months, the harness must be re-adjusted to accommodate the additional thickness of winter weight clothing.

The flight safety team went back upstairs to the main shop and inquired if Captain Hughes had signed out a spare parachute prior to his flight. He had not. Again the question was raised, "What the hell was he wearing?"

The remains of aircraft CF-101007 were found on Texada Island, its once sleek grey lines lay flattened in a charred heap of smoking twisted metal. The pieces of most military aircraft involved in a catastrophic accident crash would be strewn far and wide and bear little resemblance to its previous design. But, CF-101007 had not thundered in at a steep angle. Instead, it had fallen from the sky in a flat spin.

According to the DND Flight Safety Incident report, Occurrence Report: 32467, Voodoo 101007 was passing through 12000 feet at 380 KIAS (knots indicated airspeed) when a loud bang was heard and felt. The aircraft then yawed violently right. On investigation, the pilot had pushed the control stick forward with no effect and he observed flames coming from the right side of the aircraft at which point he ordered the crew to eject. Both aircrew landed in a heavily wooded area and had sustained minor injuries. The aircraft came to rest flat on the ground at N49° 46′ latitude W124° 36′ longitude.

A previously unreleased photo of the remains of CF-101007.

Inspection of the recovered wreckage revealed a rupture of the sixteenth stage compressor disc in the LH (left hand) engine. When the disc had ruptured it had blown apart with so much force that it had taken out the RH (right hand) engine. Without any forward speed the aircraft quickly began to fall in a flat spin, rotating clockwise from the initial violent RH yaw.

After being rescued by 442 Squadron, both of the aircrew were taken directly to the Base hospital for a thorough medical inspection. All of their clothing, from their flight gloves to their underwear and all personal survival equipment, was packaged and sent for an evaluation at the Defence and Civil Institute of Environmental Medicine (DCIEM) in Toronto, a component of Defence Research Development Canada (DRDC), that studies integrated human effectiveness, science and technology (S&T) in defence and national security. It provides the Canadian Forces (CF), government agencies, academia and industrial clients with an internationally recognized combination of expertise and research facilities. The whole purpose of sending the personal gear to DCIEM is to determine if the equipment used by the military provides for the safety and security of the user, especially when it is subjected to adverse environmental conditions such as being violently punted out of an aircraft at 400 KIAS in less than five seconds. If any piece of equipment is found to be deficient then modifications could be recommended in order to enhance its performance and the survivability of the aircrew.

DCIEM could not assess the performance of parachute issued to Capt Hughes for any stressors that may have occurred during an ejection sequence because he wasn't wearing it. It was found to be on inspection. The parachute that Capt Hughes wore wasn't a spare because he did not get fitted for one at Base Safety Systems prior to his flight. So, whose parachute was Captain Hughes wearing when he ejected out of Voodoo 007?

It is my contention that when Captain Hughes found that his personal parachute was on inspection, he was in such a rush to punch more holes in the sky that he simply grabbed the parachute of the person who had been assigned to take the flight in the first place. This would be the only logical choice. Captain Hughes would not have taken someone else's chute because anyone else may have to go for a flight.

According to Canadian Forces Technical Orders (CFTO's) pertaining to the maintenance of emergency parachutes[13] Paragraph 17 states: Parachute harnesses are designed to meet the following requirements during parachute deployment:

1. To withstand opening shock load;
2. To disperse the load throughout the harness structure;
3. To contain the body without injury or excessive discomfort.

Paragraph 18 of the same CFTO describes requirements incorporated into the parachute harness "such as adjustment, release and attachment for additional equipment and components"[14]

---

[13] Parachutes General, C-22-010-013/MF-000

and the *"proper fitting of parachute harnesses to the individual is essential to prevent injury or excessive shock loading".*[15]

Did Captain Hughes sustain his minor injuries as a result of the ejection process, landing in a heavily wooded area or by the ill-fitting parachute? Due to the violent nature of the occurrence it is unclear which process would have caused which injury. My contention is that his injuries would have minimized if he had been correctly fitted with a spare parachute.

There are many traditions in the military. Saluting, parades, beer calls. Another tradition is for the survivor of an ejection to offer a bottle of alcohol to the person who had packed the parachute. Kinda like, "Thanks for being there for me". Captain Hughes did take this traditional offering to MCpl Al Brodie. But Al turned it down stating, "If the captain hadn't taken the other parachute he may not have been injured."

Years later, I ran into Captain Hughes at the Herc Lounge, an all ranks Mess in Winnipeg. He was instructing at the Canadian Forces Air Navigation School (CFANS) and I was working in the Base Safety Systems section. After a bit, we sort of recognized each other and, just as when any two service members meet, we asked if we had previously served together. On hearing that I had been a safety systems technician with 409 Squadron at Comox, Captain Hughes asked, "Did you ever get your bottle?"

Well, I'm still waiting.

---

[14] Parachutes General, C-22-010-013/MF-000
[15] Parachutes General, C-22-010-013/MF-000

A rear view of a Quick Response (QRA) hangar with a CF-101 parked inside.

Moving Down the Line

With 409 Squadron closing there was a desperate need to move people to new places of employment. Some individuals, both technicians and aircrew, would continue working on the Voodoos in either Chatham, New Brunswick or Bagotville, Quebec until the last of the One-o-Wonders were phased out of the military's inventory while others were slated to begin work on the shiny new CF-188 Hornets. Each trade in the Canadian military has a career manager, usually a senior person of that particular trade group. Often it is a chief warrant officer for the non-commissioned personnel and a major for the officer ranks, and their thankless lot in life is to achieve a balance between the needs of the military and the requirements of the service member that will best afford a progression in both the trade and rank. Of course, these scales are rarely found to be in equilibrium and as such, a career manager was/is often referred to as a *career mangler* for their perceived uncanny ability to mismanage a member's career.

The first time I saw my career manager was in the late spring of 1984. With Canada's three Voodoo intercept squadrons closing there would be a lot of personnel movements. To ensure that everyone understood the 'Big Picture' the safety systems trade career manager came out from Ottawa to hold a mass briefing with all the technicians on the base. We were informed that with the loss of the CF-101s and with the safety systems technicians being eliminated from the Parachute Maintenance Depot (CFPMD) in Edmonton, our trade would be over-staffed in this fiscal year by eighty-five bodies. He went on to say that personnel movements were inevitable and for those who did not like where they were being posted to they would always have the other option of getting out of the military. Immediately after the mass briefing the career manager met with each individual technician to discuss which options, if any, were available. As expected some people emerged from these private discussions happy and some, not so much. When my name was called I entered the warrant's office with some trepidation. I was asked if I would like to work on helicopters. Immediately, I had visions of moving to a hard army base like Gagetown or Petawawa to work with a tactical helicopter unit. It wasn't what I really wanted but for me there was no other option.

"Where would I be going, sir?"

"How's 442 Squadron sound?"

"Pick me coach!"

> **The de Havilland CC-115 Buffalo:**
>
> **Crew** – three (pilot, co-pilot, engineer)
>
> **SAR Crew** - six (with addition of a navigator and two SAR techs)
>
> **Payload** - 18,000 lbs,
>
> **Length** - 79 ft.
>
> **Height** - 28 ft. 8 in.
>
> **Wingspan** – 96 ft.
>
> **Max speed** - 290 mph. at 10,000 ft.
>
> **Max take-off weight** – 49,200 lbs
>
> **Range** - 691 miles at 10,000 ft. with a max payload
>
> **Service ceiling** - 31,000 ft.

I wasn't moving very far, only several hundred yards down the flight line to Number 1 Hangar, the home of 442 Transport and Rescue Squadron. Outfitted with four CC-115 De-Havilland Buffalos and five CH-113 Boeing Vertol Labradors, the squadron was responsible for approximately 1.5 million square kilometers stretching from the Yukon to the 49th Parallel and from the Alberta border to several hundred miles off the west coast of British Columbia.

This is an enormous amount of territory to cover and during the height of the primary search season when the weather on the west coast of British Columbia is most foul, the squadron sometimes had more than one rescue operation deployed away from the base at the same time.

Like any self-contained squadron, it had its own hierarchy. There was a commanding officer, a separate flight leader for both the Buffalo and the Lab pilots, a lead navigator to run the navigators and a squadron chief to enforce all the rules. Aircraft maintenance was carried out by the safety systems section, an engine bay, an avionics shop and a components shop all of which were governed by both a senior and a junior maintenance engineering officer. There was also an admin group to sort out all of the burgeoning triplicated paperwork.

The squadron's personnel was comprised of a host of pilots, some navigators, a multitude of aircraft technicians along with a few flight engineers (FE's) and a bunch of search and rescue (SAR) technicians. Of these, the last two trades are unique. At that time, in order to be a flight engineer or a search and rescue technician the service member had to previously be qualified in a base trade. FE's were drawn from one of three aircraft trades: airframe, aero-engine and electrician. In the early days of search and rescue, para-rescue personnel were made up of volunteers from across the service. On the initial call for volunteers there were twenty thousand applicants of which twelve individuals were selected to endure the fifteen week course that encompassed jump training, bush lore, basic wilderness survival, mountain climbing and medical training. Medical assistants, nurses and medical doctors were later added to the fifth and sixth training courses. However, the "cost and time of employing doctors and nurses in para-rescue was proven not to be practical or cost effective and resulted in a quick end to their recruitment. Further volunteers were selected from the RCAF safety equipment and medical assistant trades.[16] Members of the RCAF Munitions and Weapons trade were also recruited as para-rescue technicians in the event there was an accident or crash involving a USAF aircraft carrying nuclear weapons.

In 1984, the Safety Systems shop in Number 1 Hangar was under the direction of Sgt Joe McCluskey.[17] He was a great boss who had many years of service under his belt, was easy to talk to and provided a wealth of knowledge to his subordinates. In the summer, when the weather was extremely hot, he would drive over to the Canex and purchase an entire box of popsicles that he would hand out to the technicians working in the hangar. The guys working in helicopter maintenance were always grateful.

Our Squadron Chief Warrant Officer (SCWO) Doug Ford was old school Air Force. And when I say old school, I'm talking Silver Dart Olde School. He wasn't a bad a Squadron Chief. He looked after his people, sort of. He was extremely authoritarian. A Chief Warrant Officer is supposed to be strict but Doug firmly believed in RHIP[18] and did not hesitate to throw his rank around. Oh, and did I mention the fact that he hated SAR techs?

---

[16] The History of Para Rescue and Search & Rescue Technicians, www.pararescue.ca/Para_Rescue/History.html., 21 November 2015.

[17] Joe McCluskey retired as a warrant officer in 1987 having completed 34 years including a tour with the Snowbirds air demonstration team in 1972. WO (ret) Joe McCluskey passed away in Comox, 20 March 2016.

[18] Rank Has Its Privileges.

One fine summer evening, CWO Ford wandered into flight servicing with his new Alsatian bitch. She was still a puppy really, not quite a year old. For some unknown reason he decided to bring her into the hangar. Who's going to say no? After all, he was the Chief. While he's standing there talking to my Crew Chief, WO Ken Christiansen the dog decides to piddle on the floor. I just happened to be walking by and CWO Ford tells me to get a mop to clean it up.

"Uh, sure Chief."

"No, you won't. Go find an aircraft to work on McMillan," ordered Ken. "Chief Ford, it's your dog and it doesn't belong in servicing. If you want the piss cleaned up then I suggest that you clean it up Chief, because my techs have snags to work on."

CWO Ford was fuming, but my Crew Chief was right. The hangar was no place for a dog and if he wanted it mopped up then he could do it. If push came to shove the puddle would have stayed on the floor until the CO came in to work the next day. Doug did find a mop and cleaned up the mess. He also never brought the dog in again.[19]

Chief Warrant Officer Ford's office was upstairs next to the Sameo's[20] office. This placed it just above our shop making it

---

[19] In the late 1980's, CWO Doug Ford was posted to a super-numeri position in Baden-Solingen. Six months after arriving in Germany he succumbed to a major cardiac arrest while walking his dog.

[20] Squadron Aircraft Maintenance Engineering Officer – the senior officer in charge of aircraft maintenance. In a Base Aircraft Maintenance facility the position would be called Base Aircraft Maintenance Engineering Officer or Bameo.

convenient for him and a detriment for us. Whenever he got bored he would wander downstairs just to see what we were doing. He wasn't really interested in what we were doing he was just killing time until the end of the day. CWO Ford came downstairs to find myself and Cpl Lorne Penny flying higher than kites. We had been modifying the ten man life rafts by replacing the CO_2 support sleeve with an improved version. This involved using a powerful solvent called toluene to remove the old sleeve and military grade contact cement to adhere the new sleeve. The two of us had started this project at 10:00 hrs. It was now 14:00 hrs. We had completed one raft, were half way through the modification on a second one and were preparing a third raft when Chief Ford wandered onto the hangar floor. He took a quick look at us before storming into the shop and called for the Warrant Officer.

"Warrant McCluskey! Do you see those two airmen out there?" he thundered. "Those men are not to be touching an aircraft!"

Seeing the condition we were in WO McCluskey immediately told us to clean up our tools and call it a day. As Lorne and I packed everything up we realized that we were so high on the fumes that there was no way in hell that we could legally drive home. We would have to wait until clearer heads prevailed. So, we walked over to the Mess to declutter our minds with a jug of draft beer.

It didn't take long for me to discover that working in a search and rescue squadron was totally different from the fighter world. From top to bottom, everyone was committed to putting forth a concerted team effort in order to save the lives of those in need, regardless of where they were or who they might be. During regular working hours the unit was tasked with maintaining a thirty minute launch time for both the standby Buffalo and a Labrador helicopter. In other words, from the time the announcement was made to "Launch the Standby Buff!" it had to be off the ground with "wheels in the well" in less than thirty minutes. In the evenings or on the weekends, when the standby crews were not actually in the hangar, this launch time was extended to two hours before having the search aircraft head out to pluck some individual from the chilly waters of the Strait of Georgia. Either way, it doesn't provide much time to have the standby crew race from wherever they are in the hangar, climb on board the designated aircraft and get strapped in before some technician runs out to monitor the start sequence.

    To provide an edge in achieving the mandated launch time, the "standby" aircraft were pre-inspected by both the technicians and the flight engineer. Once the Before and pre-flight checks were certified the aircraft was quarantined, whereby access, without the approval of the servicing Crew Chief, was denied to all personnel. So, at Oh-Dark 30 when the pager sounded off, announcing to the entire household that a SAR launch had been called, those personnel on the standby response list would jump out of bed, get dressed and try not to speed as they drove into work. Once there, the ground crew would be informed by the Crew Chief which type of aircraft had to be towed out of the hangar and as soon as the aircrew were onboard the engines would be started for another SAR launch. The only thing left for us to do was to turn on the TV, make a pot of coffee (the lubricant of all ground crew), grab a deck of cards or have a game of ping pong and wait for the aircraft's return. Sometimes these late night launches happened so fast that the aircrew didn't even know where the hell they were going until they were already in the air.

As exciting as all this activity was (and probably still is), it must be remembered that the technicians, the pilots, the navigators, the flight engineers and even the aircraft itself are only a well synchronized means of taking the SAR techs from the unit and delivering them to the search area. When a crash scene is located the SAR techs quickly swing into action. SAR techs are trained to parachute, scuba dive, climb or hoist themselves into every possible emergency situation imaginable and they are fully qualified to administer medical trauma care to the survivors. Furthermore, in the event of any unforeseen conditions, they have the survival skills and are equipped with all the gear necessary to hunker down with their patients until additional assistance can be delivered on scene. If you have an emergency when you are out in the weeds these are the professionals you want to show up.

When a downed aircraft cannot be easily located due to weather conditions or because the search area is very large, a portion of the squadron's personnel may deploy to a location that is closer to its last reported position. This affords the search team the ability to remain in the target area longer and by having the aircraft maintained by the technicians the overall workload of the flight engineers is reduced. Searches are conducted under the direction of a qualified searchmaster[21] who has the authority to use any and all resources necessary to benefit a search in progress. This includes the purchase or the rental of any civilian equipment. For example, while operating on a deployed search in Penticton, BC there was an urgent need for a large crane to hoist a Buffalo engine that needed an impromptu engine change. These mobile cranes are commonly used throughout the province and so all it took was a phone call from the searchmaster to the local BC Hydro office to secure a large mobile crane complete with an operator. Of course, we needed something on which to place the unserviceable engine once it was removed (nobody flies around with an empty engine stand while on a deployment) and for that purpose a number of mattresses were purchased from the local K-Mart. The next day a spare engine, mounted on a stand, was flown from Comox to Penticton on another Buffalo. Upon its arrival, the engine was quickly installed onto the unserviceable aircraft and the damaged engine was then mounted on the now empty stand to be returned back to Comox. In total, the crane truck was leased for three or four days and in the end, the mattresses, now soiled with various engine fluids, were bagged and shipped back to the unit.

---

[21] The Canadian military searchmaster course is intended to train qualified and SAR-experienced aircrew officers to perform the duties of a SAR Mission Coordinator or "Searchmaster" for a specific major air search operation. Ideally, candidates should have at least two to three years operational SAR experience on primary or secondary SAR aircraft. http://www.forces.gc.ca/en/training-establishments/international-training-programs-courses/searchmaster-course.page

Waste not, want not. Eventually, impermeable mattress covers were locally manufactured and these mattresses became just one more item added to the squadron's MRP (Maintenance and Repair Party) kit along with the standard aircraft tool kits and boxes of assorted spare parts.

So there I was…Riding in the back of a Buffalo enroute to Kamloops, BC on a deployed search for a missing aircraft. We had left CFB Comox with a fully crewed CH-113 Labrador and a CC-115 Buffalo along with a search master, a pay master and an eight man ground crew team. As personnel participating on a deployed search mission we could expect to be away from our home base anywhere from a week to ten days before being relieved by a fresh set of ground crew members. For the next week or so we would make the best of it, working fourteen to sixteen hour days out of the local RCMP hangar. Our accommodations were across town at a hotel and our meals were covered by per diem. The only thing we had to contend with was the weather. It must be understood that the working conditions for those on a deployed search are quite often the same conditions under which the aircraft or vessel went missing with precipitation varying from snow to drizzling rain, high winds and low light levels. This applies for both the aircrew and the ground crew although the aircrew often bear the brunt of the conditions. Working on a deployed search was a lot like working at our home unit except that there are fewer bodies to share the workload. It was times like this when the squadron's teamwork really paid off. Unlike the disparity that exists between aircrew and ground crew in a fighter squadron our aircrew would quite often ask if there was anything they could do to help us. Oh, you can't make it for supper because you're working late to fix a snag? No problem. Here's a couple of pizzas and thanks guys for all your hard work. It didn't happen often, but when it did it was very much appreciated.

We had been in Kamloops for several days when the weather turned a little bit more for the worse. The snow began to fall and precautions had to be taken to protect the aircraft. There were six fabric tubes stored inside one of the bench seats of the Labrador. Each of them were some twenty-four feet long and were used to protect the helicopter blades from icing conditions. To install them you disengaged the rotor brake and manually rotated the rotor head until a rotor blade was in line with the fuselage; at that point a technician, or the aircraft's flight engineer, slipped the cover up and over the length of the blade like a giant rainbow coloured condom. Once in place, the cover was secured at the rotor head with several straps. The rotor heads were turned again and the process repeated until all six blades were covered. If high winds were expected and the helicopter could not be placed inside a hangar the blades could be secured with special tie-down ropes to prevent them from being damaged by flapping. Of course, the blade protectors and tie-downs - along with any other protective devices - were removed before any flight operations could commence.

As with all other aircraft, the CC-115 Buffalo has similar covers and/or plugs to protect the pitot tubes, air intakes and exhausts from foreign objects, including critters, from entering the aircraft. Whereas the blades of the Labrador are covered with a protective sheath, the wings and control surfaces of a large fixed wing aircraft are not normally shielded from any sort of precipitation. The best prescribed method to prevent an accumulation of snow and ice is to simply keep the plane in the hangar. However, care must be taken when moving an aircraft out of the hangar during freezing weather conditions. When snow lands on a warm aircraft wing it can quickly melt and then re-freeze creating a film of ice that could impair the aerodynamic properties of the wing and the operation of the flight controls. To prevent this from happening, prior to a winter flight, we would open the hangar doors and allow the aircraft to cold soak before towing it out onto the flight line. When the skin temperature of the aircraft was reduced to that of the outside air the falling snow was no longer an icing problem. It was just snow. And, loose snow is easily removed.

There is another procedure that can be used when an aircraft has been exposed to inclement weather. After removing all of the loose snow, a de-icing fluid is applied to all of the lifting and flight control surfaces. De-icing an aircraft is a common core task that everyone had to do. Of course, when you're operating from someplace other than your home unit applying this fluid with equipment you're not familiar with may be a bit of a challenge. In

Kamloops, a brave individual, yours truly in this case, had to shuffle along the icy wings of the Buffalo with a manually pressurized pump fire extinguisher (commonly referred to as a piss can) to coat the leading edges and the flight controls with de-icer fluid. As daunting as this sounds, repeating the procedure on the horizontal stabilizer was a more challenging task due to the fact that it is 8.5 metres (or 28 feet) off the ground. The only way for us to get up there was by using a locally made jerry-rigged civilian cherry picker. Essentially, it was a forty-five gallon drum mounted at the end of an I-beam with a metal yoke. It had no end stops so the bucket itself could rotate a full 360°. This buckshee contraption was connected to a geared rotor atop a flatbed truck with hydraulic lines snaking all around the base much like Medusa's head.

Normally, most young aircraft technicians would jump at the chance to get up off the ground in a cherry picker but not this time. After a detailed inspection of the equipment no one had volunteered to de-ice the Buffalo so an unlucky individual was decided by drawing lots. Thank God it wasn't me! Cpl Doug Leadbeater was not so lucky. Before climbing into the drum Doug put on a crew restraint safety harness and secured it onto the lift arm. It didn't take long before he was thirty feet in the air spraying de-icer fluid from the piss can onto the top of the T-tail. I must say, it was a pretty precarious position to be in, swinging about in that non-conforming bucket. It certainly didn't help matters when the bunch of us started to throw snowballs at him.

"Hey guys! Knock it off!"

"Oh yeah! What are you going to do about it!"

Doug was an easy target and there was no place for him to go. The drum was too small for him to hide in and he hadn't finished the task of spraying down the top of the tail. But, he was bound and determined not to be hit by anymore snowballs. With the bucket swinging and the boom arm shaking it was just a matter of time before something connected. Sure enough…smack! On one of the swinging rotations the bottom of the drum came up from underneath the tail and crunched into the trim tab of the elevator.

"Holy crap! I'm going to have to report this."

Doug brought the boom lift to the ground, climbed out of the drum and walked over to the RCMP hangar to talk to our Crew Chief, Warrant Officer Ken Christiansen. Ken was an old school technician. He didn't take any crap from anyone and he was as tough as nails, and his crew loved him for it. We could only imagine how much trouble we were going to be in because of our clowning around.

"Uh, Warrant?"

"What do you want now?"

"I want to report a suspected bird strike on aircraft 454."

"Where'd you find the damage?"

"I found it while I was de-icing the top of the T-tail. It's under the trailing edge of the elevator trim tab, Warrant."

"Corporal, if I understand you correctly, for this damage to have occurred the aircraft was flying in reverse and descending when it was struck by this bird?"

"Or, a bird could have struck the tail while the aircraft was stationary on the ground. Either way, I believe it's a bird strike and that's how I am writing up the CF-349."

"Okay! That's a possibility. Write it up!"

Once the proper entries were made in the aircraft log set, the damage was surveyed by the senior airframe technician. He had no problem finding the damage as he had been throwing snowballs too and witnessed the event in question. Sure enough there was a slight, but very noticeable, six inch long dent on the underside of the trim tab. It was big enough to affect the airflow over the flight control and therefore it would have to be changed. While the inspection was taking place WO Christiansen placed a call to our unit back in Comox informing them of our snag. As luck would have it, there was another Buffalo undergoing an in-depth maintenance check and the entire elevator assembly, including the trim tab, had already been removed for inspection. The only problem was how to get the part from Comox to Kamloops as quickly as possible.

The following day, a CP-140 Aurora from 407 Squadron arrived with the new trim tab. The part was so long that it had to be gingerly passed up the crew stairs at the rear of the aircraft and fed inside the fuselage where it was somehow secured for its delivery to Kamloops. When the aircraft arrived, the process was carefully reversed until the part was in our waiting hands. With the use of the de-icer/boom lift we were able to remove the damaged component and install the serviceable one in a short order. As soon as the paperwork was completed and the flight engineer did his walk around inspection the Buffalo was sent out to continue the search.

Is there a moral to this story? Not really. Except, maybe to keep the high jinks away from the aircraft. Did Warrant Christiansen know what had actually happened? Maybe he did, maybe he didn't. We will never know.

After seven days of operating from a deployed search location we were replaced by a fresh set of technicians and aircrew. This new team would continue from where had we left off. Five days later this particular search was terminated due to increasingly poor weather conditions. To my knowledge that aircraft and its passengers were never found.

When working on a flight line you never know when or where you are going to learn something interesting. One particular incident comes to mind when MCpl Pat Burke called for myself and a couple of young riggers to help him with a snag on one of the Labs.

"McMillan! You're a pretty good safety systems tech. Do you know how to sew a window? No? Well, come with me. I'm going to show you how to sew a spotter's window on a Lab."

What the hell was he talking about? Sew a window?

The spotter's window on a Labrador helicopter is shaped like half a fish bowl. You can stick your head inside of it a look straight down below the aircraft or along the side of the fuselage which is quite handy when you are out searching for a lost soul. This particular spotter's window had a four inch crack in it. Our aircraft supply was checked and there were no spares. However, according to the CFTO's the window could be repaired using a prescribed method if the technician had successfully completed the Aircraft Battle Damage Repair course. As luck would have it, MCpl Pat Burke had not only attended the course but had also passed it with flying colours.

The three of us followed Pat out onto the hangar floor. Sure enough, the right hand spotter's window was cracked. But, how

> **CH-113 Labrador:**
>
> **Crew** - three (pilot, co-pilot, engineer)
>
> **SAR Crew** - six (with addition of a second engineer and two SAR techs)
>
> **Passengers** – up to twenty-six
>
> **Length with rotors turning** – 83 feet 4 inches.
>
> **Height** - 16 ft. 8 in.
>
> **Rotor diameter** – 50 ft.
>
> **Max speed** - 168 mph.
>
> **Max take-off weight** – 18,700 lbs
>
> **Range** - 684 miles
>
> **Service ceiling** - 10,600 ft.
>
> **Hover ceiling** – 6,500 ft.
>
> **Hoists** – two (one internal and one external)

was I supposed to sew something that was made out of a polycarbonate material?

MCpl Burke had one of the young techs go inside the aircraft and under his direction the technician used a red china marker to place a dot at both ends of the crack. A series of dots were also placed every half inch along the length of the crack on both sides.

"Thiessen, get up on the stand and hold this wooden block tight against the window. Don't push on it! Just hold it firmly against the window. Now Trepanier, take this air drill and drill a hole where each red dot is placed on the window. Don't push hard or you'll cause the crack to run longer. Start with the dots on the ends and then work your way along both sides of the crack."

Over the next ten or fifteen minutes, Cpl Robin Trepanier drilled out the holes as he was told. We learned that the hole placed at either end of the crack was called a stop drill and is placed to stop the crack from running any farther through the window. After all the holes were drilled along the length of the crack the two sides were laced together using .020 monel lockwire. Once completed the entire area was sealed over with some clear RTV silicone. In the end, the repair to the window looked like a bad suture attempt by a mad scientist. It may not have looked pretty but the window was now serviceable. What more could you ask for?

Something else that I learned in 442 Squadron was how to tow aircraft. Everyone who works in an aircraft servicing section will participate as a member of a tow crew but most safety systems techs never learned how to tow the aircraft. I wanted to learn to be a tow driver and not be relegated to riding the brakes or walking the wings or monitoring the clearance like all the other numpties, and Master Corporals Gaylor, Lessard and McGrath were instrumental my training.

Our hangar floor was painted with yellow squares to mark out in where the wheels of the plane had to go when the aircraft was parked inside the hangar. When the wheels were correctly inside these boxes it meant that the wings and the tail of the aircraft were clear of any obstructions including other aircraft. To ensure they learned how to position the plane correctly, trainees were given the opportunity to be tested on the last day of the shift. If, in the course of pushing the plane into the spot, one of the wheels crossed a yellow line it would cost you a beer that was payable to the tow crew supervisor: namely MCpls Gaylor, Lessard or McGrath. Cross three lines and you might as well buy an entire jug of draft.

Did I have to buy any beer? Of course I did. I would be lying if I said that I didn't. But it sure didn't take me long to become a qualified tow driver on both the Labs and the Buffalos. When all of our aircraft were home we would have five helicopters and four Buffalos plus all the maintenance equipment jammed inside that hangar, which made for a tight fit and some very interesting tow jobs.

In the early spring every year, millions of pacific herring migrate along the coastal waters of British Columbia to spawn.

Due to its abundance, this fish species is a very integral part of the food chain. Everything that lives on the west coast, from eagles to whales and all that is in between, is somehow connected to the life cycle of the pacific herring. On top of that, herring is also considered a valuable food source having "long been fished by First Nations on the Central Coast of British Columbia, and elsewhere."[22] Until the late 1960's, up to 250,000 tonnes of herring were harvested annually and processed into low value products such as fish meal and oil - to the point of a near total collapse of the entire fishery.[23] As a result, the federal government shut down the commercial herring fleet for four years. When the biomass began to recover in the early 1970's there was a change in the industry whereby the harvest was more focused on collecting the herring roe as opposed to the entire fish. Since 1983, catches have not been allowed to exceed 20% of the annual forecast for each spawning stock. The value of the harvest averages more than $40 million per season contributing on average $214,500 gross income per herring licenced vessel.

Obviously, the success of the herring harvest is dependent upon where and when the fish gather to spawn. This tends to be towards the end of February and into the beginning of March. The harvest season itself is only a week to ten days in length. Despite

---

[22] Historically, the Pacific herring has been an important species, simply due to its reproductive ability to generate significant species biomass. http://en.wikipedia.org/wiki/Pacific_herring.

[23] Herring spawning stocks were reduced to an estimated 15,000 tonnes coast wide. www.pac.dfo-mpo.gc.ca.

the reduced quotas, greedy fishing boat captains have been known to overload their vessels in an attempt to gain a bigger slice of the pie and in doing so jeopardize not only the vessel but the lives of their crew as well. This is where 442 Squadron comes into play.

But first, a quick science lesson.

Which provides the greater amount of buoyancy - freshwater or saltwater? Everyone knows that it's salt water. But why? It is the density of the liquid that is the prime difference between fresh and saltwater. Simply put, salt water is denser than freshwater due to the weight of the salt dissolved in the water. If an object that is one cubic foot in volume and weighs 63 pounds it will float in salt water but it will sink in fresh water. On average, salt water weighs 64.1 pounds per cubic foot while freshwater is only 62.4 pounds per cubic foot. According to Archimedes, the upward force on a submerged object is equal to the weight of the water that it displaces. Salt water weighs more than fresh water, so it exerts a greater upward force on a submerged object.[24] And, this is where the problem rests.

The captain of a fishing vessel laden with an exceptionally large catch and wallowing in the seas must always remember that in order to return safely to port, he must first stay afloat! For example, when transitioning from the Strait of Juan de Fuca into the mouth of the Fraser River the ship is moving from saltwater to freshwater. In other words, the boat is moving from a high

---

[24]Buoyancy in Salt Water vs Fresh Water for Scuba Diving, http://scuba.about.com, 06 March 2016.

buoyancy liquid into one that is low buoyancy. Now, some ambitious captains have been known to overload their fishing boats, leaving them with next to nothing for freeboard. Once that vessel enters the fresh water it is going to sink beneath the waves faster than the Edmund Fitzgerald. In the past, both the Canadian Coast Guard and 442 Squadron have responded to the distress calls of a bloated herring boat, its gunwales close to being swamped, as it began its interpretation of a submarine.

In the mid 1980's Canadian Federal Fisheries had predicted a massive herring spawn would occur off the eastern shores of the Queen Charlotte Islands in British Columbia.[25] In preparation for the lucrative harvest a large portion of the herring fleet had moved into the area and 442 Squadron, in preparation for a potential emergency, sent a CH-113 Labrador to the town of Sandspit located on the northeastern side of Moresby Island. The distance between Comox and Sandspit is 620 kilometres and most of that is over open ocean.

---

[25] The Queen Charlotte Islands are an island archipelago that is comprised of two main islands, Graham Island in the north and Moresby Island in the south, and over one hundred fifty smaller islands. On 03 June 2010 it was officially renamed Haida Gwaii in accordance with the Haida Gwaii Reconciliation Act.

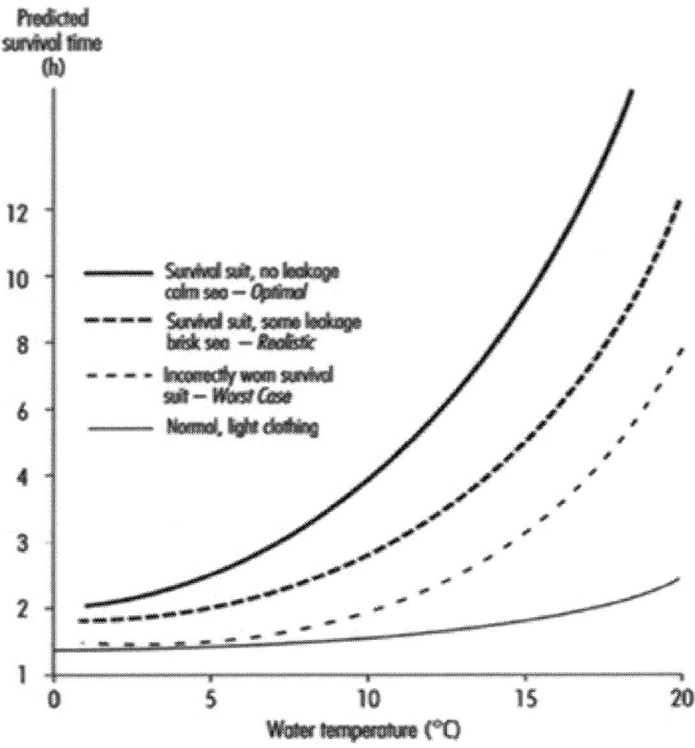

Source: Hayes 1988.

To err on the side of caution, when a Lab crew had to fly to the Queen Charlottes they would routinely land in Port Hardy, a small town at the northern end of Vancouver Island, to top off the fuel tanks. This also provided an opportune time for the crew go to the washroom and, in the winter months, put on their ditching suits. Also known as poopy suits, the constant wear immersion suits are a vital necessity to the aircrew if they are to survive a forced water landing.

Even when conducted under ideal conditions hoisting people aboard a helicopter is by no means an easy operation. To successfully lift a person into a helicopter several events have to take place. First the rescue helicopter positions itself over the vessel and the rescue sling or basket is lowered. If the individual is capable, he then puts on the rescue sling or climbs into the rescue basket before being hoisted up into the hovering helicopter. If the individual is injured or if there are multiple persons to be evacuated, a SAR tech may be lowered first to assist in preparing the patients for hoisting. During this transition period, the helicopter must remain on station so that those being hoisted don't hit anything and, more importantly, the hoist cable does not become entangled with another object.

Picture your team has been called out to rescue people from a ship that is foundering, the winds are gusting upwards 65 knots and the rain is coming at you sideways. Arriving on scene you discover that the ship's crew are in their sea survival suits, clinging to the deck and beckoning for you to save them. The fishing vessel is pitching and rolling in heavy seas. The ocean swells are bouncing the boat up and down some thirty feet at a time. This intense storm has freed the ship's outriggers from their extended positions and they are now swinging dangerously about on their own accord. Taking it all in you know that this mission will task you, your crew and your aircraft to the limit. Now imagine that this scenario is taking place at night!

So there I was... Working the night shift in servicing. The weather in Comox was horrendous and farther up the coast it was even worse with gale force winds, driving rain and forty foot seas.

We had received word from the Rescue Coordination Centre (RCC) in Victoria that one of the herring boats was caught out in Hecate Strait when the storm descended upon them and that the rescue helicopter, which had been pre-positioned in Sandspit, would be dispatched to hoist the endangered crew off of their boat. Even with the treacherous weather we were very optimistic about the mission and fully expected that it would be completed in a couple of hours. Little did we know that this particular night would be a true test of our resolve.

About ninety minutes into the rescue RCC contacted us with an update. The helicopter was on scene but there were some problems, beginning with the weather. From what we were told the rescue helicopter had been hovering over the fishing boat and a SAR tech was rigged on the external hoist. The plan was to conduct a buddy hoist whereby the SAR tech is lowered down first and then he accompanies the casualty back up to the helicopter. But with the vessel rising and falling some 30 or 40 feet at a time and the winds gusting to 45 knots trying to stay on station above the fishing boat was proving to be extremely challenging. With the wind buffeting him, and induced by the movement of the helicopter, the SAR tech hanging at the end of the cable began to swing like a pendulum. At first, it wasn't all that much. But little by little the arc had increased until the SAR tech was nearly parallel to the surface of the ocean and when he reached the end of his forward swing, he was looking at the pilots through the windscreen. That's where the second problem began.

What happens if you take a twist tie and bend it back and forth and back and forth? It breaks. Well, if you suspend a 200 pound weight at the end of a 100 foot long 3/8 inch diameter cable and then swing it from a fixed point eventually the cable will break. Unfortunately, the SAR tech - who was hanging spider-like at the end of the cable - suddenly found himself launched out into the icy cold waters of Hecate Strait.

Back in Comox, the only thing we were told by RCC in Victoria was that the external hoist cable broke and that the SAR tech had hit the water. We did not know how or why. Was it a hoist failure? Was he alive? RCC had no answers to our questions simply because they did not know either. What we did know was that the helicopter was calling "Bingo" for fuel and had to find a place to land. They couldn't make it back to Sandspit and they didn't have enough juice to reach a fuel cache on the mainland. But wait a moment! There's a wide flat rock that's clear of the surf and it was big enough for two Labs. WO Christiansen commanded that we strip down another Lab to the bare bones. The only things to be left on board would be the crew life preservers, the ten man raft, the flight engineer's stores (spare oils and hydraulic fluids) and a hand pump. With the all up weight now significantly reduced we fueled it with as much JP-4 as it would hold and with a crew of four it was launched into the rain soaked darkness. Their first stop would be at Port Hardy where they would land, re-fuel, go for a bathroom break and put on their constant wear immersion suits.

I don't know how they were able to find each other in the midst of that maelstrom but somehow the second helicopter was able to locate and land beside the first one. Once the hand pump and its hoses were bridged across the flight engineers quickly balanced the fuel load between the two aircraft. The plan was to transfer enough fuel to allow both helicopters to relocate to a fuel cache on the mainland where they would both completely fill their tanks.

Several hours later, we were still very much in the dark over the situation. Days earlier MCpl Burke had signed the independent check for an external hoist change on the afflicted Lab. Now he was extremely distraught at the thought that he had missed something on his inspection and believed that an error on his part may have killed the SAR tech. As soon as he heard of the incident MCpl Burke began pacing out on the hangar floor with one hand in his pocket and the other gripping his coffee cup. When he ran out of coffee he came in for a refill and asked the Crew Chief for any news. None? Okay. And then out to the hangar floor he went to continue pacing. I swear that by the end of the night he had worn a groove in the concrete floor. Finally, RCC Victoria called our Squadron Operations to bring everyone up to speed on the aspects of the rescue. The SAR tech was alive. After he hit the water, a Canadian Coast Guard vessel had moved in to pick him up but went right over him. As it turned out, the fisherman he had planned to rescue plucked him out of the heaving surf. After topping off their fuel tanks both Labs returned to the scene and -

as the weather calmed - they succeeded it rescue hoisting several individuals. As soon as the aircraft were safely on the ground in Sandspit those of us in 442 Sqn servicing were "stood down" and cleared to go home at 02:45 hrs local.

Aircraft accidents can happen anytime and anywhere, and this is especially with helicopters. A helicopter has been described by some as a million loosely associated parts flying together in a very tight formation. When you think about that statement it actually sounds very plausible. There are just so many components that have to operate (and cooperate) in a very coordinated manner. Everything might be working like clockwork but let Mother Nature throw you a curve ball and the result won't be pretty.

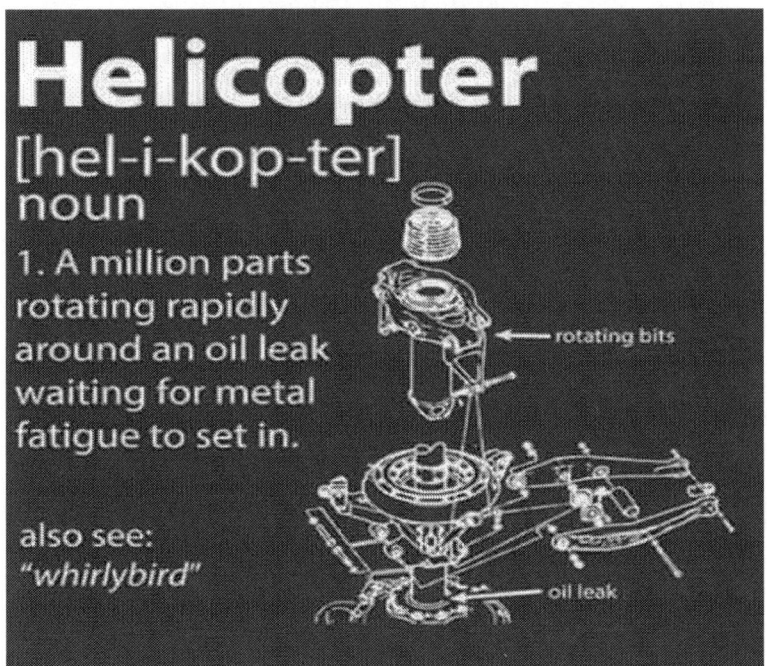

So there I was... On my way into work for night shift on a particularly windy day. As I turned the corner to pull into the parking lot at No. 1 Hangar, out of the corner of my eye I saw a Labrador helicopter sitting on the ramp. There was something that looked very odd about it. The aft rotor blades appeared to be hanging from the rotor head in a most unusual fashion.

In the early afternoon of May 11, Labrador CH-11304 was starting up for a routine OTU (Operational Training Unit) flight. On board were two pilots, two flight engineers and one SAR tech. During normal start up procedures both pilots and one engineer are seated in the cockpit, while the second flight engineer takes up a position at the rear of the aircraft to monitor the engines; and any remaining personnel are to be strapped into the seats. This particular aircraft had been recently outfitted with new fiberglass rotor blades, which were heavier but more durable than the previous metal blades. The reported winds were 25 knots gusting to 35 knots. At that time the US Navy and the US Marine Corps operated the Sea Knight which, for all intents and purposes, is the same aircraft as the Labrador. However when starting the aircraft in winds over 20 knots the Americans place the tail to the wind (as opposed to the normal position of having the nose to the wind) which aids in lifting the rotor blades at low rotational speed. On start-up, as the blades began to rotate and pass over the fuselage the engineer at the rear of the plane, Sgt Larry Brown, noted that the SAR tech was standing between the two spotter seats amid ship.

"Take a seat" said Larry.

"What's the problem? I've done this a thousand times!" retorted the SAR tech.

Seconds later a wind gust slammed into the aircraft, driving the aft blades down. The first blade from the aft head creased the top of the synch shaft[26] cover. The next blade from the forward head cleared the synch shaft as per normal. The following blade from the aft head struck below the synch shaft, cutting into the fuselage of the Lab and breaking in half. After this, each successive blade on the aft rotor head snapped as it sliced deeper into the left hand side of the aircraft. Sgt Brown, who was standing just off the ramp when this began, jumped back aboard and was now standing directly below the engines. When the first rotor blade bit into the side of the Lab the SAR tech, who had been instructed to sit down, turned and attempted to exit the aircraft. Sgt Brown received a Good Show award for having "physically restrained the SAR tech" and prevented him from receiving serious injuries. The key words being, "physically restrained". When the SAR tech was barrelling towards him Sgt Brown had to act fast. Trying to grab and hold onto him could have ended with the two of them outside the fuselage where the rotor blades were now swinging wildly around the aft pylon. Sgt Brown reacted in the best possible way that he knew how: he threw a punch that

---

[26] The synch shaft is a drive shaft that runs between the forward and aft rotor heads and synchronizes the rotation of the heads (and therefore the rotor blades) preventing them from striking each other. By all reports, a synch shaft failure in flight will lead to a catastrophic failure of the aircraft.

knocked the SAR tech down onto the ramp where he stayed until the danger had cleared.

It is truly amazing that everyone survived. According to the Flight Safety panel, "one very important lesson that was learned in the accident was the performance of the damaged fiberglass rotor blades. Unlike metal rotor blades the fiberglass blades did not break apart and depart the aircraft. In a case like this, personnel must remain onboard the aircraft, preferably away from the centre section until all rotation has stopped."[27]

---

[27] Flight Comment Magazine 1987-4.

Later that night, Labrador 304 was towed gently back into the hangar where it sat for an extended period of time. Most of the service members from across CFB Comox had heard of the accident and over the next few days many of them came to look at the damage. Eventually, Labrador 304 was stripped down of anything salvageable and crated for shipping. It was sent to a third line maintenance facility in Arnprior, Ontario where it was rebuilt.

It doesn't matter where you work in the military - everyone is responsible for keeping their workplace tidy. A tidy workplace is a safe workplace. It doesn't matter if it is just an office cubicle or it's an entire hangar, you have to keep it clean. Servicing crews are not only responsible for a portion of the hangar to clean but the crew room must also be kept up. In 442 Sqn, the crew room was cleaned every Thursday night. Depending on how filthy it was and the time available between aircraft duties, the floor might be swept, washed and waxed. Of course, the one job no one wanted to be saddled with was dunging out the crew fridge. With bruised apples, crusty desiccated sandwiches from old box lunches and moldy forgotten Tupperware containers the crew fridge was a perpetual science experiment writ large.

So there I was... Taking a break in the crew room. Most of the crew was busy working on a Buffalo when WO Christiansen suddenly stuck his head through the window hollering for someone to, "Launch the standby Buff!"

I dropped what I was doing and dashed outside. At the plane I disconnected the grounding cable, coiled it, placed it on board and took up a position off the nose of the aircraft to wait for the aircrew. The standby aircraft were still on a thirty minute posture so it didn't take long before they boarded the Buffalo.

Auxiliary Power Unit started.

#2 engine turning.

#1 engine turning.

APU stopped.

Nose wheel chocks pulled.

Thumbs up!

By the time I took the chocks back to the hangar and placed them on the storage rack the standby SAR Buffalo had already taxied across the apron to Runway 29 via Runway 18. Even with my ear defenders on I could hear their urgency as the twin turbo props pulled the plane into the air. Once back in the crew room I dumped myself back into a chair. Cpl Stacy Thiessen was sitting across from me calmly eating her supper. Elated with another successful launch, I lit up a smoke. Yes Virginia, in those days you could smoke in the crew room.

Not five minutes had passed before the Crew Chief called out again, "The launch is cancelled! They're coming back. Stacy, go park the Buffalo!" The Buff had just leveled off its flight when the search had been called off. The aircraft did a quick circuit of the airfield and was on approach for landing.

"But, I'm eating my ham sandwich," she moaned.

The sound of the props changing pitch announced that the SAR Buff was on the ground and taxiing in. We were the only unit operating that night. The apron was clear and the aircraft was coming in fast. I glanced over my shoulder and saw it moving down Runway 18/36 towards the centre pad.

"Are you going to park it?"

"I'm eating my ham sandwich," she calmly replied.

Fuck it!

Tossing my smoke into the ashtray, I went out the door, snagged a pair of chocks off the storage rack and sprinted to the designated spot barely ahead of the aircraft..

Hands up.

Left turn.

Straight on.

Arms crossed to stop.

Clenched fists for brakes.

Engine shut down.

Chock the nose wheels.

I retrieved the grounding cable from on board, connected it to the plane and then the grounding point before walking away. Normally, I would have jumped aboard to quickly do my own checks but I figured the "A plus a B" could wait since all the other trades would have to complete them too.

I walked into the servicing crew room, grabbed a coffee and re-lit my smoke when the Crew Chief asked who had parked the Buffalo.

"I did, Warrant."

"Stacy, why didn't you park the SAR?"

"Because, I was eating my ham sandwich."

Stone faced, WO Christiansen said nothing. But the look on his face indicated that trouble was brewing. Over the next two hours the snag was fixed, the checks on the standby SAR aircraft were completed and they were towed in. It was supper time. Everyone was tucking in and looking at having an early night, as soon as the housekeeping was done. MCpls Gaylor and McGrath were in the process of designating who would sweep, mop or whatever else needed doing. As we started to haul the furniture out onto the hangar floor WO Christiansen announced that there would be no clean-up tonight.

"No clean up? But it's Thursday, Warrant. And Thursday night is clean-up night."

Our Crew Chief took a $20 bill from his wallet and handed it over to MCpl McGrath commanding that he, "Take the boys over to the Mess for a *burger*."[28]

"You're sure there's no clean up tonight, Warrant?"

"Oh, the clean-up will be done. Cpl Thiessen has volunteered to do it by herself. Now, get out before I change my mind!"

You didn't have to tell us twice. Within ten minutes the members of 1 Crew had changed out of their coveralls and had their rumps comfortably planted in chairs at the Mess where they all enjoyed the *burger* compliments of WO Ken Christiansen. I don't know how long it took Stacy to complete the clean-up. From our vantage point, upstairs in the JR Ranks Club, we could see No.

---

[28] Beer

1 Hangar. Three hours later the lights were finally turned off indicating that no one was there. We found out later that the floors had been swept, washed, waxed and buffed. Even the crew fridge had been cleaned.

Our squadron was fairly small in size and as a result everyone pitched in to help each other out even if it wasn't your area of expertise. By lending a hand the squadron experienced a greater amount of esprit de corps and our aircraft serviceability rate was higher. One night when I was working in 442 Sqn my servicing crew was tasked with assisting the guys in Labrador maintenance by installing the rotor blades onto the maintenance bird. Since it was a bit of a slack evening we trooped out across the hangar floor. Each of the twenty-three foot long helicopter blades were lifted by hand up the side of the fuselage and slid into the rotor head where I dropped the bolts in to secure it. Upstairs, on that side of the hangar, was the Sameo's office. Major Ron LaGrange happened to be working late that night when he looked out to see me sitting atop the helicopter. Immediately, he came downstairs to see what was going on.

"What are you doing up there Corporal?" the Major asked.

"I'm helping to put the blades on, Sir!" I replied.

"I can see that. But, you're a safety systems tech. That's not your trade."

"I know that, Sir. There's only two airframe techs in tonight and they needed a hand. So a bunch of us are helping out. Anyone can pass a wrench."

"Good point."

A couple of hours later I was sitting on top of a very tall stool in front of the nose of another Lab. The radome was raised and power was applied to the aircraft. Cpl Dave White was working inside the SAS closet located just inside the crew door. Once again, Major LaGrange spotted me doing something else out of trade.

"Corporal, what are you doing now?"

"I'm rotating the SAS box."

"Do you know what it does on the aircraft?"

"Not a chance, Sir."

"So, why are you rotating the box?"

"Sir, Cpl White is in the SAS closet. He said that he was checking the linkages. He tells me on which axis to turn the box. I'm just helping to fix the snag and besides, anyone can rotate the box."

"Good point."

As a *"Transport and Rescue"* Squadron we would take care of any transient SAR or transport aircraft that came to the base just as 407 Sqn would look after any maritime patrol aircraft or VU33 Sqn looking after any visiting jet aircraft. Just after 409 Sqn was disbanded from CFB Comox a full squadron of F-15 Eagles from McChord Air Force Base in Washington state came up to occupy our QRA while their airstrip was resurfaced. In 1985, the US Marines came to visit. For nearly a month we had a dozen CH-53E Super Stallions and a squadron of A-4 Skyhawks out of Alameda,

California taking up a major portion of our precious ramp space. To haul all of their parts and pieces they arrived with a C-5B Galaxy that was stuffed right to the gills. We would also get Hercs dropping in on a regular basis and not just your standard trash hauling cargo variety but some of the specialty C-130s flown by our neighbours south of the 49th Parallel. There were HC-130's for combat search and rescue, AC-130 gunships, EC-130 electronic warfare aircraft and another variant used to communicate with submarines at depth. You never knew what was going to come in to visit.

"Corporal McMillan! There's a Herc coming in from the States in about thirty minutes. Find a place to put him!"

"Okay, Warrant!"

Thirty minutes later I went out and marshalled in a nice shiny C-130E flown by the New York State Air National Guard. Everything went according to plan. They followed my directions and stopped where I had indicated. When the aircrew exited from the aircraft I asked them how long they would be staying in Comox.

"Oh, about a week or so."

"Well, I can't have you sitting here for a week. How about I get you to park over there on the side of the apron so you'll be out of the way?"

"Not a problem," was the reply. I pulled out the nose chocks, they fired up the GTC plus one engine before taxiing over to the spot I had indicated and then shut everything down again.

The pilot asked me, "Do you know if a Canada Customs officer is coming?"

"Pretty sure that they are," I replied.

"Customs is coming guys! Lock it up!"

On hearing the order from the aircraft commander the American crew pulled their personal luggage off the plane and set it down by the crew door which they promptly closed, locked and then sealed with a very official looking metal band. Once Customs arrived and inspected their personal luggage the seal on the door was removed.

I had asked the aircrew why the door was sealed and they said that the gear on board was "Secret Squirrel Equipment".

One of the crew asked me, "Now that Customs is gone would you like to see inside?"

"Sure, I'm game."

The Herc's Crew Chief fired up the GTC once more to provide power for the loadmaster to open the aircraft and unload the "Secret Squirrel Equipment." Moments later he backed out an 18 foot boat attached to a small Winnebago camper. They had flown all the way from New York State just to go salmon fishing on BC's west coast. After securing the aircraft the six of them boarded their Winnebago and waved goodbye as they drove off the apron.

By the spring of 1988 the Powers That Be had me moving once again. This time I was heading east to Winnipeg, Manitoba where the summers were hot and the winters were - NOT! I was sad to leave Comox. I had made quite a few friends but I knew I would make new ones. I was eager to move on to someplace new and with the unique set of skills I had acquired in Comox I could work on anything.

By the Centre

There are those who believe that Toronto – along with all the other cities that make up the Greater Toronto Area, is the centre of the Canada. They even go as far as to refer to the area as *Central Canada*. I beg to differ. From east to west, Canada is 5,187 km (or 3,223 miles) wide and 4,627 km (or 2.875 miles) from north to south.[29] Meagan Campbell of Maclean's magazine travelled to all the centres of Canada for an article in the June 30, 2016 issue. The Canadian Cartographic Association states that the centre of Canada is located at the junction of the middle lines of latitude and longitude, which happens to be at 62° 00' 00" N and 97° 00' 00" W. For the rest of us, the centre of Canada is usually measured from east to west and it rests in Tache´, Manitoba, at 49° 42' 00" N and 96 ° 48' 35" W. It should be noted that neither of these locations are anywhere near the Golden Horseshoe along Lake Ontario.

---

[29] The Encyclopedia of Nations, www.nationsencyclopedia.com, 06 June 2016.

In the summer of 1988, I was posted to the Base Safety Systems Section at CFB Winnipeg. I may have been born on the prairies but it had been many years since I had lived there and I would soon discover that I was ill prepared for its environmental extremes. In the summer months the static air temperature would often climb to 40°C. Magnificent thunderstorms with black anvil headed clouds would build for days until they towered tens of thousands of feet high like mountains across the horizon and threatened the landscape with hard rain, golf ball sized hail and even the occasional tornado. In the winter months the temperature would plummet down to -40°C. The flat featureless terrain did absolutely nothing to stop the arctic winds from burying cars in massive snow drifts and the cold dry air would freeze-dry the earth causing it to crack open to the depth of up a metre. To top it off the wind chill would lower the temperature even farther to where any exposed skin would freeze in minutes. When the wind flowed out of the south it was often packed with moisture and when it then collided with the cold Canadian air mass, it could dump twenty to eighty centimeters of snow during the course of a storm, which has been known to shut down the city. With their roads completely buried, Winnipeggers remain in their houses while a mercenary army of plows, front end loaders and dump trucks battle to keep the transportation corridors open.

Why people insist on living on the prairies is beyond me. In the depths of winter the sun rises after you get to work and sets before you get home. The populace longs for a heat wave even if it only raises the daytime high to -5°C. Then, in the summer months when the big sky country is parched and thirsty, the wish for rain is tempered by the knowledge that any moisture other than snows in October will only increase the ravenous mosquito population.

In 1988, the aircraft operating from Canadian Forces Base Winnipeg included three CT-133 Silverstars (T-Birds) and eight CT-114 Tutors that belonged to the Central Flying School. There was also a VIP configured CC-109 Cosmopolitan (call sign Smokey One) at the disposal of the Commander of Air Command, and over in 10 Hangar, 429 Squadron had four CC-130E Hercules that were used primarily as training platforms for navigation students. The last nine CC-129 Dakotas in the air force operated by 402 (City of Winnipeg) Squadron and finally a lone CH-139 Bell Jet Ranger on loan from CFB Portage La Prairie for the ICP course put on by the Central Flying School (CFS).

Flight line servicing in Winnipeg operated out of two locations: the Hercs and Daks were flown out of 10 Hangar and everything else operated out of 16 Hangar. Each separate servicing crew had its own complement of NCO's which included a warrant officer or a sergeant, a couple of master corporals, a lot of corporals and a few privates. Aircraft servicing crews work on a shift schedule and the rotation of the shift schedule is often determined by the type of aircraft operating at the unit. Most fighter jet squadrons have two servicing crews, a day shift and a night shift that covers from Monday to Friday with a duty crew covering the weekend. Technicians working in transport or SAR squadrons tend to work longer shifts that overlap one another in order provide around-the-clock coverage.

The dedicated group of aircraft technicians in 10 Hangar worked a 7/3 -7/4 shift[30] during which they carried out all of the flight servicing checks and performed 1st and 2nd line maintenance inspections as required. The servicing section in 16 Hangar had been given the moniker "Triple T Servicing" due to the fact that aside from the helicopter (which we towed and refueled but did no inspections on) and Smokey One (which rarely flew at all), the bulk of the activity was taken up by the Tutors, the T-Birds and of course… the Transients. The Boys at Triple T were doing a fighter squadron-style shift of a week of day shifts followed by a week of nights. For the lone safety systems technician working the flight line was maddening because the technician had to cover the needs of two different hangars that operated on two different schedules. The only way to accomplish this was by working consistently with one crew in one place and whoever happened to be on duty in the other place.

With CFB Winnipeg being smack dab in the middle of the country most Canadian military aircraft transiting from one place to another would inevitably land here for fuel this included Tutors,

---

[30] There were several variations of the 7/3 -7/4 shift. Starting on a Tuesday, the shift went for seven working days followed by three days off. The next rotation started on Friday and also went for seven working days followed by four days off. To confuse the workers even more the seven working days were often divided into various day and night configurations. Three days then four nights followed by three days off. Four days then three nights followed by four days off. Servicing shifts always added variety to your life.

CF-5's, CF-18's, T-Birds and Musketeers. Many foreign aircraft enroute for training at CFB Cold Lake would include F-4 Phantoms from the United States and Germany, Tornados from Germany and the UK, as well as British Jaguars, which were used for close in ground support. I even remember seeing a few British Royal Navy Buccaneer strike fighters sitting on the apron. Yes, every day was a different day. You never knew what was going up flying or what was going to be landing, except for the CC-137 Boeing service flight which came in like clockwork six days a week.

Before I could move down to the flight line - a position that I always considered to be a plum spot - I would have to do my penance in the Main Shop. Over the next twelve months I would have to demonstrate my technical skills in the various areas of the section to the satisfaction of Sgt Perron. The Personal Equipment section issued and maintained the aircrew helmets, oxygen masks and personal mae-west life preservers; the Kits Room - commonly referred to as the Rubber Room - was large enough for the inspection of multi-place life rafts and all of the other types of survival kits; the Parachute department is self-explanatory as are aircraft Snags and Maintenance and the Liquid Oxygen (lox) building.

Having worked in 442 Squadron, I had a really good grasp of all the areas except for parachutes. Oh, I could do the job but the routine of inspecting, folding and packing personal emergency parachutes was so monotonous that it drove me crazy. It was the same steps over and over, the same physical motions, the same… sameness. And it had to be the same for obvious reasons. Parachute maintenance requirements are demandingly precise with **no deviations**, because missing something could result in a death.

Being a Bameo organization - as opposed to a squadron – meant that those of us on the bottom of the heap were just a mass of bodies. I suppose I was lucky to be in Winnipeg, as it was a relatively small maintenance organization and our supervisors did take some interest in our well-being. From what I had been told, when individuals were posted to CFB Trenton's Bameo organization they often felt as if they were the property of the maintenance officer's empire and in his realm people and planes were assigned when and to where they were required. That's right folks! As an aircraft technician, if you were posted to Trenton you were just swimming in a big pool of maintainers with no real sense of belonging and often treated as less than a number. Subsequently, the subjugated worker bees would sometimes drag their feet causing the length of aircraft inspection cycles to increase. In the mind of a maintainer, it stands to reason that "…if the boss doesn't give a damn about my welfare why should I bust my ass for him? Oh, I'll still do the job to the best of my ability but it won't be expedient." If you don't believe me ask any aircraft technician who worked on CC-130s. CFB Trenton was often referred to as the Black Hole for a reason.

There are two things that take place in Manitoba every mid-November just like clockwork. Remembrance Day and the opening of deer season. I had been on or had attended a Remembrance Day parade ever since I was in army cadets and this year, instead of parading at the cenotaph, I planned to go out to harvest my first grain fed whitetail deer. To make sure that I wasn't going to be on the parade, I duly submitted my CF-100 Annual Leave Request form in mid-August for the last two weeks in November and it was approved a week later.

Winter came early that year to Manitoba. By the end of October the leaves had fallen from the trees, the ambient temperature had dropped far below freezing and snow was drifting deep in the farmer's fields. On the first Tuesday of November Warrant Officer Bruno Dostie, the Maintenance Warrant Officer, strode confidently into the Safety Systems section with a sheaf of papers clutched in his hand.

"Cpl McMillan! Here are your parade orders!" barked Bruno.

"Uh, what parade orders, Sir?" I asked.

"For the Remembrance Day parade."

"Sorry, Warrant Dostie but I'm on leave at that time." At which point, WO Dostie promptly began to shout at me.[31]

"There's no leave granted during that time frame! The entire Base will be on parade!"

"Everybody but me, Sir. I have a signed leave pass."

"Who's the idiot who granted you leave? Show me the pass!"

---

[31] Warrant Officer Bruno Dostie always talked like this when people questioned him. But, if you were in the right, the only way you could win the argument was to hold your ground and shout back.

I retrieved my leave pass from my wallet, unfolded it and read aloud the authorizing signature…Warrant Officer B. Dostie.

Thoroughly unimpressed at the sudden turn of events, WO Dostie beat a hasty retreat back to his office to lick his wounds. He didn't like being proven wrong, especially by a mere corporal. He would need a replacement and as luck would have it he had one. Earlier that morning a fellow safety systems technician, Cpl Sylvan Deslippes walked in to work from his PMQ (Private Married Quarters) for his day shift in servicing. It was about 06:15 hrs. The wind was up and the temperature was down. Sylvan had his hands thrust deep in the pockets of his skunk jacket as he had accidently left his gloves at work the previous day. Unbeknownst to Sylvan, as he walked into the breezeway, his transgression was being observed. Seated in the dark, one floor above the entrance to Hangar 16 was Chief Warrant Officer (CWO) Genovy, commonly referred behind his back as Obi-Wan Genovy, The Man With No Life.

With nothing better to do with his time, CWO Genovy often crept into his darkened office to watch unsuspecting technicians as they came to work in the hope of spotting someone committing a dress code violation. Remove your head dress before entering the hangar – two days of extra duties. Jacket not zipped up to the height of your breast pockets or higher? That will cost you as well. Sylvan's crime? He had his hands in his pockets to ward off the possibility of frostbite. After he had completed his required aircraft checks, Cpl Deslippes was ordered to report immediately to CWO Genovy's office.

"Cpl Deslippes, why were your hands in your pockets when you came into work this morning?" questioned Obi-Wan from behind his desk.

Standing at attention, Sylvan answered, "I had forgotten my gloves at work, Sir. It is -20°C and I didn't want to get frostbite on my hands."

"Cpl Deslippes, you will proceed upstairs to Clothing Stores where you will purchase a second pair of gloves. You will then return to this office and show me the gloves and the receipt. This is so, no matter where you go, you will never be without a pair of gloves. You will have the opportunity to wear your new gloves on the Remembrance Day parade.

"But Sir, gloves are not worn on the Remembrance Day parade because it is held inside the Winnipeg Convention Centre."

"You will be replacing Cpl McMillan as a cairn guard in Norway House. You will be departing the Base from 10 Hangar at 08:00 hrs on board a Dak. Here are you orders. That will be all Corporal Deslippes. You are dismissed!"

On Remembrance Day, Sylvan boarded a frigid CC-129 Dakota at 07:30 hrs. The aircraft had been B checked and cold soaked at 06:30 hrs. As scheduled, the aircraft lifted off at 08:00 hrs for the 460 km trip. If all went well and there wasn't a strong head wind, it would take nearly two hours to get to Norway House. This would allow just enough time for the parade contingent, consisting of a bagpiper from the 402 Squadron Pipe and Drum band, four cairn guards, two wreath bearers and some 2nd Lieutenant (a coffee boy) from Air Command - who thought it might be neat to volunteer for the duty - to fall into formation, have the lone piper play the Last Post, drop the wreaths and then snag a cup of hot chocolate before climbing back aboard the venerable Dak for the trip home. The good news was that a free meal had been provided for the trip - a box lunch from the Mess hall - consisting of a cold bologna sandwich, some carrot sticks, a package of fig newton cookies, an old wrinkled apple and a small carton of milk that was now a milk-cicle.

So there I was... Working out of 10 Hangar in the summer of 1989. I had just replaced Cpl Dave Salter on 1 Crew in 10 Hangar servicing. It was nothing but open skies and bright sunshine during the day and inky blackness with hordes of ravenous mosquitoes hunting for victims at night. Regardless of any weather conditions it was far better than being surrounded by the concrete walls inside the main shop. It didn't take long before friendships were formed with many of my fellow crew members. These friendships were forged through long working hours, difficult situations and (more often than not) copious quantities of beer.

During that particular summer, northern Manitoba was stricken with a higher than usual number of forest fires that forced the evacuation of some 18,000 people from the communities in the region. Many of the main highways were blocked by smoke and fire and, as a result, the order was given to fly in the Hercs to get the people out.³² Over in 10 Hangar, we were told that until further notice all navigation training flights were cancelled and that our four CC-130s were to be immediately reconfigured for full passenger seating or max pax. To complete the reconfiguration we began by removing the custom built Nav training consoles and placing them on the hangar floor. Next, the centre stanchion posts were mounted down the middle of the fuselage and then linked together with the upper and lower beams. Then, the standard military rag and tube seats were pinned and clipped into place, followed by the pax lap belts being snapped onto the D-rings. A well-honed crew could, with a little luck, complete this reconfig in as little time as an hour, and we had four aircraft to change over.

By now the aircrew had been called to Base Operations to receive their briefings and to file their flight plans. There was no time to waste. Those who were not involved in reconfiguring the aircraft began their respective trade B checks. A couple of the aircraft also required a fuel up-lift so some technicians were dispatched to do those jobs as well. All of this work had to be finished before a flight engineer could even start his pre-flight inspection, which could take up to another two hours to complete.

In just over three hours we had completed all of the configurations and the servicing checks. Our first aircraft was about to launch for Thompson - about 750 kilometres north of Winnipeg - when we got word that a 435 Squadron Herc from

---

³² Forest Fires in Manitoba Force Evacuation of 18,000, Associated Press, July 24,1989, www.apnewsarchive.com, 20 September 2016.

Edmonton was inbound with the first load of evacuees. The City of Winnipeg was now routing a fleet of buses to the Base to pick them up and take them to their temporary accommodations. The aircraft was about thirty minutes out and our Crew Chief had already designated two individuals for the park crew. Things were about to get very busy.

Everything went as planned when the first Herc arrived. The park crew marshalled it into position. The nose wheels were chocked, the engines were shut down and ground power was applied. Once the aircraft was secured military police officers were on hand to guide the passengers across the tarmac and onto the waiting buses. After their departure we approached the aircraft to do an A/B check and the fuel bowser pulled into position off of the right hand (R/H) wing. It was then that the loadmaster asked us where he could wash out the cargo area of his aircraft. The ramp and door of the plane were already open so we went around back to take a look. I had seen some messy aircraft before but nothing could compare to what I saw that day. Most of the floor and the ramp of the plane were covered in vomit, urine and faeces. From the stench you would have thought the cargo had been livestock, not people.

"What the hell happened, Loady?" Cpl Walsh asked.

"We had them all strapped in. The take-off was normal. I figured some of them were going to be sick because they had never flown before. I had given my pre-departure brief. Handed out plenty of passports (air sickness bags) and showed them where the toilet was. We were barely ten minutes wheels in the well when somebody starts to throw up. Well, that starts a chain reaction and a couple more start to heave. Then one lady has to go to the washroom. No problem. I show her where it is and she goes behind the curtain. A couple more have to go and now I have a line up for the head. A few minutes later one guy gets out of his seat and decides he wants to take a look up in the cockpit. So, I go forward to head him off and while I'm gone some of the people decided they just couldn't wait for the shitter so they just dumped on the floor. Of course, that caused more people to start puking."

Looking at the aircraft, we knew that he wasn't lying.

"Okay, Loady. What we'll do is, as soon as the aircraft is refuelled, we'll tow it over to the corner of the hangar and we can have the fire hall hook up a hose to the hydrant."

"Thanks guys. I'll need a hand putting the seats up."

We drew straws.

While the re-fuel job was ongoing a couple of technicians, myself included, assisted the loadmaster in raising all the passenger seats. When the refuel job was done, a tow crew hooked on to the aircraft and moved it over to the corner of the hangar. Ground power was re-applied and, once the grasshopper arms were disconnected, the ramp was lowered to the ground. With a hose from the fire hall the loadmaster first washed out his precious cargo area onto the ramp and into a drain. Then he meticulously mopped the floor with a disinfectant solution, let it sit for ten minutes and rinsed it off again. With the sun beating down on the apron it didn't take long for the floor to dry.

The second plane from Winnipeg was now ready for departure but we were all concerned that every plane returning would be in the same condition as that first arrival or worse. Our trepidation grew as we learned that the next Herc was on its way in. It was one of ours: aircraft 130310. We all watched as it taxied into position. The aft door was open and the ramp was level. On engine shut down the GTC continued to run and the ramp was lowered to the ground. Inside the aircraft the passengers were still strapped into their seats. Or rather, they were strapped onto their seats. It would seem at some point the first inbound Herc had radioed to the outbound plane and informed them of their situation on board. Before aircraft 130310 had landed to pick up their passengers the loadmaster had dropped all of the passenger lap belts behind and below the seats so they could not be used. Once all the passengers were sitting nice and pretty on the rag and tube seats he ran a 5000 pound cargo tie down strap across their laps. The strap was stretched from the 245 Bulkhead at the front of the plane all the way to the back. After being hooked into a D-ring on the the floor the strap was cinched up. Comfy? Snug? Good, because you're not getting up until we get to Winnipeg. This quickly became the SOP (Standard Operating Procedure) for strapping in the evacuees. It was very fast, very secure and it sure helped to keep the planes clean.

The evacuation of the towns in northern Manitoban went on throughout the night. It would continue into the next day and over the next week. With the aircraft flying at all hours of the day the technicians began to live at the hangar. For sustenance we had the choice of enjoying the late night meals the Base laid on for us at the mess hall or someone was voluntold to do a pizza run. Other than that, the only time anyone left the hangar was to shower, change clothes or to buy cigarettes. On the third night, at about 01:00 hrs, a military police officer came through the hangar and found everyone asleep. He stopped by the couch in the crew room and shook Dave awake.

"Hey! What are you guys all doing in here?" queried the Meathead.

"We're sleeping. What does it look like?" Be quiet or you'll wake everyone up!" cautioned Corporal Duncan.

"But, what are you doing here?"

"Uh, we're flying the residents out of the north because their towns are on fire and we have Hercs landing around the clock. Now be quiet!"

"But, you can't sleep in the hangar!"

"Oh yeah! Well, you can take it up with my Sergeant!"

"Where is he?"

"He's sleeping in the office across the hall!"

"We'll see about that!"

The MP walked out of the crew room and went looking for the sergeant. Just as Dave had said the Sergeant was asleep in his office with his chair tipped back and his feet resting on an open desk drawer.

"Uh, excuse me Sergeant. But, what are you doing sleeping in the hangar?"

As you can imagine, our Crew Chief was none too pleased at being woken up by this MP. After a few quick questions, a few choice words and a heated call to the watch commander the patrolman was quickly recalled back to his section

The vast majority of the first group of evacuees who arrived in Winnipeg were housed in local motels and hotels. Once all the available rooms were tapped out the province began to look for alternatives. One place to be utilized was a gymnasium at the Red River College where hundreds of temporary beds were set up. The provincial government also provided food vouchers that were redeemable at some local restaurants. The evacuees would remain in Winnipeg for close to a month before being allowed to return to their homes after the fires had been extinguished.

Quite often CFB Winnipeg received visiting aircraft from across the continent. Some of them came in for fuel and a quick turnaround while others came in for an extended period of time due to an unserviceability. We had a USAF C-130E out of Alaska parked on our ramp with an broken generator. As a matter of course Cpl Duncan - being an aircraft electrician - volunteered to help out the aircraft's Crew Chief. A pair of aero stands were positioned on either side of the # 3 engine. Dave helped him remove the dead generator and while the USAF Crew Chief went to supply to get a new one, he mounted the generator crane onto the side of the engine nacelle. The C-130 generator weighs in at about 85 pounds and is mounted onto the engine with twelve stud bolts. The difficulty comes when trying to slide it into position while aligning all the stud bolts and the phenolic gear, hence the need for the crane.

About twenty minutes later the Crew Chief, who was a very large man, came walking back from the aircraft supply section in 16 Hangar some 400 yards away, with the generator tucked under his arm. Stopping in front of the aero stand he looked up and saw the crane mounted on the side of the engine.

Pointing at the crane with his free hand he asked Dave, "What's that?"

"It's a crane for the generator."

"That's real cute!"

He then proceeded to climb up the aero stand one-handed, took the generator out from under his arm and with balanced precision he *palmed* the 85 pound unit into position aligning all twelve stud bolts and the phenolic spline on the first go. Looking at the astonished Cpl Duncan sitting astride the engine nacelle, he said, "Would you mind putting the mounting nuts on?"

"Uh, no. Not at all" replied Dave, as he quickly began to fish the parts out of pocket.

When Cpl Duncan came back to the hangar and told us what had taken place we were in a state of disbelief. We all knew from experience that it was impossible to hold a Herc generator in one hand for any length of time, not to mention mounting it on the engine in one shot. That was until we saw how big the USAF Crew Chief was. When this giant of a man walked into the servicing section to say thanks for the help we all knew that Dave had been telling us the truth.

The majority of the technicians on the servicing crews had an average of more than seven years in the military so having a brand new private posted in to the unit became something of a novelty. It was like receiving a Christmas present from a long lost relative who you hadn't seen in years. One Friday afternoon, I was on my way home after my shift when I found this poor soul wearing his best dress uniform standing in the middle of the breezeway clutching his PLCC card. It was quite plain that this person was lost.

"Excuse me Corporal. But could you help me?" asked the young airman.

"Sure. What's your name?" I replied.

Standing at attention with his heels together, the young lad smartly replied, "Private Trent Reineke, Corporal!"

"What can I help you with, Private Reineke?"

"Uh, I'm trying to get signed in and I don't know where I have to go."

"Let me take a look at that PLCC card."

Private Reineke handed me the document and I quickly looked it over to see where he had signed in and where he still had to go. I went through the list while talking to myself, "Well, let me see. Clothing stores? It's closed. Bameo Orderly Room? They're gone. Base Orderly Room? You've done that. MSE? They're closed."

"What's MSE, Corporal?"

"Mobile Support Equipment. It's where you will go to get your 404's. That's your military driver's licence so you can drive on the ramp."

"Oh."

"Hey, I see that you haven't signed into the Red River Lounge yet!"

"What's the Red River Lounge?"

"Just follow me. The PMC should still be in his office and we'll get you signed in. Okay?"

Trent followed me over to the Junior Ranks Mess where I took him to the PMC's office downstairs. We were in luck because the PMC was still there and Trent was duly signed as the newest member of the Red River Lounge. Over the next six hours and a great many beer, I learned that Private Trent Reineke was from a small farming community in Saskatchewan. He liked hunting but was not too keen on fishing. He owned his own truck, which he called the Black Knight. Trent had just graduated from CFB Borden as an aero-engine technician and was anxiously looking forward to working on the crew. He asked me a thousand questions and got only a few answers in reply because I felt that he would learn more once he was out on the flight line.

When we were done drinking - and I knew that we were done because Trent was now passed out in his chair - I covered him up in his dress uniform jacket and pinned on a "Please Tuck Me In" note that provided his name and barracks room number. He would be safe in his chair until the cleaning staff woke him up in the morning.

Private Trent Reineke was special. He was everyone's assistant, everyone's friend and everyone's little brother. He would run and fetch tools or supplies just like a puppy and no one ever abused him. To do so would incur the wrath of the rest of the fitters and you really wouldn't want to wish that on anyone. Instead, everyone took Private Reineke under their wing to mentor him on the path to be a member of the crew and superb technician. Of course, this did not impede the crew from enjoying a laugh or two at Trent's expense.

Trent's tutelage was not without its funnier moments as well. Such as when Trent marshalled in a Herc for the very first time. He had completed his training package and was finally ready to stand out front as the Number One Man,[33] which meant he was in charge of the park job. Even if a sergeant was manning the Number Two Man position it wouldn't matter because Trent would still be the one giving the orders.

So, there was Trent...Standing in front of a designated parking spot on a warm summer day. He was wearing his ear defenders and a high visibility vest, a pair of marshalling paddles held firmly in his hands. He had prepositioned his Number Two

---

[33] Depending on the aircraft's type a start or park crew could be comprised of a single position to multiple positions. Each position will have specific tasks that it is responsible for. Regardless of how many people are involved they are all under the direction of the Number One Man. The Number One Man is responsible for the safety of the team and the aircraft during the park/start evolution.

Man at a safe place on the edge of the flight line near the corner of the hangar. Aircraft 130307 was moving down the civilian taxiway towards the military ramp. Once it crossed onto our apron Trent put his arms high in the air and pointed to the parking spot in front of himself. This signalled to the pilot that he was to proceed towards the marshaller. Once, twice, three times he indicated the parking spot and for each indication Trent went down on one knee as if he was on an aircraft carrier. As the mighty Herc drew near, paralleling the edge of the apron, Trent waited for just the right moment to have the pilot swing the nose gear over onto the angled parking line.

Timing is everything. Trent missed the mark by several feet. When he gave the indication to turn the nose wheel the plane had to make a hard left and then a right to re-align itself with the painted hash mark. Knowing that the entire crew was standing in front of the hangar waiting for him screw up the mental pressure Trent was experiencing must have been extreme. Then, just as Trent was crossing arms high above his head signalling for brakes to be applied, a hydraulic line in the nose wheel well broke.

The remainder of the park procedure was unremarkable. The GTC was running. The engines came to a stop. Trent called for ground power to be applied. Wheel chocks were put in place. The aircrew exited the plane. The only thing wrong was the growing puddle of hydraulic fluid spreading slowly all over the apron. By the time Trent had walked back to the hangar the die had already been cast.

Seeing us standing there Trent asked, "So, how do you think I did?"

Corporal Bob Whittle quickly jumped in to set the stage, "I think you might have turned him too sharply. You had better go see the sergeant."

Seeing Trent coming towards him the Crew Chief bellowed for effect, "Reineke! Get in my office!"

Nervously, Trent followed the Crew Chief back into the hangar, while listening to his tirade of expletives and accusations. He didn't know what to make of this. No one had spoken to him this way since basic training. He was beginning to believe that he had screwed up and he was in serious trouble.

"Just what the hell did you think you were doing out there?"

"I was just marshalling the aircraft."

"Well, you sure as hell don't know how to do that right! You waited too bloody long to start the turn. A turn that was too frickin sharp and it blew a hydraulic line because of your damn mistake. Now, I want you to sit here and fill out this this Statement of Responsibility and Liability form. Make sure you don't leave anything out. Not one bloody word and if you're lucky the Board of Inquiry won't take the cost of repairs out of your pay."

"What do you mean take it out of my pay?"

"Look Private, there are fifteen witnesses who all saw how you turned that aircraft. Do you think for one minute that your crew mates are going to put their careers in jeopardy and lie just to save your scrawny ass? Not a chance. It happens even to the best of us. You will just have to suck it up. Not to worry Trent. It's not too bad because they'll just set up a pay allotment and deduct the cost a little bit at a time. You'll hardly even notice it."

"Well, how much do you think it will cost?"

"With the parts, the man hours and replenishing the lost fluids…maybe about $1,500."

"Are you kidding me? $1,500!"

"Yeah, but the expensive part will be the cost of the environmental clean-up. That can easily double the cost. But, if we can get the fluid contained and off the ground before any of it gets flushed into a drain then that will save you a bunch of money."

"Sergeant, how can I help?"

"Here's what you can do…"

When we next saw Private Reineke he was taking a large bucket of dust bane out onto the tarmac where he used it to liberally cover the spilled hydraulic fluid. Using a small whisk broom he gently massaged the absorb-all into the concrete and after waiting the prescribed amount of time - as dictated by our Crew Chief - Trent swept up every crumb from under the aircraft before bagging it for disposal. After completing the job and all the associated paperwork, Trent sat down at the picnic table to have a smoke and to contemplate this turn of events. Everyone left him alone. Nobody talked to him or offered any advice. We simply went about our business of fixing the broken hydraulic line and completing the A checks on A/C 307.

The aircraft was fully serviceable in about two hours. Once the hydraulic line was fixed and the aircraft was finally signed off as serviceable the Crew Chief called for a crew meeting to be held at the Herc Lounge to discuss the incident. During the meeting it was revealed to Pte Reineke that the repair costs would not be recovered from his pay and in fact the idea was all just a joke. As he raised his glass of beer, Trent knew that he had been well played. Welcome to the crew!

To say some members of the flight servicing crew in Winnipeg drank to excess would be a gross understatement. There were many times when after working a full eight hour day shift the crew would head over to the Mess to indulge in up to six hours of alcohol consumption. Some nights we would still be sitting there when the guys from the evening crew came in to have a couple at the end of their shift. If we were not going to make last call we would simply send Trent to the Mess with a wad of cash and a grocery list. For accepting this important task he always got out of work early and a couple of free beer. Trent's only worry was that we would not show up and he would be stuck with all the beer to himself. The one thing we had to do was make sure that we left the Base before midnight because at midnight the grumpy old Commissionaire manning the front gate was replaced with a Military Police officer. After a few beers, it was quite easy to get past the "old guy on the gate" since all he did was ask what your licence plate number was. Even if you couldn't see past the hood of your vehicle if you could repeat your licence plate number without slurring your words you were good to go. And you got good at it. I could rattle mine of without even thinking about it.

"It's Seven Six Five Why Cee Eh."

"Okay, have a good night."

On the other hand, the MP's would stop you, sniff your breath, make you walk an imaginary straight line and then probably arrest you for impaired driving. Yes, quite a number of folks did drive home impaired. Were they stupid and irresponsible for doing so? Most assuredly. But they never worked on an aircraft while impaired. Yes, there were times when they came into work looking like they'd had been pulled through a knot hole backwards before being dragged over ten miles of bad road. That's when technicians would use their Standard Fitter Repair Kit and get back to the job of fixing planes.

A year after I arrived in Winnipeg a host of changes began happening across the military. Aircraft fleets were being moved, reduced and even eliminated altogether. In 1989, the Daks were

Standard Fitter Repair Kit

Contents may include some or all of the following:

1 x small bottle of Tylenol
1 x small bottle of Ibuprophen
1 x bottle of Visene
Assorted Band-Aids
Rolaids
Condoms
Breath mints
Leftover box lunch cookies
Zantac 150

retired from active service but continued to be lovingly maintained in flight condition by the boys in 10 Hangar until they were finally sold off. Sometime later in 1990 the CT-133's that had been based in Winnipeg were sent elsewhere, likely to Cold Lake. Around the same time, Smokey One, the Air Command VIP bird, was returned to 412 Squadron based at CFB Uplands in Ottawa and was replaced with two CC-142 de-Havilland Dash 8 - 100's that had previously been stationed in Germany. Eventually, the CC-130 Hercules from 429 Squadron, that had been used primarily as navigation trainers would be replaced with the CT-142 Dash 8, affectionately referred to as *Gonzo* for its large protruding bulbous radome at the front of the aircraft. For the personnel - the maintainers - the shakeup meant amalgamating the servicing crews from the two hangars into one. The Daks were retired but the Hercs were still in place and after squashing the two servicing sections together it was decided by the Boys at the Pointy End that the guys in Triple T would learn how to service Hercs and the people from 10 Hangar would learn about the Tutors. Going from Hercs to Tutors was akin to a mechanic going from a Kenworth tractor trailer to a Mazda. No problems. But from a Mazda to a tractor trailer was just a little bit more complicated.

With the arrival of the CT-142 Gonzos, the 429 Squadron Hercs were longer required in Winnipeg as air navigation training platforms. It was decided, somewhere in the upper reaches of Air Command that the best thing for Winnipeg would be to reform the base aircraft maintenance organization as a squadron.

Oh, Happy Days!

The change from a Base Aircraft Maintenance organization to a squadron meant it was no longer **Us & Them**, maintainers versus aircrew. We would all be under the same roof and be one big happy family complete with the weird uncle and the whining cousins (twice removed) who nobody wanted around. But it was a family nonetheless. Of course, this happy family concept only applied to squadron members. Those of us in aircraft servicing still had to contend with the Instrument Check Pilot (ICP) School. A lot of the instructors from the ICP School had previously served in fighter squadrons or with the Snowbirds. While most of the ICP aircrew were pretty much "max relax" there were still some prima donnas who flaunted their rank or position above the peons who were bonded permanently to the tarmac. One pilot in particular comes to mind.

So there we were…It was Christmas Eve. The only thing we had going on was a departure at 21:30 hours for a destination to the east of Winnipeg. The pilot was flying solo and had requested that his luggage be secured in the right hand seat. Whenever a dual seat jet aircraft - such as the CT-114 Tutor[34] - was flown solo the emergency seat pack from the ejection seat was either removed or it was secured into the seat pan with a special tie-down harness to prevent the component from falling out and jamming the flight controls. This same harness allowed objects such as a tool kit, a suitcase or a golf bag to be secured behind the shoulder and lap restraint harnesses.

With the Crew Chief's blessing, we had made up a punch bowl of Moose Milk - an alcoholic punch made with rum, Irish cream, eggnog and vanilla ice cream - and had some potluck appetizers to go with it. The rule of thumb was we had to wait fifteen minutes after "wheels in the well" - that's fifteen minutes after the plane's departure - before we could leave work or in this case enjoy some holiday cheer. The Tutor was already B checked in the hangar when Major C.N. Bull came to the servicing desk requesting that his luggage be tied down in the empty right hand seat.

"Not a problem, Sir. Cpl McMillan, could you tie down the Major's luggage? And MCpl Gauthier, have the tow crew cold

---

[34] The Canadair built CL-41A entered Canadian military service in 1963 as the CT-114 Tutor. It was designed as the primary pilot training aircraft and has been flown by the Canadian Snowbirds Air Demonstration team since 1971. The Royal Malaysian Air Force bought twenty copies of a single seat version, the CL-41G, that could carry up to 4,000 lbs of external stores mounted on underwing and under fuselage hard points. In appearance the Tutor was very similar to the USAF T-37 Dragonfly but was easily distinguished by its high T tail as opposed to the T-37 cruciform T tail.

soak the plane. As soon as the seat pack is tied down tow it out onto the VIP spot for a quick departure."

With all the players in motion it didn't take long for the Tutor to be prepped and towed out to the VIP spot for its scheduled departure at 21:30 hrs local. It's not that Major Bull was a VIP, it's just that the spot was right out in front of the hangar and since it was -20°C and since it was also Christmas Eve the Crew Chief decided to be nice to him. Shortly after the plane was towed into position the pilot came out and strapped in. The start crew was already standing by and soon the pilot was taxiing out for his Christmas flight down east. Once he was safely in the air the members of 1 Crew noted the time and added fifteen minutes. At 21:50 hrs it would be Moose Milk Time and until then the cards were dealt out for another game of Hearts.

The minutes ticked slowly by. Several hands had been played when someone looked out the window and saw a single light descending on a final approach. Our Tutor was back! Was it in trouble? No crash alarm had been sounded.

"Sgt Dubé, that Tutor is on final approach!"

Sgt Charlie Dubé quickly grabbed the phone and called upstairs to Ops to find out if something was amiss.

"Really? You're kidding me right? Okay, thanks for letting me know."

Click!

"Hey guys!" Sgt. Dubé shouted. "You won't believe this! That Major was not scheduled to fly down east. He's scheduled to do bumps and grinds for the next ninety minutes!"

This turn of events must have really torqued off our Crew Chief because he very rarely cursed and just as he passed on the good news we all heard the roar of the engine as the Tutor started to climb back up into the sky.

As scheduled - according to the real flight plan and not the bullshit one we were given - the Major landed ninety minutes later after completing a dozen or more touch-and-goes. A two man tow crew met him out at Spot 28, which is just about the farthest parking spot you can get from 16 Hangar. Once he climbed out of the aircraft, his luggage was removed from the aircraft and unceremoniously dumped onto the ramp. The aircraft was quickly connected to the tow bar. With the tow crew supervisor operating the mule and his Number Two man now riding the brakes they headed back for the hangar leaving Major C. N. Bull to drag his luggage down 450 metres of frozen tarmac.

By the time the pilot walked into servicing the aircraft had been put to bed and the boys were well into their Christmas cheer. As the Major signed in the aircraft Sgt Dubé informed him that a report of this incident would be forwarded to the Commandant of the ICP School. Little, if anything official, would be done to discipline the pilot. After all, in truth he did nothing wrong. It was just a shitty thing to do to another service member. Not to worry, most maintainers know how to take care of things like this. Over the next little while any time he was scheduled to go flying something was always found to be unserviceable with his plane and it did not pass its B check inspection. Oh, so sorry.

There are two sayings, well maybe three, that have always been a moral or ethical guide in the military no matter where you are working:

1. Always try to help your fellow man.
2. One good turn deserves another.
3. What goes around comes around.

When I first joined the military we had to form up in a line on payday and when you were called forward you would state your name, produce your ID card and watch as the paymaster counted out your money. Then - just to make sure there were no discrepancies - you would recount it, before signing your name to confirm that you had received the correct amount. Later on, a service member's pay was not given in cash but issued as a cheque, and later still the Canadian military was dragged kicking and screaming into the 20th Century with direct deposit. Pay cheques in the Canadian military are distributed on the 15th and the last day of the month. Depending on where these two dates fall within a calendar month payday could be close to three weeks apart and therefore household budgets could be stretched a bit thin at that time.

It was during one of these long stretches between paydays when a Raven Flight ICP school Tutor was headed almost due south to the USAF Base in Grand Forks, North Dakota. It's a short hop, only some 220 kilometers direct. There were two pilots on board, a Captain and the ICP School commanding officer, LCol Jerry Elias. Prior to start up, one of the technicians, Cpl Bloggins, took the Captain aside and asked him if he could pick him up a carton of American cigarettes. He mentioned that it was almost a week till payday and he would really appreciate it if he could help him out. The Captain said, "No problem" and the technician handed over $20. With the deal struck, the two aircrew took off for lunch in Grand Forks.

Now, I don't know the exact conversation that took place between the CO and the Captain but on their return to Winnipeg the Captain informed Corporal Bloggins that when the CO found out he was doing a favour for a maintainer he had crapped all over him saying, "You don't do favours for those guys!" Feeling sorry that he could not hold up his end of the bargain the Captain returned the twenty and fronted Cpl Bloggins another forty until payday. Thanks, Sir.

So There I was…It was a Sunday afternoon, on the same shift rotation and three weeks after the "No Smokes for You" incident. We were expecting a flight of four CT-114 Tutors returning from a weekend trip over the border. CFB Winnipeg is located across the airfield from an international airport where Canadian Customs is usually pretty busy so 99% of cross border military flights would usually receive what was termed "Courtesy Customs."[35]

---

[35] Canadian Customs Services would quite often grant the privilege of not inspecting a military aircraft for contraband on the ethical assumption that

When a shift change occurs, the members of the crew coming on shift will normally take a look at the status board to gauge what the work load will be. When he came on shift Cpl Bloggins noted that there was a four-ship flight returning from a weekend at Colorado Springs and that LCol Elias was leading the flight. A notation on the board indicated there would be "Courtesy Customs."

"Not a bloody chance," muttered Bloggins.

An hour or so later the four CT-114 Tutors arrived in Winnipeg. The park crew went out and marshalled each of them to a designated spot on the south line. But this time something was different. Once they were in position the ground crew signalled for brakes to be applied and did not place a rope chock around the left main gear wheel. I was in the Safety Systems flight line truck with an O6HA oxygen cart behind me and was parked several spots to the right of the lead aircraft. The four aircraft were sitting there with the engines idling. Several times the pilots signalled for the chocks to be installed and each time the request was denied. It was at that point that the ICP Commanding Officer motioned for Cpl Bloggins to come forward. A hand written note was pressed to the inside of the canopy.

"Why aren't we chocked?"

Bloggins responded to the pilot with his own note.

"Waiting for Customs."

---

military members would not break the law.

Initially, I did not see what was written on the notes and I had no idea that Canada Customs had been called, but on seeing the note from the technician LCol Elias immediately repositioned his oxygen mask to his face.[36] Seconds later, a Canadian Customs vehicle approached the four Tutors. The park crews chocked the planes and toggled the gear door switch to lower the main gear doors for inspection. The pilots shut down the engines and climbed out of the cockpit leaving their parachutes and any personal luggage on board. They now stood casually beside their planes waiting for the customs officer.

"Hi! I'm Officer Smith-Jones from Canada Customs. Can you tell me where you've been and for how long?"

Elias explained for the group, "We were down at Colorado Springs, Colorado. We left Friday at noon."

"Okay, so what do you have to declare to Customs?"

No one said a word except one pilot from the second plane down. He was standing by the wing holding a cardboard box.

"I have a pair of running shoes that I bought."

"That's all you have to declare? Seems like a big waste of my time for just a pair of shoes."

"Yes, I guess that's all there is. Sorry to trouble you," replies LCol Elias.

---

[36] In order to communicate while flying a jet aircraft there is a small microphone mounted inside the oxygen mask.

"Excuse me, Sir?" said Cpl Bloggins, "But, what's in the wing roots?"

A scowl crossed the CO's face as the Customs Officer politely asked, "What's a wing root?"

Grabbing the bilingual screwdriver from his tool pouch, Cpl Bloggins popped open the conformal storage panel built into the left hand wing root. Inside the compartment were three 40 ounce bottles of alcohol, wrapped in clothing to prevent them from clinking against each other.

"Is there only one of these panels per plane?" queried Smith-Jones.

"Heck no. There's one on the other side of plane too!"

"Open them up!"

The ground crew quickly complied with the request and inside each of the wing root storage compartments were three 40 ounce bottles. Two dozen bottles in total.

While eyeing LCol Elias, Customs Officer Smith-Jones declared that there was sufficient evidence to prove that the aircrew were attempting to smuggle alcohol into the country. As such, she was going to seize the alcohol and the aircraft. Unless, of course, the individuals were willing to pay their fines and excise taxes.

After the customs paperwork was all completed, LCol Elias angrily turned to Cpl Bloggins. He was not happy with what Bloggins had done and threatened that some sort of disciplinary action might be involved.

With nothing to lose but a couple of days working in the mess hall, Cpl Bloggins pointed out that if the Lieutenant Colonel had allowed the Captain to do him a favour three weeks earlier then maybe he could have returned that favour today.

To my knowledge Cpl Bloggins was not disciplined.

Those of us who had served in the Canadian Forces (CF) during this time frame suffered through many changes. With a rising federal deficit, the Government of Canada needed to reduce spending and, for those of us who have served in Her Majesty's Forces, this meant another reduction in military spending. Between 1994 and 1999, the DND budget was reduced by 23%, from $12 billion down to $9.25 billion and most importantly, there was a radical downsizing of personnel strength from approximately 90,000 to 60,000. In order to achieve such a rapid reduction, the CF offered a compensation package designed to entice those members who were soon to be retiring to leave just a little bit sooner. This Force Reduction Plan (FRP) was so effective that 14,000 members left the military and in the year 2000, the CF suddenly recognized the fact that there could now be a shortage of personnel required to conduct the necessary tasks of the Canadian Forces.[37]

The FRP was aimed at specific trades which had been identified as overburdened by senior members who were soon to

---

[37] In 2007, Canadian Forces Major John D.V. Vass presented his thesis *Retention in the Canadian Forces* to the U.S. Army Command and General Staff College in Fort Leavenworth, Kansas as part of the requirements for his Master of Military Art and Science degree.

retire or, in many cases, those who should have retired long ago. Release bonuses in the form of the elimination of pension penalties were in the offing. There were some senior members who took the bait but the vast majority remained in the fold, probably out of an institutionalized fear of retirement. The unfortunately largest cohort who left the military were those with less than ten years of service and who felt they could make more money once they were out of the military and back on civvy street.

In addition to the FRP, the federal government - in their everlasting quest to save monies - placed a three-year freeze on all promotions and annual pay incentive increases. This may have been fine if you were already a corporal but not for someone like Pte Reineke who, after four years in that rank, was on the very cusp of being promoted in one month's time to corporal (and thus receive the single largest pay increase in a non-commissioned member's career) when the brakes were suddenly applied. He remained maxed out as a full incentive private until the austerity program was lifted and only then did he finally receive his much delayed promotion to corporal. Due to the government's desire to save a few shekels, Trent, along with everyone else in the military and the federal public service, missed out while the cost of living kept climbing ever higher.

While these changes were happening across the country, adjustments were also taking place at CFB Winnipeg, including a swap in supervisors in the Safety Systems section. Sgt Guy Perron was leaving with an out-of-season posting to 419 Squadron in

Cold Lake, Alberta. His replacement was MCpl (soon to be promoted to Sgt) Sandy Scott and for a short span both of them were in the shop at the same time. This made for some interesting entertainment. MCpl Scott was now holding the reins of power while Perron watched as his oppressive regime come tumbling down around him.

One morning, at 07:25 hrs, the members of the section were standing around in the hallway waiting for the doors to the shop to be opened when MCpl Scott came up the stairs.

"Why is everyone standing in the hallway?" she asked.

"Only the Sergeant, the Master Corporals and the duty technician have keys to the shop," stated Cpl Grigg.

"Whose dumb idea was that?"

"Sgt Perron's!" we all chimed.

And by the end of the day we all had shiny new keys to the shop.

"Why is the door to the fridge locked?" asked Sandy.

"Some time ago someone on duty had lifted the change from the canteen. So now, on Sgt Perron's orders, the fridge is always locked at the end of the day."

"Is the suspected thief still working here?"

"No. He was posted out last year."

"Well, that's just dumb!"

And, the lock was cut off.

"Why is the material locker locked?"

"Someone swiped some velcro, so Sgt Perron locked it up."

"Was it the same guy who stole the canteen funds?"

"Yes."

"Well, that's stupid."

And those locks were removed too.

Personally, I think Sgt Scott took great pleasure in bringing the Safety Systems section out from under Perron's overbearing micro-management while rubbing his nose in it along the way. This by no means says that Sgt Scott let freedom reign. She ran a very tight shop. Everyone knew what was expected of them and everyone did their job to the best of their ability. Failure to perform or failure to do your job correctly as a safety systems technician meant that you were putting lives in jeopardy, which was something that Sgt Scott would not tolerate.

Sandy was also not afraid of taking a stand against the Olde Boys Club. She had come up through the ranks when women were first allowed to be in the Air Force trades, which was a tough battle in an environment that was rife with sexism and misogyny. I can remember when so-called men's magazines like Playboy and Penthouse were common in the workplace as late as 1986. But, through perseverance, Sgt Scott rose to command a shop full of dedicated maintainers.

Shortly after Sgt Scott took charge she received a call from our career manager. He was enquiring as to why I hadn't been tested for a second language ability. As an incentive to advance one's career, just being tested for the ability to learn a second language would boost a person's annual performance review by an extra half a point which could make all the difference at the promotion boards. Knowing that I needed all the help I could get, I had applied to be tested. Surprisingly, I never was. However, since I had requested to be tested, the Inquiring Minds in NDHQ wanted to know why.

"Blaine, can you come into my office please?"

"Sure thing, Sergeant Scott."

I shut down the sewing machine and walked past the parachute tables to her office. At this point in time Sgt Perron was still waiting to depart on his posting to 419 Sqn in Cold Lake and spent his days working on the other Pfaff sewing machine making hockey bags.

Once inside her office Sandy closed the door behind me. I figured that something must be pretty serious for her to shut the door. Sgt Scott asked if I had applied to be tested for a second language ability. I confirmed that I had. She then asked me if I had ever been tested to which I told her that I had not. Sgt Scott informed me that Ottawa was now wondering why I had not been tested especially after I had specifically requested it.

Opening the office door Sandy ushered me out with, "Thanks Blaine, that will be all. Sergeant Perron can I see you for a moment?"

Guy casually got up from the sewing machine and walked past me towards the office. I couldn't see what was happening as the office was situated behind me but I heard the door close heavily behind him. Closed door or not it wasn't long before their voices rose to the level of shouting. And then suddenly, Sgt Perron forcefully swung open the door office door and stormed out of the section.

I turned to see Sgt Scott speaking into the phone. Then, she called out to me from behind her desk, "Don't go anywhere Blaine! I'm going to get to the bottom of this!"

The bottom of what? I had no clue as to what the hell was going on.

Several minutes later the Sameo came into the section. Sandy invited him into her office and after a little chat they called me in. Standing before the Major, Sgt Scott asked me the same two questions she had previously asked and I gave her the exact same answers, after which she asked me if I could try to locate Sgt Perron for her. I found him downstairs having a coffee in the canteen and informed him that Sgt Scott wanted to speak to him as soon as possible. Without saying a word to me, Guy went back upstairs to the shop. About ten minutes later another technician from the section came into the canteen telling me that Sandy wanted to see me in her office.

"Sure thing. Thanks, Gary."

Back in the office, Sgt Scott stated that until Sgt Perron departed for CFB Cold Lake he would not be coming into work. The Sameo had deemed his presence to be too disruptive for shop during the transition to Sgt Scott's command.

What a load of bullshit!

As it turns out, Sgt Perron did not send me for the second language testing because he would have been compelled to give me the extra half point on my PER placing me just a bit higher in the pecking order than someone else who he favoured. Sgt Scott said that she would reschedule my testing and it would be reflected on my next PER. As far as I know there were no career ramifications for Sgt Perron's actions.

So there I was... Working in 402 Sqn servicing on a sunny Saturday afternoon. The reserves were now being integrated with the regular forces on the flight lines as part of another grand experiment whereby the squadron would eventually be 80% reserves and 20% regular forces (as opposed to the other way around). Initially, these people weren't qualified to do anything as the training package had not yet been developed, let alone approved. But, as a warm and fuzzy body, they could be utilized in all manner of tasks not requiring a signature. Assisting in parks and starts, refueling, as a ground guide during a tow job, etc. The vast majority of these young reservists were very dedicated and once a training package was developed and approved they leapt forward to achieve their aircraft servicing qualifications. As full-fledged members of a servicing crew in 402 Squadron, the reservists were treated no differently than regular force personnel by the Crew Chiefs. Tasks would be assigned on a rotational basis by availability of personnel, by their qualifications and experience level.

De Havilland CT-142 Dash 8

Crew - Eight (pilot and co-pilot, two instructors and four students)

Length –	23.63 m
Height –	7.44 m
Wing Span –	25.89 m
Max Speed –	500 km/h
Service Ceiling –	7500 m
Range –	2400 km
Max Weight –	19, 260 kg

A vast majority of 402 Squadron's pilots were reservists as well. Many of them were civilian commuter pilots flying for Air Canada. As many of them were already qualified on the civilian pattern De Havilland Dash-8, it wasn't a stretch for them to be checked out on our aircraft. The CC-142 was the very same aircraft as the civilian version. The only visible differences between it and the CT-142 were aft of the cockpit bulkhead and the large bulbous nose housing a rather large radar antennae. For the safety systems trade the real big difference between the Air Canada Dash-8's and those parked on the military apron was the amount of emergency equipment carried on board. When the Canadian military acquired the CC and CT versions the aircraft arrived with the bare minimum of emergency equipment. There was one first aid kit, the standard airline life preservers and a couple of fire extinguishers. For military operations the aircraft were soon outfitted with what would be considered to be the norm for aviation life support equipment: a basic survival kit (containing emergency rations, a stove, an emergency radio, et al), an aircrew arctic kit complete with a triple-layered SAR survival tent and extra clothing, a ten person raft, military first aid kits, aircrew life preservers and a sleeping kit. All of it was vacuum packed and sealed for its protection.

Earlier that morning, Captain C. Lou Less, the squadron's Aviation Life Support Equipment Officer (ALSEO), had requested the use of a CC-142 to conduct some ground training for a number of Air Force Reserve pilots. The Desk Sergeant had given them permission to use A/C 801. Captain Less thanked him and said that he would let servicing know when the training had been completed. The only additional request was for ground power to be applied.

"MCpl Smith! Have someone put ground power on 801 in the hangar for the ALSEO."

"Right away, Sergeant."

Over the next six hours Captain Less instructed the new Air Force Reserve pilots on his knowledge of the survival equipment. Nobody knew precisely what that was because nobody from the day shift went out to see what hell they were doing. Other than the request for ground power there was no need for any servicing personnel to attend.

Shift change for the incoming servicing crew was at 14:30 hrs. After receiving my handover from the day shift technician I checked the status board for any inbound or outbound flights. It looked like it was going to be a fairly simple night, nothing too strenuous - three inbounds with one remaining overnight and two departing, a Primary Inspection on A/C 142804. The O6HA oxygen cart needed to be refilled and there was a liquid oxygen transfer to be done prior to receiving a shipment on Monday. All pretty run-of-the-mill tasks but first I wanted a cup of coffee. About thirty minutes later the ALSEO returned to the servicing desk.

"Hi Sergeant Dubé. We're all done on 801."

"Uh, okay Sir. Thanks."

"Yeah, the life raft needs to be repacked, the emergency windows have to go back in and unfortunately we couldn't get all of the stuff back into the kits."

"Excuse me, Sir? What are you talking about?"

"We were doing some ground training. Well, that's about it. See ya."

"Captain Less. Could you wait just a minute?" requested the Crew Chief. And then he yelled, "Cpl McMillan!"

"Yes, Sergeant!"

"Get out to aircraft 801 on the hangar floor. Take a quick look and get back to me asap."

Not knowing what to expect, I quickly headed out to see what was amiss. As soon as I stepped out onto the hangar floor I was in utter shock at what I saw. The emergency equipment, all of it, was strewn all around the aircraft on the hangar floor. The basic survival kit was sitting open inside the cargo door. Both the No. 1 and No. 2 first aid kits were sitting open on a maintenance stand with a number of the sterile dressings torn open. The life raft was inflated and sitting on the hangar floor off the nose of the aircraft with the anchoring lanyard snaking its way up the crew stairs and into the cabin. The SAR tent was half assembled. The aircrew arctic and the sleeping kit stowage bags had been sliced open and contents were dumped inside the tent. The port side emergency exit was lying face down on the hangar floor - it's window cracked like a spider's web. Hastily, I turned and ran back to the servicing desk to find Captain Less still standing there.

"Well?" asked the Crew Chief.

I shot him a look of concern and asked Captain Less to wait just a couple more minutes as I checked through the pockets of my flight jacket. I was looking for my little red notebook. Besides part numbers and work unit codes it also contained a few all important contact numbers.

"Hello, Sgt Scott?"

"What's up, Blaine?"

"I need you to come to the hangar right away!"

"Is it important? We're having some people over this evening and the guests are starting to arrive. Is this for a 2J signature?"

"No, Sandy. It's much bigger than that!" I replied before relaying to her what I had witnessed. After hearing me out Sandy quickly gave me some instructions.

"Listen. I'm on my way in. If the ALSEO tries to leave have the Crew Chief call the MP's and have him detained on the destruction of military property. I also want you to call in the duty photo tech and have him take pictures of everything. I'm calling the Sameo. I'll be there in ten minutes!"

True to her word, Sgt Scott wasted no time getting to the hangar, followed shortly thereafter by the duty photo technician and Major Davies, the squadron's aircraft maintenance engineering officer. With the ALSEO in tow, the four of them went out to the hangar floor. As much as I wanted to be a fly on the wall, it would be best to remain out of the line of fire for this one and besides, I knew Sandy would fill me in on the details later. Their meeting should have taken about fifteen minutes but it lasted closer to an hour and in that time I never heard Sgt Scott raise her voice once. I have no doubt that it took some restraint on her part. Instead, Major Davies had taken the lead in the inquisition. In the end, Captain C. Lou Less was told to submit a report to the Sameo by Monday morning detailing all of the "ground training" activities which had been carried out and who was involved.

Once the scene was cleared the other technicians and myself inspected the damage that had been done to the aircraft and made the appropriate unserviceability entries (form CF-349) in the aircraft record set. With the grateful assistance of my crewmates, we gathered up all of the survival equipment and routed it to the main shop upstairs. Over the next three weeks all those who had been involved in the "ground training" presented themselves to Sgt Scott who personally instructed them in the fine art of inspecting and packing aircraft survival equipment. Rest assured that if some minor detail was not correct in each step of the procedure she would have them unpack the kit and start over. The ten-man raft must have been through the complete inspection and packing cycle at least four times. Some of the pilots were also detailed to assist the airframe techs in replacing all the one-time seals they destroyed on the emergency exits.

In total, the aircraft was unserviceable for four weeks. Hundreds of man-hours and thousands of dollars were needlessly wasted inspecting, repairing, replacing and re-installing the equipment and components. As the ALSEO, Captain C. Lou Less was fully aware that the squadron's Safety Systems section had complete sets of equipment specifically designated for training and that the section routinely conducted ground training sessions. Whatever possessed him to supervise his own training session without prior approval is beyond me.

The passenger version Dash-8, the CC-142, was a very versatile aircraft for military purposes. It had a large cargo door on the aft left hand side. The passenger seats could be moved to any position in the fuselage accommodating up to thirty or more passengers or remove them all together for carrying cargo or a combination of cargo and passengers by moving the aft cargo bulkhead farther forward. Modifying the seating/cargo arrangement is called a configuration change or a re-config. The removal or addition of any equipment must be signed for in the aircraft record set. Airframe technicians would sign for the actual seats themselves and, as a safety systems tech, I would have to sign for the life preservers contained under the seats. It just so happens that early one spring morning, at 04:45 hrs, I was called in to sign for just such a re-config job.

Rinnng Rinnng

"Hello?"

"Hi Blaine. It's Sergeant Dubé. I know it's early but I need you to come in to do a B check and sign for a re-config. The aircraft may need to depart at any minute so the sooner you're in the better." Click. The line went dead.

I arrived at 16 Hangar about fifteen minutes later and found that aircraft 802 was already out on the flight line with ground power applied. Both of the doors were open and there were two suspicious black Suburbans with heavily tinted windows parked nearby.

When accessing a Dash-8 through the crew door you will find the galley area directly on the opposite side of the fuselage. Sitting on the small work station were four large boxes of Robin's Doughnuts and two cardboard coffee urns. In the aft cargo area I saw four large Pelican long rifle cases and several smaller Pelican cases all secured to the D-rings in the floor with cargo tie down straps. Something unusual was most definitely afoot.

After completing my inspection, I went to the servicing desk to sign off the paperwork. Sgt Dubé was there waiting for me. "So, what's up Sarge?"

"A guy in Flin Flon has shot some lady and has taken a girl hostage. The local RCMP have him cornered and have asked for the SWAT team and two police dogs to be flown up to provide assistance. Most of them are in the Stevenson VIP lounge. Are the dog handlers still parked out by 802?"

"I saw two blacked out Suburbans parked out there. Looked pretty serious so I didn't check to see who was in them."

"I should have given you a heads up. Sorry about that."

Sgt Charlie Dubé was one of the good ones.

Aircraft 802 never did make its flight to Flin Flon. The local RCMP, who had tracked the perpetrator to an old cement truck drum at the local landfill, had informed him that the SWAT team and police dogs would soon be on their way north from Winnipeg. The kid never even hesitated. He threw out his weapon and came out with his hands up.[38]

By virtue of our proximity to the Air Command Puzzle Palace - squatting large on the other side of the airfield - the personnel of 402 Squadron were often used as subjects for the many trials and experimentations that would complete the requirements for some desk jockey's master's thesis. Reverse the ratio of Reg Force to Reservists to create an operational Total Force unit? Sure thing. Trial eight different styles of boots for use on the flight line. You betcha! How about wearing all the layers of $3,000 worth of your new Gore Tex environmental clothing so we can determine how it functions while carrying out routine flight servicing activities...so

---

[38] On 10 May 1993, RCMP in Flin Flon, Manitoba arrested James Philip Bridson, aged 18, for the murder of his ex-girlfriend's mother and brother. After shooting two people, Bridson took his ex-girlfriend, Meaghan McConnell, aged 13, hostage. After a 72 hour manhunt Bridson was found in an abandoned cement mixer and taken into custody. On 21 September 1994, Bridson was sentenced to two concurrent 25 year life terms.

sorry that it's now summer time and +32°C on the tarmac. Try your best not to sweat.

In 1994, a plan called Operation Genesis was hatched by Air Command and christened by National Defence Headquarters (NDHQ). It was a perfect name for the amalgamation of the air trades from thirteen trades down to three plus one. Don't quote me but I believe that when I joined the military the air technician trades were as follows: airframe, aero-engine, integral systems, instrument electrical, communications systems, radar systems, safety systems, air weapons, refinishers, machinists, metals technicians, armament (Explosives Ordnance Disposal was a specialty field within the armament trade) and photo. With the loss of so many bodies due to the FRP (plus the routine retirements) and almost no recruitment to the air trades the people at the pointy end suddenly realized that pretty soon there wouldn't be enough qualified technicians left to cobble together an aircraft tow crew. Hence, the brilliant idea of teaching everyone how to help out the other trades.

By all accounts, the air trades restructuring initiative was never intended to produce an individual who could perform as an all knowing all seeing 'Super Tech' that could fix and sign for everything. The intent was to have aircraft technicians conversant enough in the associated trades that they could work on basic systems and eventually become specialists in a particular field of expertise such as propulsion systems, hydraulics, life support equipment, etc. In essence, we were already the specialists and now we would be regressing to learn all of the common core skills. It is interesting to note that the concept the Canadian Air Force was rapidly moving towards is very similar to what the civilian aircraft trades have been doing for years. Mind you, they don't have a weapons system on board a Boeing 747. Now that the three air force trades (aviation, avionics and aircraft structures) have been fully implemented the civilian aircraft technicians are now moving more towards that point from whence we came – extreme specialization. At one time the USAF used to be even more specialized than we were. For example, in order to refill a quick disconnect lox converter a cryogenics specialist could not open the panel on an aircraft to remove it. He would have to wait for the Skin technician - the guy responsible for the overall outer surface of the aircraft - to open up the panel. Additionally, a hydraulic specialist may work on the brake system but a tire technician had to remove the wheel first. To change a CC-130 engine a Canadian MRP (Maintenance and Repair Party) could have as few as three people (an electrician and two fitters) whereas the Americans would have to send three or four times the number to cover all the tasks and signatures.

Operation Genesis was a three month crash course conducted at CFB Borden,[39] a place that I was quite familiar with, having

---

[39] Each military member on the course had more than 10 years in the service. However, the staff at CFB Borden still considered us to be just students and treated us as if we had just come out of Recruit School. No new students had attended a basic trades course in over four years. In order to keep themselves proficient the instructors taught each other the cross training package and then became certified as cross trained without any practical experience.

spent six months there on my basic trades course plus another month or so between a Special Aircrew Helmet Fitting course and a Cryogenic Equipment Maintenance course. The trade conversion course covered the very rudimentary basics of each trade. My own trade's six month safety systems course was given in two days! The entire airframe TQ3 course was pared to six or seven days. The aero-engine basic course was reduced to roughly the same length.

I was lucky enough to have a fitter as a roommate because I couldn't wrap my head around the theory of jet propulsion. He summarized it for me to its basic elements: suck, squeeze, bang and blow. When the course was over, there was an additional training package to be completed when we returned home. For myself and about a dozen other individuals, we did not have the opportunity to complete the extra training as we were all posted out of 402 Sqn.

In 1994, 435 Squadron was relocated from CFB Edmonton to CFB Winnipeg. This unit was unique in that it was the only triple tasked squadron in Canada providing air to air refueling, search and rescue as well as cargo transport, commonly referred to as trash hauling. Seven aircraft were moved to 17 Wing Winnipeg, five KCC-130HT air to air refueling tankers and two older CC-130H cargo aircraft, but the squadron didn't bring enough technicians to maintain them. As the senior corporal in the Safety Systems section I was tapped to go to the other side of the hangar. But there was a slight problem…

"Sgt Scott. So, who's this Corporal McMillan we're getting?"

"Chief Warrant Officer Kampermann, Cpl McMillan is my senior corporal. He is fully qualified in his trade and has previously been posted to a SAR squadron. He has experience working on Hercs when 429 Squadron was based here in Winnipeg. Cpl McMillan is also fully qualified to maintain the equipment in the liquid oxygen building, which will now be under your squadron's control."

"Fine. But, does he play baseball or hockey?"

"No, he doesn't Chief."

"Well then, I don't want him. I would like Cpl Snodgrass to be posted over to 435 Squadron. He used to be in Edmonton and had played on our sports teams."

"Chief Kampermann, Cpl Snodgrass was posted to 402 Squadron just last year and is not on the list. If you want to discuss it with the career manager that would be fine but I will have to object."

"Have it your way Sgt Scott. But, McMillan had better be everything you said he is."

And with that, I was posted once again.

Crossing the Hall

I was moving back to a Search and Rescue unit and I was loving every minute of it. Being a member of a SAR squadron was one of the most exciting things I had ever experienced in my military career. Why? Because, serving in a Search and Rescue squadron made me feel like I was contributing to something positive, something larger than myself. My job was much like a link in a chain: doing it to the best of my ability enabled the aircraft to launch successfully which in turn enabled it to deliver the SAR techs to their target.

Even though five of the seven Hercules in the squadron were Air to Air tankers all of them were all capable of being re-configured for hauling cargo and for Search and Rescue. When configured for SAR, the aircraft had a pair of uniquely manufactured platforms mounted adjacent to the para doors at the rear of the fuselage that provided a comfy seat with a floor-to-ceiling Plexiglas window for spotting purposes. Nothing can compare to the Lockheed C-130 Hercules as a multi task workhorse. It can be configured in so many different ways to carry so many different kinds of loads: all cargo, all passenger (pax) or part cargo and/or part pax or whatever is required to meet the mission. This capability is especially critical in Canada where the number of military aircraft in our inventory is constantly dwindling. Unlike our American neighbours, who have more types of C-130's than we have actual aircraft including: Hercs for SAR, Hercs for trash hauling, Hercs for talking to submarines and Hercs for close in air support, we simply cannot afford to operate aircraft platforms that are designed for a sole use.

As a fully staffed and kitted squadron, 435 Sqn was like a big family. Everyone worked hard and played hard. Senior staff looked after the worker bees who, in turn, put forth an even greater effort. Even the aircrew, who are normally disconnected from the technicians, began to notice the dedication and perseverance by those of us on the floor keeping the aircraft in the green on the status board. It didn't matter what the mission was, if the aircraft crapped out and couldn't be fixed a second one would have to be B checked and then have the pre-flight inspection done by the flight engineer. It could be time consuming but easily done if both aircraft have the same configuration, but this was almost never the case. The unserviceable aircraft may be rigged as 40% pax and the rest as cargo space, while the replacement may be set up as full pax. The Crew Chief would call for the checks to be done and for a Master Corporal to throw together a config crew. Everybody not otherwise gainfully employed would step up and get the job done.

This can-do attitude resulted in more serviceable aircraft and more missions being met than any other Herc squadron in Canada. In two words: ***Certi Provehendi*** (Determined to Deliver).

Being triple tasked our squadron's aircraft were always flying to the four corners of the globe. Tanker missions routinely took the aircraft to Cold Lake, Alberta or to Bagotville, Quebec for training and overseas in support of CF-188 fighters operating in theatre. The dedicated SAR bird would either be training in the local area or deployed on an actual search while the remainder of the unit's aircraft could be anywhere in the world hauling everything from soup to nuts. On some deployments a team of ground crew comprised of 2 to 6 personnel would often accompany the aircraft. If a deployed search mission was extended a dozen technicians could be sent for a week or more before a replacement crew was sent out to relieve them.

My first contact with 435 Sqn actually took place when I was still with 402 Sqn. Late one Friday afternoon Sgt Scott tasked me to escort a 50 gallon lox cart to Red Lake, Ontario. Several days earlier 435 Sqn had been deployed from Edmonton on an extended search. It's only a 275 km direct flight between Winnipeg and Red Lake, a distance that could have been covered by the Herc in about thirty minutes. It would have been much easier to fly to Winnipeg, top up the lox converter and then fly back vice the six hour one way road trip.

So, there I was... Deployed to Fort McMurray, Alberta on a search. It was the summer of 1996. We were looking for a small aircraft that had disappeared between Fort McMurray and Red Deer while being ferried to Red Deer for a scheduled maintenance inspection. The weather was bad and getting worse. The pilot had landed in Fort McMurray and, in an effort to carry more fuel, had removed all the survival equipment from the plane. As soon as the pilot had refuelled the aircraft, he lifted off and headed south. By this time the ceiling level had dropped even lower to the point where he had been seen by truck drivers flying at tree top height following the highway. I suppose no one had told him that flying by **IFR** does not mean **I F**ollow **R**oads.[40] He never arrived at his destination.

The squadron sent two Hercs for the search. In addition to our own aircraft, we had two CH-146 Griffon helicopters from 408 Tac Hel Sqn in Edmonton, a CH-113 Labrador helicopter, which was enroute to its home base at CFB Comox from a major maintenance inspection in Arnprior, Ontario and a half dozen CASARA[41] aircraft.

The searchmaster and the aircrew set up shop in the main terminal building where they had access to a multitude of rooms for meetings, large tables for the maps and a communications hub. For the maintainers, our base of operations would be a nondescript

---

[40] IFR and VFR refers to flying rules. Dependent on weather conditions and if the aircraft has the correct equipment pilots can operate by Instrument Flight Rules or by Visual Flight Rules.

[41] Civil Air Search And Rescue Association is a Canada-wide volunteer aviation association dedicated to the promotion of aviation safety, and to the provision of air search support services to Canada's National Search and Rescue Program.

civilian flight centre complete with a table for playing euchre, a phone and the all-important coffee machine. For ground servicing equipment we had a Stewart Stevenson power unit and an ASU (Air Start Unit). The one thing we did not have was a vehicle to move them around so when an aircraft landed and ground power was required for a refuelling job the whole crew was needed to drag the power unit into position. There were enough technicians on site to operate a 12 hours on and 24 hours off shift. At least that's what it was called but with the amount of daylight hours available it was more like 20 on and 24 off.

The search was into its fifth or sixth day with no luck at all. The topography of the area has a lot of low rolling forested hills festooned with ponds, lakes and streams. The trees are predominantly lodge pole pine and were likely the missing pilot's undoing. Flying as low as he was - with one eye on the horizon in front of him and one eye on the road below him - he probably missed a turn in the road and impacted on the tops of the trees. Lodge pole pine trees are very tall and slender which makes them extremely flexible over their length. In a wind storm they bend and flow with every gust of wind that hits them. So when the small plane hit the tops of the trees they simply bent under the force of the impact. The aircraft then tipped over, nose down, and slid vertically towards the ground. The forest simply closed together and swallowed him up. That plane may be only fifty or one hundred metres off of the highway and unless you were looking directly down on its location or you happened to walk off the road at that precise location chances are that it would never be found. But still, we had to try. That was our mission.

Sometime during the long summer day, one of the search aircraft had picked up a weak ELT (Emergency Location Transmitter) signal but was unable to localize the beacon. The ELT, also known as a crash position indicator, is an automatic beacon that, if functioning correctly, will indicate the position of a downed aircraft by broadcasting a signal on an emergency frequency.[42] Commercial and military aircraft have them but in 1996, most small privately owned aircraft did not as the cost was prohibitive. Unfortunately, this particular emergency frequency can be artificially created by atmospheric conditions and by hydro power lines. In the past, this has resulted in false searches being launched. To eliminate this possibility and increase the likelihood of locating the missing aircraft, the searchmaster reached out to Alberta Hydro for their assistance.

"Hello, Alberta Hydro? This is the Canadian Forces Searchmaster in Fort McMurray. We are conducting a search for a missing aircraft and we may be getting a false distress signal generated by the hydro lines. We need the power shut down between these two grid references from 18:00 to 21:00 hours."

---

[42] The original ELT frequency used was 121.5/243.0 MHz. This beacon frequency would be detected by the Copas-Sarsat satellite system which would process the coordinates to a more definitive search area. On 31 January 2009, the Copas-Sarsat ceased processing distress signals from 121.5/243 MHz beacons and began monitoring ELT beacons on 406 MHZ.

"Well, I would like to help you but I can't shut down the power between those two points. The only thing that I can do is shut down the grid."

"Okay, so shut down the grid."

"You do realize that the grid covers the town of Fort Mac and most of northern Alberta?"

"On my authority as the Searchmaster, shut down the grid!"

"Okay, it's your call."

And so…without any warning at all, at precisely 18:00 hrs, in the middle of Game Five of the Stanley Cup playoffs, the town of Fort McMurray along with the rest of northern Alberta went dark for three long hours. Prior to the power being cut we had launched a single Hercules aircraft and, as suspected, the ELT signal turned out to be just a freak harmonic. As soon as the switches were thrown the signal diminished for the allotted three hours and when the power was turned back on the harmonic was again present. Once this was verified the search aircraft returned to Fort McMurray. We did our A checks and put it to bed.

Several days later the search was called off. We packed up our equipment and headed home to Winnipeg. The flight plan that had been filed by the missing pilot had been criss-crossed many times over. Nearby lakes and ponds had been scoured using SAR techs with scuba gear. After nearly two weeks of searching, no evidence of the aircraft or the pilot were found except for the survival gear that he had removed prior to his departure for Red Deer.

Shortly after my return to Winnipeg, I learned that despite having completed the AVN trade cross training, it was determined by someone higher up the food chain that there were two weeks of additional training that the original 402 Sqn Op Genesis guinea pig crew did not receive. Therefore, I would have to re-do the entire basic AVN conversion course all over again, and not in Borden, but in the training school at CFB Trenton. When that course was completed I was home for three short weeks only to return back to CFB Trenton for the AVN CC-130 type course.

With the completion of both courses, there was an unhealthy rush inside the squadron to have all the technicians cross trained and authorized to sign for the other trades servicing checks. Any AVN technician who was qualified to complete the checks for airframe, aero-engine, safety systems and instrument electrical was referred locally as a Super Tech. I really didn't know who was doing the pushing or why but I fought hard against having technicians authorized to sign for life support equipment, especially since their knowledge of the subject was so limited and at the same time I didn't want to be signed off for those trades I felt that I was not qualified for. Simply knowing how to do the inspections without knowing why you were performing them was a waste of time. A better option would be to have the trainees shadow an experienced technician for a couple of shifts and then have them complete number of servicing inspections. If they were able to complete them successfully, their work would be signed for by the qualified technician. After another shift or two or three, the trainee would be tested by two qualified technicians before being signed off to do the flight line inspections on their own. Well, you can guess how far that idea flew. About as far as a lead balloon.

So there I was… Standing in the Crew Chief's office with my heels together, being questioned on my position of not authorizing two master corporals to sign for the safety systems servicing inspections.

"So, why won't you sign off Jim and Kevin?" asked Sgt Burns.

"I don't think they are ready to be signed off, Sergeant. They don't know the equipment or the systems. I'm afraid that if I sign them off and they make a mistake then I would feel that it would come back on me. The question would be raised as to why I signed them off if they didn't know what they were doing."

"Well, you will sign them off. There is no reason not to. They are both knowledgeable master corporals and if they can sign for rigger and fitter checks then surely they can sign for safety systems too."

"That's the point, Sergeant. MCpl Sylvestri has been a rigger on Hercs for how many years? Seven or more? And what about MCpl Fredricks? He's been a fitter for what, ten or twelve years? They both know their own systems incredibly well. But they know nothing about my systems and to sign them off would be irresponsible."

"Corporal McMillan, your concerns have been noted. You will take them out to an aircraft and have them carry out the flight line inspections for your trade and if they complete them in accordance with the CFTO's, you will sign them off. If they make a mistake after you have signed them off then it is on their heads not yours. It would be the same if you made a mistake inspecting the engines or airframe after you have been authorized. No one will be seeking out the person who signed you off. It is up to the applicant to determine if he thinks he's ready to be signed off. These two think they're ready. So, check them out and sign them off!"

Against my better judgement, that's what I did. I took the two of them out to an aircraft on the hangar floor and had them show me all the safety systems flight line inspections: the Before flight, the After flight, the shortened After & Before flight and the Primary inspection. Working off of each other and with the check list in hand they knew what to look at but they didn't know what to look for. Again, against my better judgement, we returned to the office where their UER's (Unit Employment Records) were waiting. They signed that they knew what they were inspecting and I grudgingly countersigned that they believed that they knew what they were inspecting. Are we done here? Good!

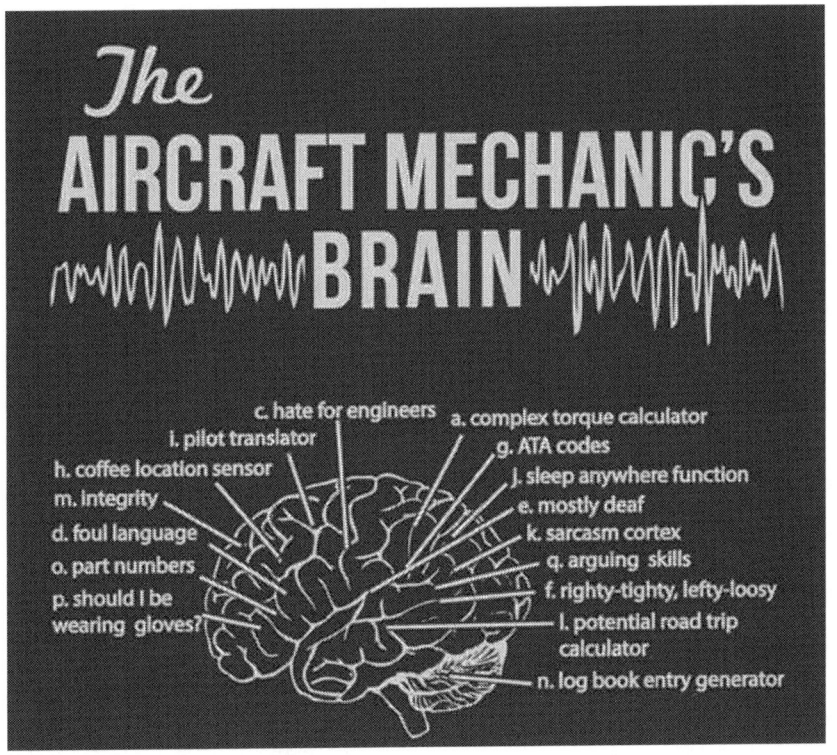

A couple of shifts later, I was in the lox building. The flight line servicing desk controller knew I was over there working on some equipment. He phoned to let me know that there was one aircraft due to land in a couple of hours and it would require an A/B check. Sure enough, about two hours later I heard a Herc taxi in. The park crew marshalled aircraft 130340 in beside 16 Hangar. Ground power was applied, the nose gear was chocked and the engines had come to a full stop. Once the aircrew departed, I walked over to the Herc, said hi to a couple of the guys and carried out my A/B check, taking note of the cargo area configuration and the lox quantity. After signing for the inspection I returned to the lox building to carry on with the equipment maintenance. Ten minutes later all hell broke loose.

MCpl Sylvestri phoned over to the lox building and demanded that I report to the Crew Chief's office immediately. I asked him what it was about and he stated that someone was suggesting that a technical charge be laid against me for failing to complete my aircraft inspection correctly.

WHAT THE HELL!

Immediately, I stopped what I was doing and headed back over to 16 Hangar. In the office, I found MCpl Sylvestri, MCpl Fredricks and Sgt Burns. Burns looked pissed off. Kevin and Jim both had a smug look on their faces.

"What's this all about?" I asked.

"Did you complete the check on 340?" questioned Sgt Burns.

"Sure, I did. About twenty minutes ago. Why?"

Kevin jumped on me with both feet, "Well, you did it wrong! And we're recommending a technical charge be laid against you for failing to carry out the aircraft inspection correctly!"

Now, a technical charge is pretty serious and has severe career implications. I racked my brain as to what I may have missed to inspect or some fault that I didn't spot on my A/B check but I was stumped. Finally, I asked, "What the hell did I do wrong?"

Now it was Jim's turn to step on me. "You didn't straighten up the passenger lap belts!" he snapped.

"I didn't have to because it isn't required on an A/B check!" I countered. "And, I'll prove it to you!"

Crossing the hall to the tech library I grabbed the CC-130 inspection cards hanging on a wall hook, quickly flipped through them to the Safety Systems A/B checklist and handed it to Sgt Burns so he could take a look for himself. After scanning the cards he handed them over to the two Master Corporals.

Now, it was my turn.

"MCpl Sylvestri, can you show me where it says that I have to straighten up the lap belts on an A/B check? It doesn't. That procedure is done on the A check, the B check and the Primary Inspection but not on the A/B check. You two guys are supposed to be qualified to do my servicing inspections and you don't even know what the hell you're looking at. Sergeant Burns, I strongly suggest that their signing authority for life support equipment be rescinded. Now, if you'll excuse me I'm going back to the lox building to complete a maintenance inspection!"

I walked out of the office leaving Kevin and Jim talking with Sgt Burns. Their qualifications were not pulled and I am pretty sure they had been told to be more careful when carrying out a cross trade inspection.

In order to be able to sign for the safety systems inspections, an individual must also be qualified to replenish the liquid oxygen system. This was something that a number of these riggers and fitters, with their greasy coveralls were not willing to risk.[43] To

---

[43] Gaseous and liquid oxygen reacts violently when coming into contact with

complete his qualifications, Sgt Burns needed to be certified to lox an aircraft. Several days before he asked to be tested, Sgt Burns had seen me out topping up a Herc. It was during a weekend night shift in the summer, but still early in the evening. I was down the flight line a ways and since it was still 30°C I was not wearing most of my PPE.[44] Yes, liquid oxygen is dangerous. Yes, a person can be seriously injured or killed if the correct PPE is not worn. But I had been loxing planes for so many years that I was pretty comfortable doing it and besides, it was just too damn hot to wear that full length rubberized rain suit.

"Blaine, were you out loxing a Herc on Spot 22?"

"Sure, Sarge. Why do you ask?"

"Were you wearing all of your lox gear?"

"Uh, no. I was wearing what I think is the minimum requirement to be safe. Gloves, a face shield and a short jacket."

"Well, next time you lox an aircraft you will be wearing the full suit. Do I make myself clear?"

"Sure thing Sergeant Burns."

The very next day on shift Sgt Burns asked me to qualify him on topping up Hercs with liquid oxygen. Not a problem, says I.

Just like everyone else that I had trained we began at the lox building by going over the properties of liquid oxygen, how a lox system works in the aircraft, the types of storage vessels, the operation of the valves and all of the safety requirements including

---

petroleum, oil and lubricants.
[44] Personal Protective Equipment or personal safety gear.

the PPE. I informed Sgt Burns that we had two aircraft to fill and asked if he was up for it.

Pointing to the water fountain I remarked, "I usually have a big drink of water before I head out. Do you want some, Sergeant Burns?"

"I'll pass."

"Suit yourself."

It was time to get dressed. As the instructor, I would not necessarily be "hands on" so I wore what I normally wore - a ball cap, leather gauntlet gloves, a face shield and my flight jacket. Sgt Burns, on the other hand, was dressed in the latest yellow rubber rain suit finery. Starting at the bottom he had shin high rain boots, bib overalls, a full length trench coat, lox gloves, face shield and a Sou'wester hat. Truly, a thing of beauty.

We hooked one of the MA-1 50 US gallon carts to a D-6 mule and headed off to Hercules 341. On the way to the aircraft I went over a few key points with Sgt Burns. "It's a simple procedure really" I explained, "There will be no electrical power applied to the aircraft. There will be no refueling of the aircraft while replenishing the liquid oxygen system. Technically, there isn't supposed to be anybody but you working on the aircraft while oxygen replenishing is under way. Check to make sure the aircraft is grounded. Once you are properly positioned off of the right hand side of the radome you ground the cart. Place a drip pan under the aircraft overboard vent hole. Open the lox servicing panel. Remove the cap from the filler valve and inspect it for contaminants. If it is clean you can now proceed with the following steps."

Warning

These procedures for filling a C-130 liquid oxygen system using a MA-1 lox cart were dredged up from my memory. They are intended to illustrate the steps I had used well over a thousand times in my career and despite being fairly accurate **they are not intended to be replace an official technical manual used to carry out the replenishment of a C-130 liquid oxygen system**.

1. Ensure the cart is electrically grounded. Using a dummy nozzle you dump the pressure from the converter. While this is happening, take the lox transfer hose and connect it to the purge point on the cart.
2. Close the vent line on the cart.
3. Open the fill/drain valve and the pressure build up valve. B. Close the pressure build up valve when it reaches 40 psi. Dump any tank pressure in excess of 40 psi. by pulling the tank pressure relief valve handle.
4. Once lox is flowing from the hose in a steady stream disconnect the dummy nozzle, place it on the cart.
5. Quickly disconnect the hose from the cart and attach it to the filler valve.

6. Maintain the cart operating pressure at 40 psi by opening the pressure build up valve momentarily once the pressure drops below 30 psi.
7. The converter is filled when lox is coming from the aircraft lox vent port in a "full and steady stream". At that time, quickly disconnect the transfer hose from the aircraft and re-attach it to the purge point on the cart allowing pressure in the hose to bleed off.
8. Open the vent valve on the cart and then close the fill/drain valve. The pressure build up valve should already be closed. When the pressure in the cart drops to below 20 psi disconnect the transfer hose and secure it on the cart.
9. Replace the cap on the aircraft filler valve and close the panel.
10. Disconnect the grounding cable for the cart.
11. Replace the drip pan on the cart in an upside down position.
12. Disconnect the grounding cable.

    I coached Sgt Burns in loxing his first Herc and then monitored him on the second one. He did quite well, actually. When we had completed topping up the second Herc the cart was now very close to being empty so I figured why not refill it instead of leaving it for the guy on day shift. It took about two hours to finish all three tasks and through it all Sgt Burns never complained one bit. He may have lost twenty pounds in sweat but he never complained. After re-positioning the cart next to the lox building we headed back to servicing where Sgt, Burns said to me, "When you're out loxing, you can wear whatever PPE you want just as long as you are safe."

"Thanks, I appreciate that."

Certi Provehendi! Determine to Deliver! 435 Squadron members were always prepared to deploy on short notice to wherever the mission took them. It could be a combat air to air refueling tasking in the Middle East or supporting NATO exercises in Europe or humanitarian relief flights to South America or even providing Search and Rescue coverage for the combat air patrols in Inuvik. That's right! Inuvik…some 200 kilometers north of the Arctic Circle in February when the static air temperature was averaging -30°C. And the reason for this little sojourn to the far north was all due to the Russians.

In February of 2000, CF-18 fighters from CFB Cold Lake were deployed to FOL Inuvik, accompanied by two Hercs from 435 Sqn, a KCC-130HT tanker and another CC-130H rigged for SAR. On our arrival, it was learned from the local residents of Inuvik that the fighter aircraft had not been there for several years. During their extended absence the USAF's fighters, based out of Elmendorf Alaska, had been intercepting Russian TU-95 Bear H bombers heading towards Canadian soil so often that they (the United States) informed us (the Canadians) that since we have an FOL at Inuvik either we defend our own territory or we would be tossed out of NORAD. Pretty strong words, but I think Ottawa got the message. Put up or shut up.

We were housed in the FOL barracks with shared sleeping quarters upstairs and various offices, a kitchen, a dining facility and storage rooms on the main floor. The CF-18 fighters were held in the secure hangars. Our two Hercs were parked down on the civilian apron and we had the use of an office in the air terminal for our servicing crews. Sometime in the past, CFB Cold Lake had all the AMSE they required either flown or trucked in to Inuvik. Ground power units, air start units, portable heaters, towing vehicles of various sizes and of course, most of it was geared towards the CF-18's. We were given a D14[45] towing mule, a ground power unit and most importantly a pair of Herman Nelson heaters. We found that the air temperature in Inuvik was so cold that the engine oils were becoming as thick as molasses. Our flight engineers asked the fitters if they could find some means of keeping the oils more liquid than solid. At first the aero-engine techs thought that if they simply ran the APU and cycled the warm bleed air alternately from one engine to the other, this would be enough to keep the oils from becoming viscous. However, by the time one engine was slowly warming up the previous one was rapidly cooling off. It was a never-ending battle that was simply wasting fuel, so it was decided that we would take two Herman Nelson heaters, place one in front of each wing between the two engines and feed an air duct directly inside the cowling. It was an ingenious plan but Mother Nature was a bit fickle. The wind

---

[45] The D14 mule used for moving heavy aircraft like the Herc weighed 22 metric tonnes and sat two people. It could crab and opposable steer.

picked up and the temperature dropped even lower. So we tapped off an extra hose and funnelled it back onto the heating unit thereby using some of the air to keep it warm too. After we had the whole thing rigged up it looked like a pair of octopi were attacking the Herc. At least the engine oils were kept warm and more importantly we didn't break any seals.

So there I was… In the pitch black of an Inuvik afternoon Cpl Denis "Longshanks" Lemoine and I were tasked to apply ground power on one of the Hercs. We called him "Longshanks" because of his long fingers. The ground power unit was inside the hangar at the top of the hill behind a roll up door. The power in the hangar was turned off so the door had to be raised with a manual pull chain. "Shanks" and I drove up the hill to the hangar and I dropped him off. He would have to make his way through the darkened building while I drove all the way down to the flight line and then go back up the hill to the rear of the hangar on an access road. I returned to the roll up door and backed in just as Denis started to raise it.

Looking out through the windshield I saw a medium sized furry something loping through the snow on the other side of the access road. It had an odd shuffling sort of gait. I quickly switched the headlights from low to high and back again. Whatever it was stopped directly in front of me and stood up on its hind legs.

"Holy shit! It's a wolverine!"

"Denis! Hey Denis! Get in the friggin mule!"

"What?"

"It's a wolverine! Get in the mule right now!"

While yelling out the back window desperately trying to get "Shanks" back inside the vehicle I kept an eye on this hairy beast not thirty feet in front of me. Finally, Denis heard me and climbed onto the back of the D14 mule. Looking through the windshield he asked, "What the hell is that?"

"It's a wolverine, Denis. Now, get the hell inside before it eats you!"

The whole time that Denis was trying to wedge his way into cab through the back window while wearing his $3000 Air Force blue winter multi-layered Gore-Tex snowsuit the beast, still standing on its two hind legs, was dodging and weaving in the light of the headlights like a prize fighter in the ring.

Watching the wolverine I could just imagine what was going through its twisted evil little mind. "Well, I know it's big. And it's got some crunchy blue bits on the inside. Nah…there's too much gristle." And with that, the wolverine continued on its way.

I spent ten days in Inuvik before being returned to Winnipeg. The squadron would continue its operations for another three weeks supporting the CF-18s from Cold Lake in making the Canadian military's presence known and deterring the Russian air force from encroaching on Canadian airspace.

There are a lot of competitions that take place in the military. Shooting competitions such as the Canadian Armed Forces Small Arms Concentration and organized team sports focus on honing the skills of the individual or the small group while major exercises like Maple Flag in Cold Lake or Rim of the Pacific (Rim Pac) are designed to train large multinational forces to work together. For those of us employed in the SAR world there is an annual SAREX competition. For years it was viewed by many as just a SAR tech family reunion however SAREX is designed to test all aspects of a squadron's team because search and rescue truly is a team effort. There are eleven Department of Defence trophies up for grabs over the course of five events: search, rescue, parachuting accuracy, medical and maintenance. The aircrew compete in the search category with the pilots, and depending on the type of aircraft could include a navigator, flight engineers and a loadmaster. They are tested for their ability to deliver the SAR techs accurately to the target area in a timely fashion. The SAR techs themselves push the envelope in the rescue, parachuting accuracy and medical events, which leaves technicians to pamper their aircraft, especially while under the judge's magnifying glass during the maintenance event. There is also the Bell Ringer Trophy, which is a parachuting accuracy competition for SAR techs over the age of forty; the Diamond Trophy - awarded to the team with the highest average score in the five main events; the Cormorant trophy - for the best helicopter rescue; the Mynarski Trophy - Canada's highest award for excellence in the field of air search and rescue; and of course there is annual trophy for the Best SAR tech, given to the individual who most exemplifies the motto: *"That Others May Live."*

While posted to 435 Sqn, I participated in three SAREX competitions. In 1997 and again in 1999, I was a member of the competition team when 435 Sqn captured the Best Maintenance Team trophy.[46] In 2002, I volunteered and had been selected to be on the team again. However, there had been a last minute reduction in the number of team members allowed and I was given the option of being RTU'ed[47] or assisting as a member of the general duty team – The Ramp Ratz. That sounded like fun so I decided to take Option 2. This proved to be a great decision as we had all the benefits of working on a flight line while on temporary duty with none of the stressors of being under the competition microscope.

So there we were… The Ramp Ratz were busy marshalling aircraft in Gimli, Manitoba. Aircraft flown by the participants included two CC-130 Hercs, one CC-115 Buffalo, a CH-149 Cormorant, a CH-146 Griffon from CFB Cold Lake Base Rescue, three American C-23 Sherpa, a hockey sock full of CASARA aircraft and two Sikorsky HH-60 Blackhawks from the 210th Rescue Squadron of the Alaskan Air National Guard (AKANG). These two aircraft had been enroute from a maintenance overhaul in Pennsylvania to their home base in Alaska when they were tasked to stop in Gimli to participate in the international Major Air Disaster (MajAid) portion of the of the exercise.

---

[46] Sarex 1997 was held in Gimli, Manitoba and Sarex 1999 took place at CFB Comox, BC
[47] Return to unit – sent back home.

With more civilian airlines now utilizing a northern polar route to cross the globe the logistics of a single country responding to a crash in the high arctic could prove to be difficult. Therefore, it is imperative that there is international cooperation and coordination of emergency response personnel. For this reason some aspects of the annual Sarex are dedicated to training the aircrew and the SAR techs in response to a major air disaster. Obviously, if an airliner ever did crash in some distant northern corner of the country the proper response would be to drop in as much emergency equipment and rescue personnel as quickly and as humanly possible. Currently, CFB Trenton maintains four MajAid Kits at the Canadian Army Advanced Warfare Centre.[48] These kits are "designed to sustain 320 people for 48 hours"[49] and contain tents, food, generators and sleeping bags. Basically, everything you can imagine from soup to nuts are in these kits.

To assess the ability to deliver a MajAid kit on time and on target, the test involved CFB Trenton (which was totally in the dark about this) receiving a call to deploy a MajAid kit to a

---

[48] The Canadian Army Advanced Warfare Center (CAAWC): "Supports the generation and deployment of combat ready forces through the conduct of parachute-related training and aerial delivery operations." CAAWC is the only national school with an operational task. It is responsible to have two officers on two hours and two six-member teams on four hours notice to move in support of Major Air Disaster Operations (MAJAID). MAJAID is a joint Air Force/Land Force operation. It involves parachuting into an aircraft crash site with survival equipment and supporting the efforts of the SAR TECH's by providing shelter and sustenance to survivors.

[49] Defence Home, Overcoming the tyranny of time and distance: Major Air Disaster SAREX 2013, www.forces.gc.ca/en/news/article, 12 December, 2016.

location identified only by a set of GPS coordinates. The technicians would have to complete a B check and increase the fuel load if necessary, the flight engineer would have to complete his pre-flight walk around inspection, and the air movements unit would have to secure the MajAid kit on board the Herc. Once loaded, the aircraft quickly departed for the following grid reference: 50.6328 N 97.0589 W. The flight was programmed and there would only be enough time on scene for the team to make two passes over the target area, one to check the drop zone and deploy the drift indicators, then a second to check the drift before descending to make the actual drop.

The steadily increasing drone of four Allison T-56 engines announced the arrival of the MajAid Hercules. It was late. There was barely enough time for both passes. On the first pass the drop zone was surveyed: red, yellow and blue crepe paper drift indicators fell to the earth. On the following approach the door was up and the ramp was level. At 500 feet above the trees we could see the drogue chute streaming behind the aircraft. Three, two, one... the ADS locks were slipped and the 100-foot diameter extraction chute deployed pulling the MajAid kit out as the aircraft began to slowly climb upward. But the release was premature and the palletized load missed its mark coming down fifty yards inside the tree line. The good news was that on inspection, the kit survived the drop. Having just completed a 1600 km mission in under three hours, the Trenton Herc banked, waggled its wings and headed south-east for its return trip home.

It was pretty impressive watching the massive parachutes pull the load out of the aircraft. Members of the media were there, as well as some local citizens who had played the role of casualties in another scenario. Some were even taking pictures of the operation as it unfolded. It wasn't a security breach by any means but with the two Blackhawks sitting on the tarmac I decided to have a little bit of fun.

MCpl Glen Swanson and I spotted the AKANG Crew Chief, who was a great bear of a man, and told him what we wanted to do. He said that he would love to help us out but unfortunately, as much as he liked a good joke, he wouldn't be able to keep a straight face. He told us to seek out the aircraft captain because he had a terrific poker face. So Swanny and I drove over to Ops where we found Captain Nuoc Mam. He was slightly built but tough as nails.

"Hey, Captain Mam. Could you help us out?" I asked.

"Sure. What do you guys have in mind?"

Over the next couple of minutes, Swanny explained what we wanted to do and to whom we wanted it done to.

"Any problems?"

"No problem at all. I'll be glad to help out. And besides, this is going to be fun."

From just outside Ops, we watched as Captain Mam approached a member of our Ramp Ratz team who just happened to be taking some pictures out on the apron.

"Excuse me Private. What do you think are you doing?" asked Captain Mam.

"Just taking some happy snaps, Sir."

"You didn't happen to take any pictures of my Blackhawk, did you?"

"Sure did, Sir! It's a great aircraft. I wish Canada had some."

"Well son, that's a problem. You see, last night we re-mounted a pair of low profile AN-10-A digital wave compasses. They allow us to transition across the far north back to our home base in Alaska. Now, I know that it doesn't sound like a real big deal to you but to our Department of Defence they are still kinda Secret Squirrel. I hate to say this but I can't allow any photos to be taken of them."

"Shit!"

"Since you're a pretty good kid, tell you what I'll do for you. How many frames do you have left on that disposable camera?"

"Three, Sir?"

"Okay, that's not too bad. I want you to take those three frames. I don't care what you take a picture of but finish the film. Then, give me the camera. When I get back to Alaska our military intelligence unit will process the film. I'll get your personal info and I will send you all the pictures except for the ones of the Blackhawk and the negatives. It's either that or I have my Crew Chief over there, take the camera and destroy it. Your option, kid."

"Damn! I might as well take pictures of my boots then!"

And just as Private Yankmy Chain was about to take three very lovely pictures of his size 10 combat boots Captain Nuoc Mam says to him, "Just kidding ya, son. Those guys over there put me up to it."

Private Chain looked over at us. "You bastards!"

I guess you had to be there.

Swanny and I had been on several deployments together and regardless of the conditions - be they working, housing or environmental - the trip was always enjoyable if we simply followed his mantra. One year, we were paired up as roommates for Operation Boxtop in Thule, Greenland. Thule is an American military base - built on Danish soil - that is 1,207 kilometres above the Arctic Circle and 1,524 kilometres from the geographical North Pole, but only 680 kilometres from Canadian Forces Station Alert.

For that reason, Thule is used as a staging area to re-supply CFS Alert. I had never been there, but for many who had spent any time working on the Hercs, Thule was like a second home to them. The aircraft were flying 24/7 with three servicing crews working the standard 12-on and 24-off shift rotation. During our shift - we would start at 06:00 hrs work until 18:00 hrs and then report for duty at 18:00 hrs the following day – we would launch and recover six or seven aircraft. If you think it sounds confusing, try working this shift when the sun barely drops below the horizon because AM or PM it all looks the same. But the food was decent, the booze was cheap and there was extra pay on top of it. Life was

> "There is no such thing as a bad TD trip. They're all good. It's just that some are better than others!"
>
> **MCpl. Glen Swanson**
> **435 Sqn.**

good! But, for some people it doesn't matter how good it was there was always be something to whine about.

There was this new guy who had been posted in to the squadron just a few months before deploying on this trip. For lack of a better name let's call him Corporal Bloggins. He had been posted to 435 Sqn from CFB Trenton and was working in servicing on 2 Crew, so I never met him before going to Thule. Once in Thule, all squadron members were expected to work as a single crew. Each crew had a sergeant or a warrant officer as a Crew Chief, a couple of master corporals and maybe a dozen corporals who were divided into two teams. Each team would take turns handling a launch and a recovery.

So, there I was... It was 07:15 hrs. I was reading a novel and enjoying a fine cup of purloined coffee. My roommate, MCpl Swanson, was still fast asleep in his rack when I heard a commotion out in the hallway. Someone was, quite literally, banging off of the walls and making a whole lot of noise doing it. I stole a quick look out the door and spotted Cpl Bloggins stumbling about.

Not wanting to wake up Swanny, I gently called out, "Hey Bloggins!"

"What the heck do you want!" he shouted back.

"Get the hell in here!" I whispered.

It was quite obvious that Bloggins was still drunk from the night before. I thought that if I could get him to sit down and have a coffee, it wouldn't be so much to sober him up as to keep him from waking the entire top floor of the North Star Inn. As soon as Bloggins dumped his ass into a chair I handed him a cup of coffee. Over the next twenty minutes I tried my level best to have him keep his trap shut lest he wake up my roomy. The last thing I needed was a grumpy Master Corporal who was shorted on his beauty sleep. Too late! Bloggins' constant bitching and whining about the working conditions, the meal hours, the lack of darkness and anything else that came to mind finally roused Glen from his slumber. With one eye open, he mumbled something to the effect of, "What the hell is going on?"

"We have a guest, Master Corporal!"

From beneath his blankets Glen realized who it was and called out, "Is that you, Bloggins? Bloggins, if you're going to stay, then stay. Just shut up!"

With a loud snort, Cpl Bloggins stumbled to his feet and exited our room. A couple of hours later everyone including Bloggins was attending the mass brief. He was barely awake and I'm pretty sure I could see the fumes that were still oozing out of his pores. At the brief, we listened to a USAF Major and a Danish site manager talk about the amenities, the Do's and the Don'ts, the dangers and the safety procedures in the event of any urgent events.

All good? Great!

Right after the briefing all the Crew Chiefs got together to decide which team would be working and when. The members of 435 Squadron got the luck of the draw. We would be going in at 18:00 hrs which gave us time to grab something to eat and then rack out for a few hours before heading up the hill to the flight line. The extra rest would later prove to be a real asset as the shift wore on through the twilight of the midnight sun.

By 17:00 hrs the crew was out on the road in front of the North Star Inn ready for the ride up to the flight line. Everyone was dressed in layers of our blue Gore-Tex consisting of thermal underwear, work dress pants, wind pants, work dress shirt, flight jacket, intermediate jacket, nylon socks, wool socks, mukluks, gloves, a nomex face mask, toque and a combat scarf. In my go bag I had my parka, a set of heavy weight pants, a half read novel, a deck of cards, a set of liar's dice, some crossword puzzles torn out of a Winnipeg newspaper and my university text books for a little light reading. Inside the crew servicing area there was an office for the Crew Chief and a larger room for rest of us. A quick glance at the status board told us what was inbound, outbound or on the ground. Four Hercs. Three in the loop and a spare. The round trip from Thule to Alert was about five hours including loading, unloading and servicing checks.

Busy, busy.

Our Crew Chief, Warrant Officer Bob Rex, had divided us up into two teams and I drew the short straw. I was working with Bloggins as a park/start team. Just great! Thanks for nothing!

There was a shout from the office.

"Start Crew! McMillan and Bloggins! Launch 339!"

And, off we went. I was the #2 man, driving the line vehicle and pulling the ground power unit. Bloggins acted as the #1 man on the headset talking to the aircrew and monitoring the start sequence. In a few short minutes aircraft 130339 was rolling out for another ninety minute flight to CFS Alert. After the start Bloggins jumped into the cab of the vehicle and immediately started bitching about how he was feeling. Tired and achy with a head like a ten pound Smartie. Well, life's rough pal. That's what you get for getting juiced last night. The point is, I really didn't want to hear it.

Almost an hour later a Herc returned from Alert. It would require an A/B check, a refuel and the internal fuel bladder would have to be filled as well. The turnaround had to be done quickly because there was another aircraft landing in a little over an hour. As I worked to complete my inspections there was a persistent whiney nattering sound in the background that underscored the droning of the ground power unit. Once again it was Cpl Bloggins. When are we going for supper? Are you cold because I'm cold? I should go get my gloves. Is that toque authorized? We didn't need them in Trenton! And on. And on. And on.

When the turnaround was completed the other team came out to launch the aircraft, freeing us up to go for supper.

In the truck, Glen asked, "Ever have a Thule omelet?"

"Nope. I've heard about them but I've never had one."

"Then you are definitely in for a treat."

The infamous Thule omelet: Imagine using four or five beaten eggs, adding in whatever kitchen scraps you have left over - be it sausages from breakfast, bacon, diced hot dogs, scavenged chicken parts or chopped up leftover hamburgers - plus onions, peppers, olives or maybe even some cooked broccoli. Then, pile on an outrageous amount of mixed shredded cheese. When the eggs are close to being set fold it in half and cook it until the cheese starts running out of the sides. Voila! A Thule omelet!

"Holy crap, Glen! It's the size of a dinner plate!"

"I told you it was big. And it's good, too!"

"Look Glen. I have a problem."

"And, what would that be?"

"It's Bloggins. The guy is such a bloody whiner. Nothing is ever good enough for him. He bitches about everything. We just started working here and already I've had enough of his attitude. I'm telling you right now that if I have to work with him anymore I'm gonna push him off a wing!"

"C'mon, he's not that bad."

"Okay then. After we're done eating and we go back up to the flight line, you work with him 'cause I'm not!"

"Not a problem."

Back up on the flight line, Swanny and Cpl Bloggins handled a launch followed by a recovery. I stayed out of the way and did what I had to do. WO Rex informed us that one of the planes was coming out of the rotation and the spare was going in. Those of us not involved in the ongoing evolutions went out to prep the spare aircraft. By the time we were done the other team had finished off the start and park jobs and we all headed in to warm up. Back inside servicing I overheard Glen talking to the Crew Chief in the office.

"Uh, Warrant Rex. We have a problem."

"What is it, Master Corporal?"

Warrant Rex listened intently to Mcpl Swanson's concerns and said, "I'll see what I can do." Later on in the shift Glen was informed that Cpl Bloggins was being swapped out with a guy on the Greenwood crew that was having a bit of an issue with his shift. Once the two technicians were reassigned to the different servicing crews there were no longer any conflicts.

There were a couple of us Thule newbies on the crew and on our next day off Glen decided to play tour guide for the bunch of us. He signed out a 4x4 crew cab truck from the user section and, after carrying out the acceptance inspection to ensure that it was full of fuel and had the mandatory survival kit on board, we all climbed in for the 5¢ whirlwind tour. From the Base we headed out towards the Ballistic Missile Early Warning System or BMEWS. I really can't say how far it was but we had been on the road for at least an hour, passing by an emergency shelter about every kilometer. Each of these storm shelters contains emergency survival equipment and a communications link back to the Base switchboard for anyone who may get stranded on the road by one of Greenland's vicious hurricane level storms.[50] We drove to a point where we could see in the distance a massive phased array radar on top of the mountain after which Glen turned the truck around and we headed towards Mount Dundas, also known as Beer Can Mountain. Near the base of this peak we found an Inuit hunting camp. It looked pretty sparse: a couple of old buildings, one of them with a chimney. Somebody may have been around, I don't know if they were but there was a bolt action Enfield rifle resting next to the door and a number of sled dogs chained to the ground nearby. Someone in the truck wanted to go see the dogs but it was ill advised: Inuit sled dogs are treated as working dogs, and they usually get fed only after they have done their work. Chances are they would have torn the dumb schmuck to shreds.

"Hey Bloggins! Ya wanna pet a puppy?"

After three weeks of flying around the clock, CFS Alert was once again re-supplied with all the goods required for another six months. There had been a week or so of dry lifts and two weeks of wet lifts - dry lifts being cargo and wet lifts being fuel.[51] It is

---

[50] There are five weather condition ratings in Thule. From Storm Condition Normal where all base activities can be conducted to Storm Conditions Alpha through Delta, with Delta being the worst when no pedestrian or vehicular travel is allowed. If there was any doubt, in March 1972, during a Storm Condition Delta, winds were measured at 207 mph.

[51] In the fall of 2014, the Boxtop mission was carried out by three CC-130J Hercules and a CC-177 Globemaster III which airlifted over 412,000 pounds of dry goods and about 1 million litres of fuel in two weeks.

during this resupply mission that personnel posted to the station on a six-month deployment are rotated out and their replacements rotated in. For myself, I was simply glad to have the opportunity to experience a Boxtop mission.

In October 2002, the Canadian military participated in a major military exercise at Marine Corps Air Station Cherry Point, North Carolina. In total five hundred and some odd Canadians took part in the exercise with about one hundred of them working directly at Cherry Point.[52] It was a massive exercise with Canadian infantry soldiers and US Marines conducting beach landings, fighter aircraft doing combat air patrols, some Secret Squirrel communications, helicopter insertions and air-to-air refueling. That's where 435 Sqn came in. We would take one KCC-130HT south to North Carolina with two sets of aircrew and a single servicing crew.

It was going to be a great trip. We were all senior technicians and there wasn't a whiner in the crowd. We had a great Crew Chief, WO Don Charlebois, to lead us. WO Charlebois had been on an advance party and had already scoped out Cherry Point - the working environment, places to eat, etc. He even had our rooms booked for when we arrived!

And that's when the problems began.

---

[52]MCAS Cherry Point is staffed by 50,000 Marines. At nearby Camp Lejuene there are 80,000 Marines. The entire Canadian military is half their combined total.

On our arrival, our Herc tanker was marshalled over to the in-ground refueling pits where the refueling pump and hose was right beside us - I know, how cool is that! We were met by a couple of members from Canadian HQ detachment. Immediately, our two navigators caught a ride back to some distant parking lot on the other side of the flight line to retrieve the rental vehicles. Each set of aircrew would have their own transportation, the Crew Chief would have one and the ground crew would have yet another. Next came the room keys. Everyone got their own room ... except for the ground crew who had no rooms at all, at least not the ones that our Crew Chief had booked for us. No, those reservations had been booked under another FinCode (financial coding) and so the organizers of this little soiree had cancelled the rooms. By the time they tried to re-book our rooms on Base they were no longer available.

So, where in the hell were we going to be sleeping for the next twelve nights?

"Oh, don't worry," said Captain Paper-pusher. "I have secured some fine accommodations for you off Base. They're about a dozen or so miles down the highway in the next town. But, not to worry, it is a *USMC approved* motel."

Thanks, Captain. That sure makes me feel very comfortable.

"Here's the address. Just head on down there. Get settled and I will be along with the FinCode."

After we had done our A checks and put the plane to bed, we headed off the Base with WO Charlebois leading the way. Twenty minutes later, we arrived at a single story off-grey motel that advertised: cable tv and full kitchenettes with every room with additional parking round back. As an added bonus, it was within walking distance of the Piggly Wiggly supermarket. A comforting fact was the knowledge that in many American supermarkets, right between the pasta and the junk food, there is an aisle that would be fully stocked with every kind of alcohol that you would ever want to sample.

As we waited at the office for the Captain from Air Command to show up with the golden credit card a couple of us noticed that the front office resembled a movie theatre ticket booth. There was a slot for you to pass your monies and for a key to be passed back to you. What was really interesting was that this slot dipped down at least four inches into the counter top and was so narrow that you could not pass a key through if it was on edge: a nice security feature because if a key on edge couldn't get under the pass, neither could the barrel of a gun. Another security feature we noticed was the office attendant was protected behind a double set of ½ inch thick bulletproof sheets of Lexan with a dead air space in between them. This begs the question: If this motel is an approved accommodation of the United States Marine Corps and if Marines stay here on a regular basis who does the attendant need this level of protection from? With our room keys in hand we began to discover what *USMC approved* was all about.

First, there was an interesting and underlying odour that permeated each room. It wasn't foul or putrid or moldy. But it was persistent and the smell in each room was distinct in its own right.

Second, were the two double beds. Well, that was nice since we now had to double up. Except for Monica, as the only female member of the ground crew team she had a room to herself. Come to think of it, I believe the Crew Chief had his own room too. RHIP.

Third, the facilities, including the bathroom and the full kitchenette with all the appliances, were surprisingly clean for a *USMC approved* motel.

Fourth, fifth and twenty fifth was the fact that we were on TD in North Carolina, so we were pretty confident that we could handle anything thrown at us. See you at the morning brief!

So there we were... One hundred and thirty plus Canadians sitting in a very large air conditioned auditorium listening to an impeccably dressed United States Marine Corps Lewtenant Colonel give us his welcoming speech and some very important advice for those of us not familiar with MCAS Cherry Point.

"First of all, on behalf of the Base Commander and his staff, I would like to welcome y'all to Marine Corps Air Station Cherry Point. From this location we operate and support a variety of fixed wing aircraft for two carrier groups. I am sure that you will recognize the Harriers, F/A-18's and the EA-6B's. We have fifty-four KC-130B's on the base and we also fly the COD[53] out of here to ferry personnel, equipment and stuff out to the carriers."

Holy Shit! Fifty-four Hercs. That's more than twice what the Canadian military has in its entire fleet. And, they are all "B" model tankers.[54]

"I want to go over some important safety factors for being at Cherry Point," continued LCol Flattop. "Are there any runners in the group?"

Not one Canadian hand went up.

"Okay. Are there any golfers among you? C'mon don't be shy."

A dozen or so arms were now raised.

"That's great to see. Our Sound of Freedom golf course is an eighteen hole PGA rated course, which I can assure you, will provide a unique golfing experience. For those of you who have never golfed in North Carolina there are some basic safety protocols that you need to follow. If your ball lands within three feet of a water hazard take a drop. We have 'gators on the Base. You will also take a drop if your ball lands in a pile of leaves. There are four species of poisonous snakes on the base including rattlesnakes, copperheads and cottonmouths. Any questions so far? No? Okay then, moving on."

"I would invite y'all to take a look around the area when you are off duty. We have some activity centres with pool tables and

---

[53] Northrup Grumman C-2A Greyhound.

[54] On the mission to USMCAS Cherry Point we were informed that there were fifty-four KC-130B aircraft, which were first introduce in 1959, assigned to that base and they were in the process of upgrading their fleet from B models to J models in one single leap.

pinball. There is the Enlisted Members and the Officers Clubs as well. I would ask that if you are walking around the Base to stick to the sidewalks and the roadways. You will notice that the trees have been trimmed back from the walkways as we have several species of poisonous spiders that love to build webs in the branches. Any questions so far? No? Okay then, moving on."

"One thing that does come to mind. You'll be operating your Cee One Thirty from out of the hot refueling pits and in the event we have hurricane there may not be a location where we can tie down your aircraft."

In true Canadian fashion our Aircraft Commander replied, "Not a problem, Sir. If there's a hurricane we'll just fly to someplace safe and come back later."

"Okay then. Good to see that you have a plan. Fail to plan - plan to fail. Uh rah! If there is nothing else that concludes my briefing. Ladies and gentlemen, welcome to MCAS Cherry Point."

My crewmates all looked at each other. What the hell kind of place is this? Hurricanes? Go for a walk and you could be poisoned or eaten. Piss off a Marine and they'll probably kill and eat you too!

Working at Cherry Point was one of the best TD missions I was ever on. The aircrew were great, the technicians were amazing and our Crew Chief was exceptional. WO Charlebois had us split down into two smaller teams so we could operate on the TD standard of 12 on and 24 off. Covering a twelve hour shift is not really a problem and during our down time we were able to explore the flora and fauna of the local area, Naturally, the most interesting flora and fauna can always be found on a road trip to the local Walmart. Surprisingly, not all Walmart stores are created equal. Some are large. Some are small. And those South of the 49th Parallel carry enough guns and ammo to ward off the Zombie Apocalypse.

So there we were... Glen, Monica and myself were scrutinizing the sale items in Walmart. It was a very large Walmart - almost the size of a Canadian Costco. It had everything that you could imagine and then some. Everything from garbage bags to guns. Glen was looking for some kind of folding luggage cart, I was looking at fishing equipment and Monica was in full blown shopping mode. And why not? She was flying home in a Herc. It wasn't as if there would be a weight restriction on her luggage. After wandering about the store for about an hour Glen and I met up outside.

"Seen Monica?"

"Yeah, she said she would be out in twenty minutes. She's looking for some kinda electronic adapter."

Sometimes when you leave a department store such as Sears, The Bay or Walmart there is this annoying sound alerting you to the fact that something in your bag of purchases was not degaussed. Usually it's a small item of high value or an item that is prone to being shoplifted. Sometimes there is an accusatory recorded voice that accompanies the annoying sound which goes something like this:

"BING BONG! Attention Shoppers! There may an item in your possession that has failed to be scanned. Please return to the customer service counter."

In Canada most people would simply ignore the warning and just keep on walking but not so in North Carolina.

At the sound of the warning announcement Glen and I turned around just in time to see the outer doors slam shut followed by the inner doors slamming shut as well, effectively containing the bewildered shoppers in a man trap. We weren't the only ones to turn around. The armed security officer, who was standing nearby, also turned towards the doors and unsnapped his pistol!

And there was Monica, locked in between the two sets of sliding doors mouthing all sorts of obscenities!

Along the wall between the two sets of sliding doors was a single door that now opened up. Another armed guard motioned for a shopper to come into the adjacent room. One at a time each shopper was directed into the room where their purchases were confirmed against the receipt and on completion, if everything was kosher, they were allowed to exit from the room directly to the parking lot. It took twenty minutes before Monica was sprung from Walmart.

Life was pretty sweet in our *USMC Approved Motel*. We made our own breakfasts and had communal dinners. In the evening we would sit on the tailgate of the rental truck and have a few beers. Or quite a few beers. The high volume of beer consumed was largely due to the fact that American beer is not as strong as Canadian beer.

One night, as we stood around sipping and telling jokes, we were approached by an elderly gentleman from a room just a couple of doors down from ours. Were we too loud? Were we being disrespectful? No - on both accounts. He was just coming over to say hi.

"Y'all in the service?"

"In the Canadian Air Force."

"I'se figured so on accounts you'se all got that accent. So, what are y'all working on?"

" A Herc tanker."

"Y'all got those new anti-missile flares and tinsel stuff?"

"Uh, yeah chaff and flares."

"Yeah, my son's in the Marines. He sez that just about all the planes have dem these days. 'Course, I never had them on my C-130."

"Oh, really? What did you have?"

"Well, y'all still have them monkey harnesses?"

"A crew restraint harness?" Troy replied.

"What he said. **So there I was**… Standing in the jump door of my Herc with a flare gun in my hand looking for missiles coming up from the jungle floor and if I saw one I would fire off that flare gun just as fast as I could while the pilot was jerking that plane all over the sky trying to stay away from the SAM's!"

"Did it work?"

"I'm here ain't I?"

"When were you on the Hercs?"

"Back in Viet Nam. It was the spring of '68. During the evacuation of Khe Sahn!"

"Well, that qualifies! Wanna beer?"

"Sure thing."

After twenty-two years of dedicated service to Canada I decided to call it quits. I had been across the globe and back, seen my fair share of trouble and had been in my fair share of trouble too. My knees and my feet were now permanently damaged from the years of walking on concrete with government issued inadequate footwear and I wasn't getting promoted anytime soon because of my persistent need to call a spade a spade and a shovel a shovel. The final straw came one day when a tow crew was tasked to pull a Herc out of the hangar. It was an unrestricted tow meaning there were no obstructions or hazards on the flight line and once the aircraft was out of the hangar, the tow crew NCO i/c could reduce the tow crew down to the minimum manning requirement.

"Okay, you're clear Kevin!" I indicated to MCpl Sylvestri with a thumbs up.

"We'll take it from here," replied Kevin. "Do the housekeeping and we'll see you inside!"

And with that the Herc was taken one way while Pte Bloggins and I headed back into the hangar to finish the job.

"I'll get these two drip trays, you can get those two."

"I don't do drip trays."

"What are you talking about, Bloggins? You heard MCpl Sylvestri. It's called housekeeping and everyone does drip trays. So grab a mop, clean those two trays and put them on the rack."

As Bloggins walked across the hangar floor he called over his shoulder, "Sorry, if you want them done then you do them. I don't do drip trays and I have to go to the can!"

Shocked at what I had just heard, I informed him of the obvious, "Well, Private Bloggins! Your two drip trays will be waiting for you when you get back!"

Grabbing a mop from the mop cart, I dunned out my two drip trays and placed them on the rack before walking into Servicing. I was infuriated that this snot-nosed brat had the gall to tell me to get stuffed. He even flipped me the finger when he walked towards the washroom. Sure, I was only a corporal but I had twenty-plus years in and he was only a private so he should have done as he was told. In fact, if I had beaked off at some corporal when I was a private I would have found myself mopping out all of the drip trays in the hangar every day by myself for a week.

"Who didn't do their drip trays?" demanded MCpl Sylvestri.

"I did mine, Kevin. I told Bloggins to do his two and he said that he didn't do drip trays."

"Really? Where is he?"

"He went to the washroom."

Just then Pte Bloggins sauntered into the Servicing section. He had no idea of the shit storm that was about to hit him.

"Private Bloggins, why didn't you mop out the drip trays as Corporal McMillan asked?"

"I don't do drip trays."

'Well Private, mopping out drip trays is considered to be a housekeeping chore that everyone is responsible for and that everyone is required to do. Now, I suggest that you get back out to the hangar floor and you mop out your drip trays before you get into more trouble."

Bloggins replied, "I don't do drip trays, Master Corporal." And then he turned his back on Kevin before walking towards the crew room.

Everyone in servicing thought that Sylvestri was going to blow a gasket. This kind of blatant insolence was enough piss anyone off - but it could really send Kevin into orbit.

"Sergeant? Are you going to do something about this?"

Now, the desk sergeant had been standing behind the servicing desk while this little drama played out in front of him. Whether or not he was paying attention to it was another matter as things can get a bit hectic in servicing.

"Do something about what?"

"Bloggins was told to mop out a couple of drip trays and he is refusing to do so!"

"Well, did you ask him nicely?"

"You're kidding right? He's a private. Cpl McMillan asked him to do two drip trays and he refused. I told him to go and mop them out and he…"

"Just hang on a second Kevin. McMillan, Downey and Baldric! Three forty-one just landed. Park it out on spot twenty-one. It will need an A check and a fuel load of 40K."

Getting up from my chair I said, "Sorry Sergeant. I don't really feel like parking Hercs today."

"What are you talking about?"

"Tell ya what, I'll park Hercs when Bloggins starts mopping drip trays!"

And with that, the three of us walked out of servicing.

The pilot taxied A/C 341 on to the military ramp and found no one coming out to park him. He knew where he was to go but there should be a marshaller and someone pulling a power unit out to greet him. It's not like he couldn't park himself. They do it all the time when they're away from the unit. But, they're not away from the unit so where in the hell is the park crew?!

"Ops – 435 Servicing?"

"Go ahead Ops."

"Do you have a park crew for Three Four One?"

"Uh, negative Ops. We're swamped at the moment. Spot Twenty-One please."

With a possible crew mutiny on his hands, or at the very least a work to rule situation, the desk sergeant came out from behind the servicing desk to regain control of the situation. Spying Pte Bloggins in the crew room, the sergeant ordered him and MCpl Sylvestri into the office where he made it abundantly clear to the Private that the next time he failed to follow the directions of any supervisor that he would be facing an immediate orders parade. Once it was settled and Bloggins went out to mop out the entire rack of drip trays, the three of us went out to do our inspections on aircraft 341.

After some heavy consultation with my Better Half, the decision was made to finally pull the pin. I informed my Crew Chief and started my release process. However, someone, somewhere, thought that I may still be of some value to the military. In a last ditch effort to retain me, someone from the career manager unit in Ottawa called and asked if I would accept a posting to CFB Cold Lake in Alberta.

What kind of medication was he on?

I asked him why - after being stationed in Winnipeg for fifteen frozen years - would I want to go to CFB Cold Lake, which is just another frozen wasteland?

"Well, we had this guy who took his release last year and with your qualifications it would dovetail perfectly with what is now lacking in that Section!"

"So, where would I be working?"

"You would be going to the liquid oxygen building."

"Oh. So, you want me to replace Gord Bell?"

"Do you know Gord Bell?"

"Know him? Hell, I trained Gord Bell when he was a remuster in 442 Squadron. Last year, Gord told me that after twelve years in Cold Lake he wanted to be posted back to Comox and when you turned him down he decided to pull the pin. So, here's the thing,

Sir. I have spent fifteen frozen years in Winnipeg. My in-laws live in Ottawa and both are in poor health. If something was to happen to them I don't want to have to drive four hours in the middle of winter just to get my wife onto an aircraft. Are you sure that there are no AVN positions available in Comox in the coming year?"

"No, there is nothing available in Comox for a couple of years!"

"Well Sir, I guess my release will stand. Thanks for your help."

And with that, the die was cast. I would spend the next six or seven months getting my affairs in order: selling our current house and going on the final house hunting trip, returning all of my military clothing and equipment to supply, finalizing the financial stuff. There were a million and one things to do and a loose timeline for getting it all done.

Despite the fact that this was something that both my wife and I had decided was the best course of action, I nevertheless felt deep in my heart that by leaving the Forces I was letting my fellow crewmates down. That they wouldn't be able to get on without me. That my expertise was still needed. And I was sure of it because just recently, one of the cross-trained aviation technicians had made a huge error on the lox building.

Cpl Bloggins had been told to carry out the necessary preparations to receive a new shipment of liquid oxygen. It was a simple job. All he had to do was fill the 500 hundred gallon tank and all the 50 gallon carts from the 2500 gallon tank. This was done by opening some valves and closing others to allow the liquid oxygen to flow through the network of pipes. As part of the AF9000 program a step by step check list had been created outlining the order in which the valves had to be closed and opened. Foolproof, right? Well, not for Bloggins. He failed set the valves as directed and, as he sat inside the nice warm building merrily waiting for the tank to fill, the liquid oxygen was quite happily following the path of least resistance, bypassing the 500 gallon tank and filling the catch basin. I'm not talking about five or even twenty gallons but hundreds of gallons liquid oxygen was now pooled behind the small protective concrete dam. When Cpl Bloggins finally detected his mistake he quickly adjusted the valves to direct the lox into the 500 gallon tank.

One would think that after such an occurrence, a person would review the procedures to ensure that it never happened again. Not Bloggins. Several weeks later he was tasked to fill a couple of 50 gallon carts and again forgot to close the transfer hose vent valve. At least this time he was standing nearby and was able to stop the flow after only ten or twenty gallons had been lost.

The creeping disaster of having people who had no concept of working in a liquid oxygen building was weighing heavily on my mind and there was nothing that I could do about it. I was afraid that eventually someone was going to make a catastrophic mistake. In fact, during a Base-wide exercise the Base Fire Marshall pointed out to the Base Commander, "If there is a fire at the lox building we do not attend. We evacuate the base." Which stands to reason as 3100 US gallons of liquid oxygen with the explosive potential of 80 sticks of dynamite per US gallon equals for one big smoking hole.

In June of 2003 my wife held a surprise birthday celebration for me. Late into the night and after many beers, I brought all of my concerns to the attention of my good friend Terry. I have known him since our trades training in CFB Borden and Terry was always one to provide some wise council.

"Let 'em bloody well sink!" he said. Or, words to that effect.

"You've done your best at keeping this ship afloat long enough. You and I both know that the unit is going to make some mistakes but they'll come around. You can't always be their life jacket. So, cut them loose. They'll come close to drowning but in the end they'll learn how to swim without you keeping their head above water."

Thanks Terry.

Starting Two" - MCpl Bill Stamper giving hand signals during a start procedure on a TD mission.

435 Squadron postscript - The days of the 435 Sqn Hercules are numbered. There has been an ongoing issue in obtaining parts for the refueling pods. The Canadian Armed Forces will cease to have a *tactical* air-to-air refueling capability after the year 2020. With the arrival of the new Fixed Wing SAR aircraft all of the Hercules will be re-tasked to a strictly transport role. It is unknown if some Hercs will be retained by 435 Sqn.

Just for Shits & Giggles

For as long as military forces have existed anywhere in the world its members have always searched for a means to relieve the stressors of the job. Some people do this by being active in sports, either individually or as a team. Some people will focus on activities with friends or family. Some tend to drink more, although I don't think the service members today are indulging nearly as much as my generation did. And there are some who get rid of their stress by carrying out a few pranks. Usually they are harmless in nature and rarely vindictive, although retaliatory pranks can get out of hand. Call it getting into mischief or just "boys being boys," but servicemen love to joke around. Some people like a good joke and can roll with the punches - give as good as they get - while some do not cotton to pranks at all. What follows is a number of the practical jokes that I was either a victim of, a party to or aware of during my twenty-seven years in the Canadian military.

During Basic Training at CFRS Cornwallis there wasn't much time to level any jokes but we did manage to have a little bit of fun. It was when you were soundly asleep that the personal devils came out to play.

When I went through Canadian Forces Recruit School no one slept on their bed from Sunday to Thursday night for fear of disturbing the picture perfect rack ready for the morning inspection. You would sleep on the floor or under your bunk or pass out against the laundry room wall while polishing your boots but the last thing you would do was sleep in your bed. Occasionally, a guy might risk sleeping **on** his bed but never **in** his bed for fear of wrinkling the sheets. On the weekend, it was a different story because everyone savoured the pleasure of actually laying on their bed and there wasn't a hospital corner in sight. Realistically speaking, a person's bed was the only thing that you could mess with. It took little time to disrupt and just as much time to fix. No harm, no foul. Right?

One popular prank involved short sheeting someone's bed. If you haven't heard about it or experienced it, short sheeting involves taking the upper sheet and folding it in such a way that when the occupant climbs into bed their feet only go half way down the bed. It's a cheap prank and it only works once or twice. Besides, there's no sense in doing this in Cornwallis because no one ever sleeps in their bed. The joke could go undiscovered for a week or until the next sheet exchange.

No, it was much more fun to mess with a guy while he was sleeping on his bunk on the weekends. An individual asleep on his bunk just begs to be wrapped up in either toilet paper or paper towels. The choice is yours, but be aware that although paper towels are stronger, toilet paper is much more plentiful. With one person standing on either side of the bunk it's a simple process of passing the roll over and under the bed frame until the Sleeping Beauty is mummified. Of course, stops and starts are inevitable if the sleeper turns over in the night. But, if successful, you can completely cocoon a person in about twenty minutes.

Taking a nap on a Saturday afternoon was always gratifying. But, if you occupied a lower bunk you had to be prepared for the unexpected when you woke up. For instance, you take an empty pop bottle and fill it with water. Now, take a sock or the corner of someone's underwear and stuff it into the end of the bottle like a cork. Hide the bottle under the sheets and blankets of the upper mattress with only the sock hanging down. Now, imagine you're in the process of waking up from a well-deserved nap. Things are kinda hazy and in your still sleepy state as you look up and see a sock hanging above your head.

"What the hell is this?" you mumble as you pull on the sock.

Seemingly, out of nowhere, water pours out onto the drowsy individual. Well, you're not so drowsy anymore.

If you have someone who is a sound sleeper you can always try the shaving cream trick. You know: you put some shaving cream in a guy's hand then you tickle his ear as if it's a bug. The involuntary reflex is to swat the bug away which causes the guy to smear shaving cream all over the side of his head. Childish, but a nice gag all the same, especially when four or five other people are watching. Please be careful. The first time I was a victim of this stunt, the prankster had placed a lot of shaving foam on my hand and then he faked the bug near my eyes. Even flushing my eyes under running water didn't address the stinging sensation for quite some time.

It is a given that the stupidity level of a prank will increase exponentially with the consumption of alcohol. I remember one particular practical joke that happened towards the end of basic training. Our course was soon to be over and we were now down to twenty-three members in the squad. By now most of us had a single bunk space. Some of us were even lucky enough to have a single bed without an upper bunk. One such individual was Bronco Horvat who, on this particular evening, had been able to consume more than his four beer allotment and was happily passed out in his rack. The rest of us impaired idiots decided to have a little fun so we picked up Bronco's entire bed and placed it on top of the lockers separating his bunk space from the next. Bronco was totally oblivious of the fact that he was now elevated some seven feet above the barracks floor. With our task completed, we sought refuge in our respective bunks.

A rule of thumb states the first person to fall asleep is usually the first person to wake up. And that's exactly what happened on this night; Recruit Horvat awoke before anyone else and, needing to relieve his bladder, he simply rolled out of bed only to quite unexpectedly fall some distance to the floor. He had no idea what had happened but he was definitely now wide awake. It was funny at the time but in retrospect he could have broken an arm, a leg or worse.

In the military, as with many other working environments, quite often there are colloquial names for otherwise common objects and unless you are in the know you can find yourself on a fool's errand. The joke usually goes something like this:

"Private!"

"Yes, Master Corporal?"

"I want you to go to the Tool Crib and sign out a left hand torque wrench extension handle. Be quick about it because we need to finish this job by the end of the day. And make sure that it has been correctly calibrated in angstroms!"

"Yes Master Corporal!"

There are a great many of innocuous things that you can send **The Innocent** to fetch. In talking with some long-serving military members some of the all-time favourites came to light:

- The key to the Supply Tent
- Forty feet of hangar line
- A sky hook
- Tobacco for the Bosun's pipe
- A bucket of prop wash
- Gas for the rifles
- Oil for the port running light

- A long weight
- A box of variable frequencies

The vital element to sending someone to get something that doesn't really exist is ensuring that the item must have some sense of plausibility. For a newly hatched airman agog with the operations of an active flight line going to supply to fetch forty feet of hangar line to secure the aircraft in stormy conditions sounds real enough as does a bucket of prop wash to clean the bugs off of the propellers during a primary inspection (PI). Mind you, there used to be a product known as prop wash and it was used exactly for that purpose. In reality, the same goes for the gas for the rifles.

When the Canadian military was issued the FNC1A1 as its standard battlefield rifle, the users were instructed that the weapon was a semi-automatic, self-loading, magazine fed, *gas operated* rifle. Semi-automatic means one round is fired for each squeeze of the trigger. Self-loading is simple, in that after a round is fired, a new round from the magazine is chambered into the breech. Magazine fed is self-explanatory... but gas operated?

Yes! Some of the expanding gases from the detonation of the gunpowder are used to drive the gas piston rod back against the breech block carrier. The breech block carrier and the breech block moves to the rear extracting the empty casing and picks up a new round from the magazine during the forward movement. Everybody knew that the entire operating cycle was dependent on the gas. But, to the uneducated - or even the marginally educated -

it does sound accurate enough to fool them. This is how I was once sent to the Quartermaster to get a long weight.

"Oh, really? What's that?"

"Well, you know the pull through for your rifle?"

"Sure, it's two pieces of brass separated by a piece of cordage used to pull the cleaning rags through the barrel."

"Well, a long weight is bigger. It's the pull through for the 50 cal. machine gun. We call it a long weight because it has a long brass weight on the one end."

"Makes sense to me. I'll be back in a bit."

And confident in my quest, off I went to see the Quartermaster.

"What are you here for?"

"They sent me to get a pull through for the 50 cal."

"Oh, you're looking for a long *wait*!"

"That's right. A long *weight*."

"Hang on. I think I've got one in the back."

So while the Warrant Officer hunted around in the back of the store room I stood and waited at the front counter. And waited and waited and….. I think you get the point.

So there I was… It was a particularly miserable rainy day in Comox. There was a Voodoo in for periodic maintenance. The ejection seats had been removed from the aircraft and the explosive charges were placed in a secure locker. The seats could now be stripped of their components and hardware. Once they were fully disassembled the ejection seats were to be cleaned, inspected and then repainted. Individual components were also disassembled for cleaning and inspection. When all the parts were verified as serviceable the ejection seats were re-assembled as a complete unit at which time the manual functions of the RPI lap belts and the shoulder harnesses were tested.

We had a relatively new person working in the shop: a technician from the Base Safety Systems section upstairs who had been assigned to us for some con-train. C*on-train* - or contact training - was the process of rotating technicians through the various units to expose them to different aspects of the trade. For example, our aircraft had ejection seats and the CP-140 Aurora does not. Technicians from Base Safety Systems would come to our section to gain experience and a working knowledge of the emergency egress system. Having new personnel in the shop was like blood in the water and the sharks were circling. Seizing the opportunity to have a bit of fun, MCpl Ian Neilson told the newbie that the best method to clean off the crud that had built up on the lap belt fittings was to steam clean them because "the warm moisture would soften the dirt making it easier to brush out." To add a wee bit of credence to his statement, Neilson even went so far as to say that this was listed in the CFTO's as an alternate method of cleaning.

"Okay. Where do I get the steam from?"

"At the steam plant of course. I want you to take this waste paper can. It will hold just enough steam. Go over to the steam plant, have the steam fitters fill it up and then bring it back."

"Yes Master Corporal."

Undaunted, off to the steam plant she went, a metal waste paper can in her hand, wearing her work dress uniform and the requisite skunk jacket to keep out the driving rain. It was an impossible task for sure, and because it was so impossible, you would think that she would have realized that it was a bullshit task from the onset. Once she got to the steam plant she told the manager that she needed a bucket of steam to clean some aircraft parts. Despite the ludicrous request the manager decided to help her out. First, they found something to act as a lid. Then, they had the girl wrap her skunk jacket around the can to insulate it from the rain. With the plant workers' assistance, hot steam from a low pressure line was vented into the can. When the can was warmed up the lid was positioned just right as steam continued to circulate in the can.

"Now!"

The con-train technician pushed the lid down tight and wrapped her jacket tightly over the top before heading back to our section in 7 Hangar. Dodging puddles and traffic, it was a quick 400 metre dash through the downpour. Soaked to the skin she burst into the shop ran over to MCpl Neilson and yanked off the lid allowing the smallest wisp of steam to gently waft up towards the ceiling.

"Screw you, Master Corporal!"

It does not matter where you are employed, when you are the new guy on the crew you can expect to be subjected to a few pranks. This is a test of your character and if you break, or go whining to management that the boys are picking on you, they will never leave you alone or worse, never be there to lend you a hand. When my father started working on the log boom at the local sawmill, a common practice was for one person to knock the hard hat off of the new guy's head just so another person could "help out" by spearing it with his pike pole. By the end of the week his hard hat looked like it was made out of Swiss cheese. Other pranks included removing the seat off a person's bicycle so he would have to ride home standing up. Another involved bolting a lunch box to a table. Through it all he never broke and he gave as good as he got, thus proving that he was a worthy addition to the crew.

When I started working on the flight line at CFB Winnipeg I had to divide my time between two separate hangars. At 16 Hangar I was responsible for servicing the seven CT-114 Tutors, the three CT-133 Silverstars and a CC-109 VIP Cosmopolitan (unofficially known as Smokey One). Over at 10 Hangar, there were four CC-130E Hercules and seven CC-129 Dakotas. To assist the safety systems tech in shuttling between the hangars, the shop possessed a red, single-speed Peewee Herman Special bike, complete with a large wire basket on the front for carrying parts. It was the responsibility of the technician to secure this noble steed in the shop at the end of the shift.

"Okay boys! Where's the bike?"

They certainly were an inventive bunch, I'll give them that. I would find the bike up in a tree or suspended from the ceiling in the middle of the hangar with .040 monel lockwire or zap-strapped to the front of a towing mule and my all-time personal favourite, "According to my watch, it should be over Thunder Bay right about...... now. Strapped down on the ramp of aircraft 310."

After a couple of shifts of putting up with these shenanigans, I was welcomed as a part of the crew. Now, I must point out that this was the crew working in 10 Hangar, the Boys in Hercs and Daks. The people working at Triple T Servicing in 16 Hangar - like Cpl Tim Brown - were far too uptight for some harmless clowning around.

I knew that I was now a member of the crew and that I had paid my dues because all the pranks stopped. But there was one guy in 10 Hangar, Cpl Nick Craig (better known as Fang for having only one front tooth) who thought I deserved even more of his juvenile attention. Fang was relentless. His pranks ranged from filling my lunch bag with leaves, grass or just plain garbage, to hiding the keys to the work truck. He was taking great pleasure in trying to piss me off, but through it all I kept my cool. After all, I had already run the gauntlet and was a member of the crew in good standing. All of this did not go unnoticed by our Crew Chief. Nick was finally called into the office and informed that if he continued the Crew Chief would turn a blind eye to any retaliation on my part. Sure enough, Nick did not disappoint.

So there I was... On an extremely hot day on the tarmac in front of 10 Hangar. The thermometer was pushing 40°C. I had just finished and signed for an A check on a Herc, and was looking forward to taking a break from the persistent heat, to just sit in the shade with a cold drink and have a smoke. But, where was my flight jacket? It wasn't on the back of the chair where I had left it. It wasn't in the crew room nor in any of the other places where the guys would hide a co-worker's belongings.

This wasn't a lunch bag or a coffee cup, although they too had gone missing in the past only to turn up in the last place one would suspect. This was my flight jacket. An item that, for an aircraft technician, was very hard to come by. The new gore tex environmental clothing that would eventually be issued was still in the larval stage of development and would not be making an appearance on the flight line for another five or six years. Until then, the clothing worn by the servicing crew members was a real hodgepodge of whatever was comfortable and protective from the elements. It was also a source of personal pride with every rip having been personally sutured like Rambo's battlefield injury. Sure, we looked like a rag tag bunch of aircraft mechanics, but as long as it was clean, the Crew Chief didn't mind what we wore. Besides, this was the flight line, a place for sweaty coveralls and scuffed boots and not Base Headquarters with its strict adherence to wearing your best dressed uniform. Unlike those, who had creatively acquired their flight jackets, I had been issued my flight jacket when I was in 442 Squadron. It had distinctive crests sewn on the shoulders and the pockets held outdated memos, a couple of blank supply vouchers, a length of .032 monel lockwire, a bunch of zip ties, a Ziploc bag containing a coil of witness wire and lead seals. I also had a small notebook containing a list of WUC (work unit codes), a list of NSN part numbers, the CSN/Autovon phone numbers for all the liquid oxygen buildings across the country as well as some personal contacts. There were a couple of pens, my fitter repair kit (even though I wasn't a fitter), a blue Bic lighter and my cigarettes.

Poof. Gone. Vanished.

Twenty minutes of searching around the hangar in all the usual hiding spots turned up nothing. Then I noticed Fang with a shit-eating grin on his face.

"You look hot and bothered. Maybe you should just chill out!"

Just the way Fang said "chill out" made me suspicious. It was a clue, if there ever was one as to the whereabouts of my jacket. Sure enough, I found my jacket rolled into a tight ball and crammed into the freezer section of the crew fridge. What an asshole!

A couple of weeks went by. In the middle of shift the crew had decided to have a barbeque after work. Just before lunch, somebody - I think it was Cpl Whittle or Cpl Rollie Walsh - was cutting up onions for the barbeque when I overheard someone wish Cpl Craig a happy birthday.

"Actually, it was yesterday. My wife made me a black forest cake and I brought a piece to work to have at lunch. I might even let you look at it!"

Glancing at the aircraft status board, I saw there was an arrival at 11:30 hrs. Perfect timing. The stars were aligned, so it was now time for a little reciprocity.

When aircraft 130306 arrived, the park crew marshalled it in to place. GTC running. All engines stop. Ground power applied. Chocks in. GTC stopped. As the aircrew de-planed the servicing technicians began to swarm over the plane like ants on a sugar cube and the park crew began the re-fuel job. The standard fuel load for our Hercs was 42,000 pounds. Cpl Nick Craig was in the Flight Engineer's seat conducting the re-fuel. He was going to be there for a while. His job was to watch the gauges and balance the fuel load between the various tanks and the wings. To achieve a balanced load of 42,000 pounds he would be putting 8,400 pounds in the outers, 7,600 in the inners and 5,000 in the auxiliary tanks.[55] This would give me plenty of time to complete my A check and head over to the cryogenics building. It was time to make an introduction… of sorts. I was going to introduce Nick Craig's monstrous wedge of black forest birthday cake to Mr. Liquid Nitrogen.

The boiling point of liquid nitrogen (LN_2) is -196°C; that's the temperature at which the liquid changes back to a gaseous state. Although liquid nitrogen does not support combustion, it does

---

[55] A C-130 Hercules has eight fuel tanks and can hold over 60,000 lbs of fuel. In each wing is an outer, an inner, an auxiliary and an external tank under the wing. The new J model Hercs are manufactured without the external fuel tanks. However, the Royal Australian Air Force is having them installed on their C-130J Hercs.

displace oxygen in enclosed spaces, and it will burn exposed skin on contact. I'm sure that everyone has seen the science experiment whereby a fresh rose or a banana is immersed in LN_2 and after it is taken out the item is easily shattered like a crystal glass. Make no mistake, liquid nitrogen does not care if the item exposed to its properties is a rose, a banana, your hand or a five-inch wide four layer slice of homemade black forest cake; given enough time the water molecules inside the cell structure will solidify, expand and rupture. Fracturing the structure's integrity is now quite simple. All you have to do is drop it.

"What the hell are you doing with my cake?"

I was caught red handed. The frozen block of rich homemade chocolatey confection was balancing precariously in my gloved hand.

"This cake?"

"Yeah, my birthday cake! Put it down!"

"Okay."

From shoulder height, I slowly rolled my hand over allowing the cake to fall to the floor where it shattered into a jigsaw puzzle.

"You bastard!" Nick roared as he advanced towards me with clenched fists.

"Corporal Craig! Get to my office. McMillan! Clean up that mess!"

It was the Crew Chief and he had witnessed the whole thing. Like many good Crew Chiefs, he knew the pulse of his workers and for the most part he let them sort out any issues on their own.

He had known all about the personal attacks that Cpl Craig had persistently launched against me and had already counselled him against continuing his activities. It was when Fang's actions turned violent that he was obligated to step in. For Fang, it was just desserts.

Did you know that when *monotony* and *boredom* are paired with *location* and *timing* the result can be a constant stream of laughs?

There was an aircraft electrician on our servicing crew named Jan who was quite the prankster. Her favourite joke was to go out to a Herc and climb up behind the main gear wheels where she would lay in wait for some unsuspecting rigger to come out to do his B check which involved opening up the main landing gear door. To open up the door, you first have to disconnect the gear door linkage by passing your hands through two small access panels. That's when Jan would spring into action. When the poor bastard reached in to undo the linkage, Jan - who had been quietly waiting on top of the main landing gear - would grab him by both wrists and pull him roughly in towards the fuselage. I swear that she scared some guys to the point where they damn near wet themselves. Jan was so good at this trick that she could scare the same guy twice on the same aircraft!

First, she would surprise the technician on the port side and then after he watched her head back to Servicing, he would continue with his inspection. As soon as he wasn't looking, Jan would slip back as quick as a cat and crawl up behind the starboard side gear door to scare the crap out of him again. It got the point where some riggers would look around to see where Jan was before they even went to do their checks and if they couldn't see her, they would pawn the job off onto some other poor unsuspecting technician.

Here's another favourite: take a coin - a quarter will work but a loonie is better - and pick a place somewhere in the crew room that looks like a spot where a dropped coin could have rolled into position. Now, glue the coin into place with a puddle of super glue and put a bead of super glue all around the edge of it. Make sure that the entire crew knows about it except for the cheapest guy on the crew. You can now be entertained for the next couple of shifts watching this guy waste every spare moment trying to pry it off the floor without anyone noticing.

You can also take a length of duct tape and wrap up your buddy's lock on his locker. Make sure you wrap some up on yours too just to deflect any suspicions. So, you come into work and find your lock all wrapped up. No problem. You simply pull out your Buck knife and cut it off. Two days later, when it happens again you simply cut it off. But now, you're seeking some revenge.

Your cautious inquiries point to your good friend, Cpl Bloggins working on 3 Crew. So, at the end of your shift you wrap up his lock in a massive tape ball. When you next come to work you discover your lock layered with tape, then lockwire and then more tape. The simplest solution was to get the bolt cutters out of the tool crib and take off the whole damn lock.

The "Locker Wars" - as harmless as they appeared to be - were getting out of hand. Lockers that were sequentially placed according to the Squadron Chief's orders were shuffled around or even moved into different rooms. It was an unwritten rule that you could put men's lockers into the women's change rooms but never women's lockers into the men's change rooms simply because most of the females on the crew were far above this childish behaviour. One technician came off the flight line at the end of night shift to find that his locker wasn't even in the hangar. He drove home in his coveralls only to find his locker waiting for him in the driveway of his PMQ. Coincidently, he was posted to another Base and it was his last night of work on the crew, so he left the locker in the backyard.

Finally, the Bameo got wind of our shenanigans and, although no real property damage was being done, the ongoing Locker Wars were deemed to be a huge distraction from the work at hand. Therefore, the Major issued an edict that there would be no more Locker Wars and any person caught messing around with a locker would be severely punished.

It was on the following day - or maybe the following Monday - when the servicing crew came in for day shift. As per normal, the technicians arrived at the hangar, got changed into their coveralls, checked the status board, grabbed their tool pouches and headed off to perform the necessary B checks. Everyone that is, except for MCpl Roy Reis. Roy's locker was nowhere to be found.

"Shit! Well, I'll look for it later."

MCpl Reis grabbed a tool pouch and headed for the hangar floor to do his aircraft checks. Once all the checks were completed, the hangar doors were rolled open for the tow crews to haul the flyers out to the apron. Roy was on his way back into the hangar when he spotted his locker suspended from the roof trusses some thirty feet above the hangar floor and directly in front of the Bameo's office window. Using a cherry picker, MCpl Reis raised himself up to the level of his locker and proceeded to get changed in the bucket…when…*Click*

Upon hearing the sound behind him, Roy turned around in the bucket and found himself facing the Bameo, who was now standing in the open window.

"MCpl Reis?"

"Yes, Sir?"

"Is that your locker?"

"Yes Sir, it is."

"Didn't I issue an order that there was to be no more of this Locker Wars bullshit?"

"You did indeed, Sir."

"So, how in the hell do you explain this?"

"Well Major…It's quite obvious that the guys on night shift didn't get the memo."

"I want you to get that locker down on the ground where it belongs right now!"

"Right now, Sir?"

"Right now, Roy!"

MCpl Reis calmly closed his locker and locked the door. He raised the cherry picker up about five more feet and, after taking a quick look below, pulled out his side cutters.

Bink. Bink. Bink. SMASH!

The force of the locker dropping thirty feet to the hangar floor split its sides wide open. Roy's personal belongings and some aircraft parts that he had squirrelled away for an emergency repair spilled out in a wide arc across the hangar.

"Roy, you could have gotten some help."

"Yes Sir. But, you did say right now, Sir. Have a good day."

The Current State of Affairs...
As I see it

It's time to wax philosophically about poor decisions and missed opportunities.

I was a member of the Canadian Armed Forces from October 1982 until August 2003 - with an additional stint in the Air Reserves from October 2003 to September 2008 - and in that time I was a witness to a great number of changes within the military, some of which I consider beneficial and others not so much. There were changes in policy objectives, changes in uniform and changes in tasking. Those policy objectives which I have found most disturbing were the ones involving massive reductions in personnel and equipment. My experience regarding the combat arms trades or the navy is limited as I was not directly involved with those elements. However, the reduction of equipment and personnel in the air force has been ongoing for quite some time and did affect me directly. These reductions began in September 1969 with Prime Minister Pierre Trudeau's new NATO policy that dropped personnel levels stationed in Europe from 10,000 to 5,000 members and the number of CF-104 squadrons in Europe being cut in half to three.[56]

---

[56] In Retreat: The Canadian Forces in the Trudeau Years, pg. 156.

This new policy reflected the Prime Minister's "own known lack of interest in NATO and to save money".[57] Before being elected as the Prime Minister, Pierre Trudeau served in Lester Pearson's cabinet as the Minister of Justice. In that role, he would have been well aware of the growing militant factions in the province of Québec. It is my contention that once he became the Prime Minister, Pierre Trudeau used the opportunity to not only save money but to have extra troops available if the shit ever hit the fan back home.

And, sure enough it did!

In 1970, the home grown terrorist actions of the Front de Libération du Québec (FLQ) forced Prime Minister Pierre Trudeau to enact the War Measures Act, which suspended civil liberties across the country and placed openly armed Canadian Forces troops not only in the major cities in Québec, but in the nation's capital as well. For Prime Minister Trudeau, having troops who had just recently been repatriated from Europe on hand was quite convenient. After the FLQ Crisis had ended cutting back on the Canadian military became a means for each successive government, regardless of political party affiliation, to save federal tax dollars. However, this targeting of military spending was nothing new. It had begun well before the FLQ Crisis.

We all know the sad tale of the Avro Arrow. In 1953, RCAF Wing Commander R. Footit was sent to search countries in the Western Alliance for a suitable all weather interceptor aircraft to

---

[57] In Retreat: The Canadian Forces in the Trudeau Years, pg. 154.

replace the Avro built CF-100. The RCAF had specific performance requirements (AIR 7-3) that the selected aircraft had to meet or exceed. According to the AIR 7-3, the new aircraft must be able to operate from a 6,000 foot runway, have a range of 600 nautical miles, be capable of speeds up to 1.5 Mach and carry advanced weapons at 50,000 feet while pulling 2G's. A number of Western alliance aircraft were considered. "Footit's examination team looked at the F-101 Voodoo in the USA during their searching tour and it was quickly decided that it fell short of their requirements. They could not have realized that this aircraft would be issued to the RCAF after the Arrow Project had been cancelled and scrapped."[58] The AV Roe company designed and built five aircraft that were designated the CF-105 Avro Arrow. Incorporated in its design were concepts that would not be found on fighter aircraft for many years to come such as quick disconnect fittings to facilitate faster engine changes and an internal weapons bay, features that are now standard items the most advanced of today's fighter aircraft. But the Progressive Conservative government under Prime Minister John Diefenbaker, which had campaigned vigorously against "rampant Liberal spending" could not afford both the anti-aircraft Bomarc missile system and the Avro Arrow. Suffice to say, George Pearkes - the Conservative Minister of National Defence - recommended that the Avro Arrow be scrapped. Surprisingly, the new Bomarc missile system was installed at only two locations: North Bay,

---

[58] Avro Arrow, pg. 13.

Ontario and La Macaza, Quebec. With a range of only 640 km, the Bomarc missile system was defending the most populated (and the wealthiest) areas of Canada while leaving the rest of the country completely exposed. Let's just say that with hindsight being 20/20, the popular opinion within the military community was that the decisions made by federal politicians at that time were not necessarily in the best interest of the country.

Another poor government decision regarding the military was the decommissioning of CVL 22. The keel for the vessel was laid down in 1943 but construction was suspended in 1946 following the end of WWII. It sat in a British shipyard for six years and work resumed in 1952, once the Royal Canadian Navy agreed to purchase it. Five years later CVL 22 was commissioned as HMCS Bonaventure, Canada's last aircraft carrier. Manned by a crew of 1,200 personnel, the Bonnie was armed with four 3 inch/50 twin mount guns and eight 40mm Bofors guns. With a squadron of F2H-3 McDonnell Banshee fighters and Grumman CS2F Trackers on her flight deck, the Bonnie was truly a jewel in the Royal Canadian Navy's crown.[59]

In late October 1962 the HMCS Bonaventure was moving swiftly through the north Atlantic ocean. When President John F. Kennedy asked Prime Minister Diefenbaker for assistance in stopping the Soviet ships from reaching Cuba our head of state refused to increase Canada's military alert status. Officially, Canada had nothing to do with the initial US naval blockade of

---

[59] HMCS Bonaventure, Wikipedia.

Cuba but the Minister of National Defence and Rear Admiral Dyer deployed the Bonnie, along with her escort ships, to conduct *anti-submarine training manoeuvers* through the mid and western Atlantic. This decision allowed the US navy to proceed south to block access to Cuba[60] and during one of these *training patrols* the Canadian fleet discovered a Soviet submarine operating within five hundred miles of Halifax.[61]

In 1966, HMCS Bonaventure underwent a midlife update at Davie Shipyards that lasted eighteen months and cost $18 million. In 1968, shortly after the project was completed, the Bonaventure was removed from the naval inventory. Citing "budget cuts" during the unification of the Canadian Forces the federal government effectively removed a high profile presence that underscored Canada's maritime sovereignty.[62] In 1970, CVL 22 was sold to a Taiwanese scrapyard for $1.6 million but no one actually witnessed the Bonnie being cut up and a rumour had been floated that the "Taiwanese had swapped the Bonnie for an aging carrier of a similar class".[63] It would be nice to envision her still afloat somewhere but I highly doubt it.

Federal monies that are used to purchase any equipment for the Canadian military have always been highly scrutinized. Canadian citizens, unlike our hawkish cousins South of the 49th

---

[60] Canadian Navy during the Cuban Missile Crisis, Canada's Naval Memorial.
[61] Cuban Missile Crisis: Diefenbaker, Harkness and Kennedy, Valour Canada, Military History Library
[62] In Retreat, pg. 44
[63] In Retreat, pg. 46

Parallel, are quite apathetic toward their military and have no idea as to the amount of funds required to purchase major pieces of equipment. It would also appear that the federal government purposely waits too long to purchase any new equipment in the hope that the taxpayer won't realize money is being spent. This action often results in the purchasing of marginally serviceable equipment at an exorbitant cost. In order to be effective the replacement of rolling stock (trucks, armoured vehicles, etc.), aircraft and combat vessels must be planned out well in advance of their expiration date in order for the new equipment to be online and more importantly, for the troops to be trained in its use.

Our current submarine fleet consists of four aged Upholder/Victoria class diesel electric vessels. They were constructed for the British Royal Navy in the early 1980's and were retired from that service in 1994 after which they had been left to wallow, unloved, tied up to a dock. Then, along comes the Canadian government - under Prime Minister Jean Chrétien - looking for a deal to replace the outdated Oberon class subs that had been afloat since the 1960's. This time the British reeled us in for the incredible amount of only $750 million for all four boats! Absolutely outstanding! However, since their arrival in Canada the subs have been plagued with deteriorating welds on the hull, electrical problems, fires and flooding. All of the vessels have had to undergo extensive re-fitting at an exorbitant cost just to use our Mark 48 torpedoes. Ask any naval person if they would like to serve on a Canadian submarine and you'll more than likely be told to "Go pound fucking sand!"

Do we need submarines? Sure, we need them just to have a fully functional navy that operates *above* and *below* the surface of the ocean. But, the federal government had better get its act in gear when it comes to acquiring this very expensive equipment. Here are some questions that bear consideration:

1. Why is the federal government always purchasing old and outdated or not enough new equipment for our military?

2. Why does it take years of endless studies to finally decide to purchase equipment that is nearly obsolete or has to undergo immediate upgrades just to be compatible with our allies when it is finally delivered?

3. How does the Canadian federal government rationalize decisions when it comes to equipment procurement?

4. And, why are so many of our senior military staff turning into just a bunch of "Yes Men" who shrink at the thought of saying *NO* when Parliament dictates what is best but in reality it may not be?

These are the kinds of questions the members of the Canadian military have been asking for years and should also be of extreme interest to the Canadian public. I firmly believe the taxpayers need to how the Department of National Defence is mis-spending their money. Here is a case in point:

From 1958 to 1979 the Boeing aircraft company built 1,010 copies of the 707 airframe in fifteen variants. In 1970-71, the Canadian Armed Forces acquired five new copies of the venerable Boeing 707-347C, designated the CC-137 Husky. It was a lovely aircraft designed to haul personnel and cargo over great distances around the globe. But, the CAF also used their Boeings for transporting people and equipment on short hops across the country on a daily basis. On Monday, Wednesday and Friday a CC-137 would take off from CFB Comox at about 08:00 hrs and over the course of the day it would cycle through take-offs and landings at Vancouver, Edmonton, Winnipeg, Trenton, Ottawa, Greenwood before finally ending its journey in Shearwater. At each stop the passengers would disembark, the aircraft would be refuelled, the passengers would climb back on board and then it would lift off towards the next destination. Not only was this hard on the landing gear but the airframe structure itself was subjected to stressors each time it was pressurized and de-pressurized. On Tuesday, Thursday and Saturday the Boeing flights reversed their course now flying from east to west with the flight terminating back at CFB Comox. In 1995, three CC-137 Huskies were retired and replaced with the A310-300 Airbus, designated as the CC-150 Polaris. The remaining two Boeing 707's continued to operate as strategic air to air refuelers until 1997. When they were finally taken off strength they ended up as spare parts for the USAF Northrop Grumman E-8 Joint STARS programme. A fitting end for any aircraft.

Now, here's the rub. In the late 1980's, Field Aviation in Calgary had taken possession of a Boeing 707 from some other country that had not paid their bill. Field Aviation was in business to maintain aircraft, not fly them and they wanted to get the plane off of their apron. But wait! Here comes a Canadian Armed Forces CC-137 in for yet another 3rd line maintenance inspection with more than a hundred times the operating hours than the one they had just acquired. So, Field Aviation approaches the Canadian military with a sweetheart of a deal: for the price of the other country's outstanding bill, let's say it was $1 million dollars, they would completely retrofit the much newer aircraft including a paint job to seamlessly match the rest of the Canadian fleet or we could spend ten times the amount to fix the old one. Which option do you think NDHQ decided on? That's right – fix the old one because any acquisitions would have to go through Parliament and there is more money than God in the budget for maintenance.

Chalk up another poor decision for the Boys at the Pointy End! And if you think that was bad here's another one.

In the early 1980's Canada purchased 138 F-18 Hornets from McDonnell Douglas to replace two hundred CF-104G Starfighters, sixty-six CF-101B Voodoos and one hundred and thirty-five CF-116 Freedom Fighters. That's four hundred and one airframes. Yes, quite a few had been written off by this time, especially the CF-104's, but I would hazard a guess that there were at least three hundred aircraft that were still operational.

Maybe it's the new math but there is something not quite right with this equation. How can you replace three hundred units of three different platforms with less than 50% of only one model? Yes, the F/A-18 Hornet is a multi-role aircraft capable of doing both air to air and air to mud missions even on the same flight. But regardless of the type of mission in which the aircraft is employed, when a major fault is discovered the entire fleet is supposed to be grounded until each aircraft is thoroughly inspected and certified as serviceable for duty. Well, you can't do that when you are operating only one aircraft type because your nation would now be defenceless.

So, what do you do? You simply change the rules to keep your country safe. You ignore the problem. Pretend that it may not be there and that will you take care of the issue on the next major inspection. While you're at it, how about telling the aircrew that you're going to play Russian Roulette with their lives over the aircraft's serviceability?

"Uh, Captain Smythe-Jones, we've had a problem with a sticky widget in the flight controls. Currently, there is a fleet-wide inspection to be done but NDHQ says we don't have to do it until the next primary inspection. Since nothing has happened so far so you should be good to go flying. Oh, now you don't want to go flying?" Imagine that!

I also have a real problem with the actual number of aircraft purchased. Of the original one hundred and thirty-eight CF-18 Hornets purchased, approximately twenty of them have been lost to accidents.⁶⁴ The remaining one hundred and some are not nearly enough fighter aircraft to protect a country the size of ours, never mind the fact that the F/A-18 is designed to be a carrier borne aircraft. It has no range. According to sources, the listed combat radius is only 330 miles (537 km).⁶⁵

In my opinion, the decision to purchase the F/A-18 Hornet as a sole fighter was a huge mistake. For the defence of Canadian airspace we would have been far better off not having all of our eggs in one basket. If the total number of aircraft to be purchased was fixed at 138 units, the better choice at that time, would have been to retain a dedicated intercept capability by purchasing fifty McDonnell Douglas F-15 Eagles and keep the remaining eighty-eight as F/A-18 Hornets. Or, split the numbers 50/50, I don't care. The F-15 Eagle is designed as an all-weather

Aircraft Costs per unit

F-18	$35 m each	(1977)
F-15	$10.7m each	(1977)
138 - F-18	for $4.8 b	(1977)
Or		
88 - F-18 plus	$3.1b	(1977)
50 - F-15	$535m	(1977)
138 a/c	$3.635 b	(1977)

---

⁶⁴ McDonnell Douglas CF-18 Hornet, 09 March 2017.
⁶⁵ Combat radius is the maximum distance an aircraft can fly while carry a full load of ordinance.

interceptor with a combat radius of 1,222 miles (1,967 km). That's four times the distance that of F/A-18 for an interdiction mission. The F-15 Eagle is operated by the US Air Force as well as Japan, South Korea, Israel, Saudi Arabia and Singapore. So why not Canada?

There are both drawbacks and benefits to having a mixed fleet. Two different supply chains is more expensive and the initial training of aircrew and technicians is costly as well. On the plus side, having the correct platform to perform a tasking such as intercepting any intruders *before* they overfly your sovereign territory is extremely useful. And, still having aircraft available to defend your country if a fleet-wide inspection is called is even better.

Due to the fact that Canada did purchase an aircraft with such a limited range the question is: How do you provide cover for a country the size of Canada with so few fighters that have such a small combat range? By building Forward Operating Locations (FOL) of course! Fighters from CFB Cold Lake are routinely deployed to various northern and western locations while aircraft from CFB Bagotville are sent to the north and eastern locations. In 1994, FOLs were built in Yellowknife and Rankin Inlet. Each FOL site can house up to 200 personnel and shelter six fighters - with aircraft servicing equipment, some spare parts and other necessities being prepositioned. [66] Even before the FOLs were built, the rotation of men and machines to other locations was, if

---

[66] Canadian NORAD Region Forward Operating Locations, 11 March 2017

nothing else, just to make an appearance and wave the flag. Comox, Inuvik, Goose Bay, Gander and Greenwood were all visited repeatedly for short periods of time. The permanent FOLs were constructed through 1995 but, as with everything else connected to the military, budgets were slashed to the bone leaving all essential expenditures, like the air defence of the country, strictly curtailed.

Purchasing military equipment that does not meet the needs of the country is also nothing new. Ask anyone who has served in the Canadian military and they will all tell you the same thing: it's the curse of the "Toos" as in too little, too late and too expensive. Some recent notable cases include the Upholder class submarines, the LSVW (Light Support Vehicle Wheeled) and the CH-146 Griffon (Bell 412) helicopter.

Western Star Truck in Kelowna, BC was awarded a contract in 1992 to produce a light wheeled vehicle for the Canadian Army. Among other things, the military requested that the vehicle be equipped with an eight-cylinder engine but the prototype vehicle offered by Western Star only had a four banger. This was just one of "more than 200 major deficiencies"[67] and as a result the vehicle twice failed to pass the military's acceptance trials. When NDHQ requested that the vehicle be accepted the engineers at LETE[68] refused to capitulate. Push came to shove and in the 1994 Federal Budget the LETE facility was closed as a cost saving measure.

---

[67] Tarnished Brass, pg. 122.
[68] Land Engineering Testing Establishment in Orleans Ontario

With LETE now closed, the LSVW prototypes were sent to the Nevada Automotive Test Center where, no big surprise here, they were found fit to operate in Canadian conditions. Interestingly enough, the contract to evaluate the LSVW at the Nevada Automotive Test Center was paid for by Western Star Trucks. Can you say: *Conflict of Interest?*

The Government of Canada's dogmatic insistence of having Canadian content has always been a detriment to acquiring any new equipment for its military. In 1993, another major military equipment contract worth $1.293B was awarded to a sole source. A hundred new *civilian* helicopters would be purchased to replace the entire existing *tactical* helicopter fleet used by the army. The three helicopter fleets to be replaced were the venerable Twin Huey, the Kiowa and the heavy lift Chinook. These three fleets totalled one hundred and nine aircraft. Once again, somebody in DND/NDHQ planned on doing more with less.

The Bell 412 was built by Bell Textron in Fort Worth, Texas and then shipped north to be assembled at the Bell Helicopter plant in Mirabel, Quebec like a life size Hasegawa model kit. In appearance, the Bell 412 - designated as the CH-146 Griffon - looks a lot like the CH-135 Twin Huey but with a four bladed main rotor. However, it is inconceivable to think that a military variant of the off-the-shelf (OTS) Bell 412 could double as a Chinook. According to the stats, the Boeing CH-47 Chinook is a tandem rotor aircraft that operates with a three-person crew, a max takeoff weight of 50,000 lbs and can carry combinations of (up to)

55 troops, 24 stretchers and cargo to a maximum of 24,000 lbs. The Griffon also operates with a three-person crew, but that is where the similarity ends. The CH-146 is a four-bladed single mast rotor aircraft that can carry ten troops and has a max takeoff weight of 11,900 lbs. The DND's 1993 Statement of Requirements (SOR) called for the new aircraft to be able "to carry a 3,100 pound load over a distance of 100km."[69] As previously stated, the Griffon has a max take-off weight of 11,900 lbs. "This includes the aircraft's 8,000 lbs and 2,000 lbs for fuel, leaving a small lift margin of 1,900 lbs; a far cry from the 3,100 pound requirement."[70]

But, is the CH-146 Griffon capable of completing the missions it is tasked to do?

The answer is…only some of them.

In 2008, the Chief of Defence Staff, General Rick Hillier, ruled out taking the Griffons to Afghanistan due to the fact that they were underpowered. This was also the conclusion of defense analyst Martin Shadwick. In 2009 he stated, "Its engines are fine for most domestic requirements in Canada and a more moderate temperature, but (the Griffon) doesn't really have the horsepower to reach its full potential in a place like Afghanistan."[71] The investigation into the fatal crash of aircraft 146434, 50 miles NE of Kandahar, concluded that "operating the aircraft at that altitude,

---

[69] The RCAF's (other) Whirlybirds (Part 2)-NAOC, 20 March 2017
[70] The RCAF's (other) Whirlybirds (Part 2)-NAOC, 20 March 2017
[71] Bell CH-146 Griffon, 14 March 2017

temperature and weight meant that it was not the correct helicopter for that mission."[72]

With everyone - the users, the analysts and the CDS - all saying that the Griffon was the wrong aircraft, why is it that no one in Parliament would listen to them? Obviously it was a political decision, as then Defence Minister Peter MacKay defended the use of the Griffon saying, "I believe the Griffon is a superior aircraft, well maintained, it's a utility helicopter that serves our interests both in Afghanistan and for the purposes in Canada."[73]

When shopping around for a new helicopter I don't know if the folks at DND/NDHQ even considered the Sikorsky UH-60 Blackhawk. This was the aircraft that the US military establishment selected to replace their Bell UH-1 Hueys. The Blackhawk has a four person crew (two pilots and two Crew Chiefs/gunners). It weighs 10,640 lbs dry and has a max take-off weight of 23,500 lbs. It can carry 2,640 lbs internally (11 troops or six stretchers) or an external load of 9,000 lbs in a combat radius of 368 miles. It can be outfitted with an external stores support system (ESSS) allowing it to carry additional fuel or up to 10,000 lbs of armament. For added safety, it has run dry transmission gear boxes which are designed to continue operating without fluid for a minimum length of time in order for the aircraft to land safely, as well as ballistically tolerant components and crash worthy

---

[72] Bell CH-146 Griffon, 14 March 2017
[73] Bell CH-146 Griffon, 14 March 2017

systems. The list of advantages goes on and on. In every single category the Sikorsky Blackhawk out performs the Griffon and yet again the Canadian government bought an inferior product for its military.

Let's not forget that the CH-146 Griffon was supposed to replace the Kiowa, the Twin Huey and the Chinooks. But, wait a moment. Don't we have Chinooks? We do now! But, just for fun let's try to follow the *ON* and *OFF* history of the CH-47 Chinook in Canada.

In the mid 1970's, the Canadian Armed Forces purchased eight CH-147s from Boeing-Vertol. These aircraft were split between 447 Sqn, CFB Namao in Edmonton and 450 Sqn, CFB Uplands in Ottawa. According to the records the first one, A/C 147001, was never delivered as it had crashed enroute due to mechanical failure. It would be replaced with A/C 147009. These heavy lift tactical helicopters operated quite successfully in Canada, supporting major military exercises and aiding in specialized missions such as the recovery of radioactive portions of a downed Soviet satellite.[74] Only one Chinook was ever lost in Canada. In Rankin Inlet, the rotor blades on A/C 147002 struck a light pole while it was taxiing. The aircraft was completely destroyed by the ensuing fire, with three fatalities.

In 1991 someone made the decision to eliminate the Chinook fleet from the inventory. In an article entitled *There's No Lift Like*

---

[74] Aircraft 147006, 114007 and 147008 from 447 Sqn were deployed to NWT for Operation Morning Light in January 1978.

It, author Ken Pole wrote "the government of the day, on the advice from the Department of National Defence, retired its original Chinook fleet as an economy measure."[75] In my opinion, there is no reason why the military would voluntarily retire anything serviceable. Realistically, the government of the day needed to save X-amount of monies from the federal budget. Once again, the quickest and most painless means to cut the federal budget without upsetting John Q Taxpayer was to excise it from the Defence department. But hey, there is no sense in putting a viable aircraft platform out to pasture when it can be sold to a qualified buyer and recoup some monies. The seven Canadian CH-147 Chinooks were picked up by the Royal Netherlands Air Force who delivered them back to Boeing Industries so they could be upgraded to the CH-47D standard. Five years later, Canadian soldiers in Afghanistan would be hitching rides from the Dutch in these former Canadian Chinooks.

    I don't know how much money the Canadian government saved by removing the Chinooks from the inventory or how much revenue was generated from their sale to the Netherlands. But, I do know that there was soon a desperate need to have our own heavy lift helicopters. In December 2008 the Canadian Forces took possession of six US Army CH-47D Chinooks already in the Afghan theatre at a cost of $292 million. The average age of the airframes was already forty years and they had been upgraded to the CH-47D standard in the mid 1980's. In August 2009, it was

---

[75] There's No Lift Like It, Ken Pole, Helicopter Magazine, 29 May 2007

announced that Canada would purchase fifteen new CH-47F Chinooks at an estimated cost of $2 billion. Delivery of these aircraft began on 25 June 2013 with the first new Chinook, A/C 147303, being handed over at a ceremony in Ottawa. As for the six Chinooks in Afghanistan they were put on the auction block. If there were no takers, the plan was to use them to augment Canada's SAR fleet, but that was not to be. On their return to Canada, A/C 147201 was placed on display at 8 Wing Trenton and A/C 147206 was mounted as a gate guardian outside 450 Tactical Helicopter Sqn in Petawawa. Two of the aircraft were beyond repair and were scrapped while the last pair of Chinooks were sold back to Boeing.[76]

Doesn't it seem to be an awful long way to travel, and at a great expense I might add, just to end up back were we had started?

In a 2015 defence study paper, Michael Byers wrote:

"the crisis in defence procurement presents both a challenge and an opportunity for Canada's next government - to rebuild the military from the ground up and do so in a way that addresses the country's actual needs. To make the right choices Canada's next government will need to engage in a fully and publically informed foreign and defence policy review. It will also need to be bold in order to overcome vested interests and ingrained ways of thinking."[77]

---

[76] Canadian Chinook helicopters now at museums, David Pugliese, Ottawa Citizen, 10 December 2016.

I have read the defence study paper from cover to cover and I feel that it is an excellent piece of work that is well worth reading. The paper shows that there is at least one person who has taken a huge step away from the shuttered cubicles of NDHQ and has applied a large dose of common sense towards the issue of what may be the best means to re-equip Canada's poorly stocked military pantry. Byers makes a number of recommendations for the different branches of the Armed Forces including the Coast Guard. In the coming years it will be interesting to see how many of them, if any, are applied in whole or in part.

Recommendation #2 - "Cancel the planned procurement of F-35's and extend the CF-18 fleet with thirty or forty F/A-18 Super Hornets."[78]

This has already been partially implemented. The purchase of the F-35 Lightning II has been put on hold pending (yet another) review to determine which fighter aircraft is best suited for Canada. In the interim, eighteen F/A-18 Super Hornets were slated to be purchased as a stop gap measure. To carry out another review is simply a waste of money because there are only so many fighter aircraft being currently manufactured in the world and the mandarins in NDHQ have had their eyes on them for a long time already.

The process of acquiring any piece of military hardware should include or maybe even begin with our elected officials

---

[77] Smart Defence, pg. 8.
[78] Smart Defence, pg. 19.

listening to the end users of the equipment. When the best option is presented, Parliament should simply pay the bill. The only problem with this idea rests with the lack of common sense in the selection process.

When the selection process to replace the CF-104 and the CF-101 first began, one of the contenders was the General Dynamics F-16 Fighting Falcon. "Ultimately, the Canadian government opted to buy 138 F/A-18's, mainly because this aircraft was bigger and had two engines giving a supposedly better survival rate with engine failure."[79]

If the F-16 was dropped from the competition in favour of the F/A-18 because of its lack of range and the fact that it had a single engine, why is it that we are now opting for a single engine fighter once again? Have the physical dimensions of our country changed? Have we built more military air bases across the nation from which single engine fighters can safely operate? No and no! This is an opportunity for Canada to once and for all move away from the single fighter types before the military gets saddled with an aircraft that doesn't suit its needs for the next forty years. Yes, Canada needs an air superiority aircraft capable of conducting long range interceptions but we also need an aircraft that is best suited for close air support/ground strike to protect not only our troops but those of our allies as well.

---

[79] Cancelled Orders, The Ultimate F-16 Site, 17 April 2017.

Recommendation #3 – "Acquire a fleet of 40 - 50 BAE Hawks (or similar plane) for training, aeronautics and close air support."[80]

These aircraft could replace the leased Hawks already used for training fighter pilots as well as the aging CT-114 Tutors used by the Snowbirds Demonstration Team. The new planes would also be available for close air support, should they be needed when Canadian soldiers are deployed on peacekeeping or other missions. Subsonic planes like the Hawks (which come in a ground-attack version) would be better protect troops on the ground than supersonic fighter jets because of their ability to fly low and slow.[81]

If acquiring an aircraft for the sole task of ground support is a real objective I would strongly suggest that the RCAF chase after the Americans to purchase some of their A-10 Thunderbolts. For those who do not recognize the name, the Fairchild Republic A-10 Thunderbolt II (lovingly referred to as the Warthog) is, by all accounts, the most capable sub-sonic close support aircraft around. It has ten hard points for external stores and a 30mm hydraulically driven seven barrel Gatling type cannon whose only job is to chew through armoured vehicles.

For quite some time there has been an on again off again movement in the United States to replace the Warthog, probably put forward by the American military industrial complex. The first

---

[80] Smart Defence, pg. 20
[81] Smart Defence, pg. 20.

time was just prior to the first Gulf War in 1991 when the A-16 (essentially the A-16 is an F-16 with a GPU-5 gun pod slung underneath it) was slated to take over the close air support role. But that aircraft was not available for issue by the time the US forces were deployed to the Middle East sandbox. Currently, the push is to replace the A-10 with the F-35. I say good! Let them ditch the A-10 for that overpriced piece of garbage. But when they do, Canada had better be prepared to take a big step forward and buy up as many of the Warthogs as we can. Since the average RCAF pilot is probably the craziest can-do hot shot in the sky, I simply cannot imagine what he or she could do with an A-10 Warthog in a battle.

An example of just how outrageous Canadian pilots can be took place out over the Mediterranean Sea in the late 1970's. A squadron of CF-104 Starfighters from CFB Baden-Soellingen, Germany were competing in a multi-force exercise against the US Navy. The Canadian jets were being used to simulate a missile attack and the object was to get as close as possible to the aircraft carrier. An aircraft carrier battle group covers many hundreds of square miles and has a layered defence of increasing difficulty all designed to protect the all important aircraft carrier located in the very centre.

So, a Canadian fighter pilot meets up with his American brethren in the Mess...

"There's no way ya'll gonna get close to that carrier!" says the Yank.

"Betcha a beer that I can?" replies the Canuck.

"Yer on!"

The following day the CF-104 driver heads out over the Mediterranean and just after take off he quickly drops down below the height of the search radar of the outlying picket ships. With the throttle pushed all the way open, he weaves his way through the fleet until he spots the prize. The aircraft carrier! Approaching from astern, the pilot gains some altitude before rocketing down the length of the flight deck and then drops down off the bow to skim back over the waves.

Over the guard frequency he hears, "What the hell was that!"

"Hmm, I guess they didn't see me."

The Starfighter pilot climbs to regain some altitude and banks his plane into a tight turn. Once he is lined up with the aircraft carrier he throttles back and then lowers the aircraft flaps and landing gear to make a "dirty" pass over the ship. After clearing the flight deck the flaps and landing gear were raised before making the supersonic speed run back to Base.

Let's face it; in comparison to our G7 and NATO allies - with our limited resources and manpower - today's Canadian Armed Forces can no longer be, militarily speaking, the best at everything. Therefore, I strongly believe that a choice must be made by NDHQ to pick one or two areas for our troops to become the world's leading experts. Why not turn the RCAF into the best damn ground support force in existence? A ground support force that is so powerful that in the time of war our allies will request us to be there in that role? To do that, the Canadian government must first convince the taxpayers to loosen the purse strings because it just might be important to spend some monies on defence as opposed to $10 a day daycare. In short, one day I would love to see several Canadian squadrons of HH-60 Pave Hawks accompanied by A-10 Thunderbolts and, dare I say it, AH-1 Bell Super Cobras or AH-64 Apache gunships. With Canadian pilots flying these aircraft in a ground support role we would be able to effectively protect any and all allied ground forces while striking fear into the hearts of our enemies.

With respect to the Royal Canadian Navy, someone has to educate those who are occupying the ruling seats in Parliament of the fact that the navy cannot wait until a ship is in the scrapyard before planning to build its replacement. As of this writing, June 2018, Canada does not have any support and supply ships operating on either coast. There is an ongoing process to cobble together some interim vessels, most notably a Joint Support Ship (JSS). According to the Royal Canadian Navy website there are two JSS vessels that are currently in production, the HMCS Queenston and the HMCS Châteauguay, that will provide underway support to naval task groups, limited sealift capabilities and support to operations ashore.[82] Construction of these vessels was to begin in 2017 with a delivery date - barring the standard delays that always prevails in the Canadian shipbuilding industry - of 2020 and 2021 respectively. With no support ships that are

---

[82] Royal Canadian Navy, 21 April 2017.

currently operational, a commercial vessel, the container ship MV Asterix, has been converted for military use at the Davie Shipyard in Lauzon, Quebec. It will be crewed by both military and civilians: civilians will operate the vessel, while military members will handle communications and navigation as well as the loading, off-loading and at-sea replenishment of goods including all ammunition. In my opinion, it's just another cocked up arrangement brought about by the inattention of the federal government.

Now, while the keels for the two new JSS vessels were in the process of being laid down, the Canadian government literally missed the boat on yet another golden opportunity. France had built two Mistral class helicopter aircraft carriers, complete with a wet well for amphibious landing craft, for the Russian Federation. However, France cancelled the deal when Moscow invaded, and then annexed, the Crimea region of the Ukraine. With two brand new vessels to sell, France went looking for someone, preferably an ally, who would benefit from the addition of these multi-use vessels to their fleet. Canada was approached as a potential buyer, but we turned the deal down. According to the public records, in 2015, people inside the defence department "advised the former Minister of Defence not to buy the two Mistral Class amphibious vessels because of how their cost might affect the multi-billion dollar national shipbuilding strategy - even though the ships would have provided a new and needed capability for the Canadian Navy."[83] In all likelihood it was Deputy Minister of Defence John

Forster who had advised the Minister Jason Kenney and the departing CDS, General Tom Lawson, not to buy the two Mistral class ships because of our stretched resources. Six weeks later, the new CDS, General Jonathan Vance, urged Minister Kenney to reconsider France's offer, stating that the versatility of the French vessels would "directly contribute to the desire for rapid, deployable and far-reaching projection of state interests, which could result in positive influences both domestically and internationally."[84]

Did we purchase these two vessels? Not a chance. A federal election had been called. So, while Canada stepped back instead of stepping forward, France went ahead and sold both of the ships to Egypt. That's right, Egypt! A country whose GDP is thirty places below Canada was able to purchase the ships for the paltry sum of $1 billion.

Was this another case of bureaucrats making decisions on equipment they know nothing about? I believe so, and this same situation repeated itself with the choice of the new Fixed Wing Search and Rescue aircraft (FWSAR).

While I was stationed in 442 Sqn, Air Command had observed that the CC-115 Buffalo was pushing beyond twenty years of age. With this in mind, the notion to replace the Buffalo with a Herc was floated about. Not a bad idea really. The Herc is bigger, faster, can haul more stuff (which is most important to the SAR techs

---

[83] Canadian Broadcasting Corporation, 08 February 2016.
[84] Canadian Broadcasting Corporation, 08 February 2016.

who are always wanting to carry more gear) and can stay aloft longer. These are all admirable features but the Hercules cannot go as slow as or turn as tight as a Buffalo. These two important points were pressed to the boys in Air Command and to prove the point, a SAR Herc from 435 Sqn came out to Comox. The objective was to have the Buffalo fly into areas where the squadron routinely conducted searches. The Hercules would observe the flight path of the Buff and try to follow only if the Aircraft Commander determined that it was safe to do so. It didn't take long before the observers onboard the Herc realized that CC-115 Buffalo could be replaced in CFB Summerside, PEI (which was soon closed with fixed wing SAR operations moving to CFB Greenwood, NS) and in CFB Trenton but not in Comox, where contour flying a CC-130 through the narrow coastal fjords and mountain valleys would be just too hazardous. In the 1990's, the CC-130 Hercules replaced the CC-115 in all SAR squadrons across the country with all remaining Buffalo flight operations being consolidated on Vancouver Island.

As the Buffalo continued to age gracefully, the need for a new FWSAR increased exponentially. The existing supply chains for Buffalo components began to dry up and Item Managers quickly had to get creative to find the necessary parts to keep the planes aloft. From what I was told, it was some very resourceful technicians in 442 Sqn who began to search out the location of all DeHavilland's DHC-5 Buffalo aircraft around the world and from there pursue the global market to find the components needed to keep their planes airborne. Egypt, Kenya, Ecuador, Mexico and others were all contacted. It is to their credit that the Buffalos have lasted as long as they have.

Each successive federal government has promised to push forward on acquiring a new fixed wing SAR aircraft, and each successive federal government has found some excuse to drop that particular line item from the federal defence budget. However, this did not stop Air Command from continuing to work on the project. Over in the Glass Palace a team of individuals were quietly researching all the available options. This new aircraft had to be STOL (Short Take Off/Landing) capable, it had to be big enough to carry all of the SAR technician's gear, and it had to have a ramp to make it easy for loading and unloading. It was preferable that the proposed aircraft have a pressurized cabin which would allow it to climb above 10,000 feet without the aircrew having to use a pressure breathing oxygen system. As a matter of course, several Fixed Wing SAR options were investigated. The top two choices were the C-27J Spartan and the Casa C-295M built by Airbus.

The Alenia C-27J Spartan, also known as the baby Herc, is equipped with the same engines as the C-130J Hercules. It operates with a three person flight crew. The cargo compartment is 3.33 m wide x 2.25 m tall which can hold 60 troops or carry a maximum payload of 11,500 kg for a range of 1,759 km.[85] Besides the United States, this aircraft is currently operated in various

---

[85] Alenia C27J Spartan, Wikipedia, 15 June 2017.

configurations by fourteen different nations around the world including Greece, Italy, Morocco, Romania, Peru and Zambia.

The next contender was the Casa C-295M. It uses a Canadian built Pratt and Whitney power plant but it does not have an APU (auxiliary power unit). It operates with a two person crew and the 2,000 cubic foot cargo area can hold 75 troops or 9,250 kg of cargo. Its speed is 100 km/h less than the Spartan and when fully loaded it has a maximum range of 1,455 km. The C-295M also has a global presence, operating in fifteen countries including Mexico, Egypt, Spain, Jordan, Finland and Uzbekistan.[86]

In regards to Canada's fixed wing SAR fleet replacement a few other ideas were suggested. One was that the Fixed Wing SAR duties currently being carried out with the Hercules fleet could continue in the rest of Canada but in British Columbia the Buffalo fleet would be retired and SAR duties would be carried out only with the CH-149 Cormorants. Now, the Cormorant helicopter does have a 1,000 km range but its speed is only 60% that of the Buffalo. Someone had also suggested purchasing a fleet of Dash-8 Q400's but this aircraft does not have a ramp which would allow for easy loading or unloading. Yet another camp had suggested that since the Buffalo is such a great SAR platform, why not build new ones? A great idea. Viking Air Industries in Victoria, BC owns the rights to the DeHavilland Buffalo and had proposed building the CC-115 NG (Next Generation) with all the modern conveniences, including a glass cockpit. However, there

---

[86] Casa Cargo Lifters: C-212, C-235 & C-295, Air Vectors, 15 June 2017.

were two drawbacks. First, the Royal Canadian Air Force really wanted a pressurized cabin (which the Buffalo does not have) and second, Viking Air did not have a working copy of its proposal in operation and the need for a FWSAR replacement was so desperate that NDHQ could not wait for a new conceptual aircraft to be realized.

Sometime in 2002 or 2003, before I retired, both the C-27J Spartan and the Casa C-295 visited the military apron in Winnipeg, albeit not at the same time. It was an unofficial looksee. High ranking officers from Air Command came to give them the once over, on the QT of course. Members of 435 Squadron, especially the SAR techs, were actually encouraged to climb on board and have a closer look. As aircraft technicians, we also had a curious fascination to see what was what.

In my opinion, the Spartan is by far the better choice for the FSWAR programme. The cabin area may not be as long as the C-295 but it is much wider and has more vertical clearance. In fact, on the C-295 if you were over six feet tall your head would almost be brushing against the ceiling. Take one step left or right of centre and you would have to duck your head. Most SAR techs are pretty robust, so I would think that they would find this aircraft to be cramped.

The C-27J Spartan can fly farther and faster with more equipment than the C-295, meaning it would take less time to get to a target area and be able to deliver the SAR techs with all the gear that they could ever ask for. There is also a commonality of parts with the C-130J so the supply costs should be less because you would be purchasing more of the same parts and equipment.

In 2006, some of the primary bidders accused the Canadian military of rigging the selection process to favour the Spartan by tailoring the Statement of Requirements (SOR) in its direction. In other words, stipulating that the aircraft must have a rear loading ramp would immediately disqualify the DeHavilland Q400 as it does not have a ramp. Maybe they did rig the competition and maybe they didn't. It certainly didn't help their cause when in 2012 "the top brass pitched the Harper government on buying surplus American C-27J's."[87]

The announcement of which aircraft would be the next Fixed Wing SAR was delivered at CFB Trenton by the Minister of National Defence, along with the Minister for Public Works and Lt General Michael Hood. Together, they announced that the Airbus C-295 would be the next SAR aircraft. This announcement took many people in the military by surprise simply because it was quite obvious that when comparing the two aircraft against each other the Spartan was the better choice for Canada's SAR requirements. However, Allan Williams, the former head of military procurement, said "the military has to know and has to be told that their job is to define the requirements for the equipment's needs and it's the Government's job to hold an open, fair tender and pick the winner. I have no doubt that the Air Force wanted the C-27J. But, that's why it's incumbent on the Assistant Deputy

---

[87] Globe and Mail, 15 December 2015.

Minister of Material and the Minister (of National Defence) to safeguard the process and protect the military, actually, from themselves."[88]

I think the bureaucrats simply wanted to put the military in its place! Is this the plane you want? Well, guess what? You can't have it because I said so!

I do not understand the logic behind Allan Williams' statement. When the users of the equipment do the research and say - This is what we need and this is the best option - why is that someone who has never flown a plane, fired a crew-served weapon or served on a warship gets to decide which is the best item for the user? You would think that a Minister of National Defence - either past or present - would have understood this.

It is my sincere hope that the people of Canada will someday begin to realize that their country's professional army, navy and air force can no longer sustain the current level of operations without a substantial increase in defence spending that will bring Canada in line with the recommended 2% of GDP. For years the Canadian military - at the behest of the federal government - has been shaving monies from its various budgets and finding unique ways of making equipment last longer. Ships don't put to sea as often or for as long, large military exercises lasting several months and involving entire battalions are often just now localized training road moves and fighter aircraft are cocooned to extend their flying hours beyond the normal life expectancy.

---

[88] CBC, Power in Politics, 07 December 2016.

It's quite obvious how the activities of the navy and the army can be curtailed but how does one cocoon an aircraft? And why?

I'll answer the second part first. If you place a portion of your aircraft fleet into long term storage you are effectively extending the overall life of the fleet. Look at it this way. If you have 100 aircraft and each aircraft can only fly for 20 years that gives you 2000 flying years. That means you will have to replace the entire fleet in 20 years and that is an expensive proposition. But, if you only fly two-thirds of the fleet and have the other third in long term storage those flying hours are now held in suspended animation, thus extending the overall life of the fleet by a third. This pushes it up to 27 years. Toss in reduced flying schedules due to the loss or lack of personnel (aircrew) and reduced fuel budgets the life of the fleet is extended just a little bit further. Reduce the number of aircraft per squadron or even close a squadron or two and those fighters can be placed in storage as well. Of the 138 CF-18A/B fighters originally purchased there are about 100 left in the inventory and of those about 25% to 30% are in long term storage. Of course, this also leaves only 75 fighters or less for the defence of the entire country!

Long term storage? It's simple. You just wrap them up...so to speak. And this is how it's done. An aircraft is flown to a long term storage facility where a series of procedures are then carried out. First, the aircraft is defueled. The ejection seats and all explosive charges are removed. The survival equipment is removed, inspected and then placed into storage. "Lifed" items -

those items that are serviceable only for a specific length of time - and any components that will be due for inspection while the aircraft is in storage (plus any components that could be used to keep the supply system afloat) are removed from the aircraft and inspected. The hydraulic systems are drained and filled with a preservation fluid. The engines are removed, torn down, inspected, re-built, run-up and then boxed. The wings and the empennage are removed. Once all of this is done, the major components of the aircraft (the fuselage with the cockpit, the tail section and the wings) are shrink-wrapped before being placed in a great big air-tight box. In the past these boxes were just giant wooden crates, but now they are most likely constructed out of a form fitting molded plastic much like some monstrous Pelican brand case that can be pressurized with nitrogen to keep out any contaminants.

Once the aircraft is inspected and crated it is quite literally shelved. The whole box is lifted up and placed on a shelf. Prior to the arrival of the next aircraft scheduled for storage, the first plane to be shelved is taken down and brought back up to flight status, complete with all modifications and upgrades. When the next fighter is due in, the next one on the shelf is put back together and prepped to depart. And so on and so on and so on. The transition from aircraft in to aircraft is usually so seamless that the pilot delivers one fighter and a few hours later flies back home in another.

This process is not new: the RCAF had been boxing and shelving the CF-116 (aka the CF-5) Freedom Fighter for years before a number of them were upgraded and sold to Botswana in the mid 1990's.[89] Unfortunately, the reduction in the number of fighter aircraft in operational service and the successful preservation of the rest of the fleet for a rainy day has allowed successive governments, both Liberal and Conservative, to forgo investing in any new aircraft. And, the politicians, have become so comfortable with this process that at this point in time they have no option but to purchase new fighters at a much higher cost.

The Members of Parliament from the past 30 years should hang their heads in shame for allowing the Canadian Armed Forces to shrink in size and rust into the dust. At every turn there has been a Parliamentary Committee made up of individuals who are hyper-focused on studying all of the geo-political and national economic ramifications of a much needed military acquisition. It's almost always been a case of not seeing the forest for the trees. These committees so busy studying all the angles that by the time they finally make the selection the costs per unit have skyrocketed to the point that the original amount required is now cut by 50%. Case in point…the much vaunted F-35 Lightning II.

In developing the F-35, the American industrial machine looked for partners to buy into the project. That is to say, if you pony up some monies for the cost of the Research & Development

---

[89] A total of thirteen CF-116 aircraft were upgraded by Bristol Aerospace in Winnipeg prior to the sale to Botswana, ten CF-5A single seat and three CF-5B dual seat. It should be noted that in June 2016 Botswana was looking to replace their F-5's with Saab JAS 39 Gripen aircraft which has, by some accounts, the same performance or better than the CF-18 Hornet.

they will sell you the final product at a reduced price. Canada, along with the UK, Italy, the Netherlands, Turkey, Australia, Denmark and Norway, bought into the project.[90] Rising costs and project delays have given the Canadian government good reason to rethink its commitment to the project. While awaiting yet another investigation as to whether or not Canada has a requirement for a stealth fighter, the federal government proposed purchasing eighteen Super Hornets from Boeing at a cost of $6.4 billion dollars.[91] This was to be an interim measure that would take the pressure off of the current fleet. In other words, the current fleet of CF-18 fighters would be reduced even further with those aircraft having the highest number of flying hours being retired from active service and additional aircraft being added to the cocooning list.

You would think that this would be a great place to start rebuilding Canada's Air Force but nothing is ever that simple.

In the fall of 2017 Boeing launched a trade war against Bombardier claiming that Bombardier was being subsidized by the Canadian government and as a result was able to offer their new C Series passenger jets for a discounted price to Delta Airlines. Naturally, the US Commerce Department sided with the American company and slapped an exorbitant tariff of over 200% on all C Series jets bound for airline companies in the United States.[92] In

---

[90] According to the Globe and Mail Canada has already invested approximately $455 million in the Joint Strike Fighter programme.
[91] The Globe and Mail, 17 September 2017.
[92] CBC News, 27 September 2017.

retaliation, Canada's Prime Minister, Justin Trudeau, pointed out that the fighter deal with Boeing was all but dead. "We won't do business with a company that's busy trying to sue us and trying to put our aerospace workers out of business."[93]

That still left the RCAF desperately needing some replacement fighter aircraft while waiting for the Powers That Be to pull their collective heads out of the sand and finally decide which fighter aircraft was best suited for the country. Of course, the list just got a lot slimmer due to the falling out with our American brethren. But still, there were still options to be had.

Option A – Purchase used F/A-18's from another country until a competition to replace the entire fleet of Canadian CF-18's is launched.[94] Currently, the Royal Australian Air Force is flying the same F/A-18 model that is used in Canada and is scheduled to acquire the F-35 Lightning II. I do not think there is anyone in the world who puts more flying hours on their aircraft than Canada so if we do purchase a number of the RAAF's Hornets they will more than likely have some life left in them. This is not a bad idea but not really a great one as all we would be doing is prolonging the inevitable complete collapse of Canada's fighter aircraft fleet.

Option B - Look for an aircraft that is already currently in production and is in operation then get in line to make the purchase. The question remains, "Which plane is best suited for Canada?"

---

[93] CBC News, 27 September 2017
[94] CBC News, 27 September 2017.

If we ignore the American fighter aircraft manufacturers which are the largest players by far, the remaining countries include the Eurofighter consortium, Sweden and France. Yes, Russia, China and India manufacture their own fighter aircraft, but I can't see Canada purchasing aircraft from them for obvious reasons. Offerings from the first three include the Eurofighter, the SAAB Gripen, and the Rafale.

The Eurofighter Typhoon is a state-of-the-art twin engine, high performance multi-role aircraft. It is capable of flying at over Mach 1 without the use of afterburners and has a service ceiling of 65,000 feet. The range is 2,900 km with a combat radius up to 1,389 km depending on its configuration. While the Typhoon is not a 5th generation stealth aircraft, it was designed to have a lower radar cross section and is constructed of 80% composite materials, making it less visible on radar than our current CF-18's and roughly equivalent to the F/A-18 E/F Super Hornet.[95] The Typhoon currently serves as a front line fighter for the United Kingdom, Germany, Italy and Austria. It has also been ordered by Saudi Arabia, Kuwait, Oman and Qatar. That's nine different countries with many others looking at purchasing it for their fleets. I dare say that if the RCAF ever decides that they want these in their hangars they had better get in line soon.

The Swedish built Saab JAS 39 Gripen is a delta wing single seat fighter that is very similar in size, shape (except for the canards on the forward fuselage) and performance to the General

---

[95] Ottawa Citizen, 16 April 2014.

Dynamics F-16 Fighting Falcon but is significantly lighter in both the dry weight and max take-off weight. Like the F-16 it is also a single engine aircraft and utilizes a F404-400 turbo fan engine derivative built under licence by Volvo. This is the same engine currently mounted in the CF-18 Hornet. As for armaments, the Gripen has a 27 mm Mauser cannon with 120 rounds and eight hard points on which it can carry a wide variety of air-to-air and air-to-mud munitions. The biggest drawback in acquiring the Gripen is the single engine. This had been cited as a deciding factor in Canada's initial selection of the F-18 over the F-16 and for that same reason I believe the Saab JAS 39 Gripen should not be considered for purchase for the RCAF.

From France comes the Dassault Aviation built Rafale. It is a single-seat, twin-engine multirole aircraft. Like the Typhoon, the Rafale is not a true "stealth fighter" but it is designed to have a reduced radar cross section and infrared signature. It can be equipped with a wide range of weapons and is intended to perform air supremacy interdiction, aerial reconnaissance, ground support, in-depth strike, anti-ship strike and nuclear deterrence missions. The Rafale is capable of flying at 1.8 mach at a service ceiling of 50,000 feet. The Rafale, when fitted with two conformal fuel tanks that are mounted on the upper surface of the aircraft along the wing root and the three drop tanks, has a *combat radius* of over 1,800 kilometers - a distance that is three times greater than the CF-18[96]. The Rafale is currently being flown by France,

---

[96] Dassault Rafale, Wikipedia, 10 November 2017.

Egypt, Qatar and India. So why not Canada? Other nations seriously considering purchasing the Rafale are Finland, Malaysia, Poland and the UAE. In fact, Malaysia - which had once flown the Canadair Tutor as a ground strike aircraft - may be purchasing a number of Rafale fighters to replace their Russian built Mig-29's. Once again, why not Canada?

In 2005, the Rafale was considered as a replacement for the CF-18 but there were some concerns about its capability to operate with NATO forces. According to CBC reporter Terry Milewski, Dassault Aviation has been making an aggressive bid to sideline the F-35 by offering to transfer technology, create jobs and share billions of dollars in business if Canada buys the Rafale fighter.[97] Dassault's Vice President, Yves Robins, stated "the Rafale will be Canadianized", with major components being manufactured in Canada and with the rights to the intellectual property (the source codes to the aircraft's computer system) Canada would be able to adapt and update the aircraft throughout its lifespan.[98] In October 2017, Reuters Business News reported that Dassault Aviation's CEO Eric Trappier "viewed the possibility of selling Dassault Rafale fighter jets to Canadian government as an opportunity for strong cooperation between Canada and France".[99] It would be my

---

[97] CBC News, F-35's French rival pitches 'Canadianized' fighter jet, 18 March 2014,
[98] CBC News, F-35's French rival pitches 'Canadianized' fighter jet, 18 March 2014.
[99] Reuters Business News, Dassault CEO not yet considering alternative engine suppliers, 11 October 2017.

hope that the Canadian government does not dither any longer and selects a new fighter soon before our airspace is undefended.

A Final Word...or Two

As of this writing, Canada's political battle for new planes, ships and other large pieces of equipment for the military rages on. And most of the fight takes place behind the scenes and out of the view of the general public. What is most disconcerting to me is the plight of the people involved, the actual members of the Canadian military, from the newest Private all the way up to the Chief of Defence. What I have witnessed and experienced in recent years is the total apathy of the individual members and how their attitude has changed from enjoying a career to **"it's just a job."** There is so much more consideration now towards the promotion of the health and well-being of the individual or the "self" that there is almost no unit cohesion. In other words, people are in it just for themselves. Gone are the days of Squadron Pride and Regimental Competitiveness, of putting in extra hours - and without any expectation of compensation I might add - just to get the job done, of having members turning out en masse just to watch their unit compete in a hockey game or celebrate a promotion, of going to the Mess after work to reinforce the bond with your crew mates by having a drink or two or three. And, when the phone rang and a crew member asked his co-workers to help him move out of his apartment that was on the top floor of a six story building with no elevator, nobody ducked out from the job unless they were bleeding profusely from their eyeballs or their own mother was on her death bed. In the past - after your immediate family - your obligation was to your Crew, the Squadron and finally the military as a whole and because of this the military, the Squadron, the Crew and your immediate family looked after you.

I could easily regale you with tales of unit resolve and dedication, but if you have served in the military before the 1990's then surely you have experienced this Esprit de Corps. It's sad to say, but I don't think much of this Esprit de Corps exists in Canada's modern-day military except for in the combat arms where your very life depends on unit cohesion. Oh yes, service members will surely pull together to get a job done but after the job is done everyone will go their separate ways.

Everyone knows that change is inevitable and a person either has to accept change and adapt to it or the change will run you over like an outdated Leopard tank. The Canadian Forces pursued this philosophy by directing everyone to take part in a Change Seminar. Somewhere around the winter of 1996 or 1997 it was our turn and, as dutiful airmen, the members of 435 Sqn braved the -20°C temperature and a raging blizzard that had shut down the entire city of Winnipeg to attend a seminar facilitated by an American who was paid an exorbitant amount of money by NDHQ. Her claim to fame was that she had been an assistant to US Senator Sam Nunn. Collectively, we couldn't have cared less if she had been an assistant to His Holiness the Dalai Lama because we knew that her discussion would have no real impact on how we did business either on the Crew or in the Squadron. In other words, the Change Seminar was bullshit and a huge waste of our time. But, since we had to attend the session as per the orders from our Commanding Officer, we did so with bells on.

Don't get me wrong, she did have a valid point. Changes in your life can be a good thing and if nothing else they will get your life out of a rut. Shake things up a bit as it were because variety is the spice of life. So, take a different route home from work, mow your lawn in the opposite direction, avoid the rush and shop for those Christmas presents in July or have breakfast for supper, which happens to be a family favourite. All of these variations in your daily routine can and will make your life more enjoyable. But change for the sake of change does not easily translate to the military. There are rules that apply to what we do in the hangar and on the flight line, rules that have been developed through years of trial, error and even some accidents where individuals have been injured or have lost their lives.

Not all change is good. When asked, we tried our level best to explain to this Change Expert that many of the tasks we are confronted with could not be changed. But it was this notion, this concept, this reality that there were some places where change was not an option that the facilitator could not wrap her head around. The session closed with both sides agreeing to disagree.

Let's have a little discussion about military wages and dispel a few myths at the same time. When it comes to pay and benefits, the members of the Canadian military are among the highest financially compensated armed services in the world. The pay and benefit allowances make up a hefty portion of the Defence

Department's budget. According to NATO's data, half of the Canadian Armed Forces budget is spent on salary - soldiers, personnel and pensions - which is 15% more of the total Defence budget than what the Americans and British spend.[100]

Despite what the general public thinks and what some of my relatives might believe:

1. Canadian Forces members **do not** receive free rations and quarters! Members who reside on Base have meals and accommodations deducted from their pay. Those members who reside in the PMQs or Private Married Quarters pay for housing at close to the local market rate.

2. Canadian Forces members **do not** receive pay and benefits tax-free. Canadian Forces members have the maximum allowable in personal income tax deducted for all categories of taxation; income earned, Canada Pension Plan and Employment Insurance.

When I enrolled in 1981, I was paid about $8,460 per annum before deductions. This was increased after I had completed basic training, then raised after I had passed my Level Three trade qualifications (TQ3) and raised again once I was promoted to the rank of corporal. Other than pay increases through promotions, Canadian military members also receive a pay incentive increase each year on their enrolment date. Non-Commissioned members (NCO's) have four step increases past the base rank, and Commissioned Members (Officers) have ten step increases beyond

---

[100] Canada's military among the highest paid in the world, Toronto Sun, 30 October 2014.

the base rank.[101] In other words, once you are promoted you will get an initial pay increase from your previous rank and a step higher in pay each year for the next four years. Once a member has reached the maximum number of incentives the pay level is now fixed until the individual is promoted to the next rank.

Not all military trades are paid at the same rate. For the NCO's there are three different pay fields that reflect the trade they are employed in. These pay fields are called Basic, Specialist 1 (Spec 1) and Specialist 2 (Spec 2). The combat arms trades all fall under the Basic pay field except for the ACISS trade (army communications and information specialist). The aviation trades are all now Spec 1. Some of the naval trades are Spec 1 as are some medical trades. There are a handful of trades that are Spec 2, namely Flight Engineers, Non-Destructive Testing Technicians, Marine Engineers and Search and Rescue Technicians. There are also allowances that are added onto a members' pay depending on the circumstances of where they are employed. For example, pilots and other aircrew that hold a flying position receive an aircrew allowance, personnel who leap out of aircraft on a regular basis receive a jump allowance, a ship's diver would collect a diver's allowance. Surprisingly, back in the 1980's and '90's SAR techs did not receive Spec 2 pay. They only received Spec 1 pay, but they also were given the aircrew allowance, the jump pay and, if they were a qualified diver, the diver's pay. So all things being

---

[101] National Defence and the Canadian Armed Forces Pay Rates, 12 December 2017

equal a SAR tech corporal would collect about $600 per month above the standard pay field plus an additional $250 for each of the three allowances. Now, they receive Spec 2 and a SAR Crew allowance which is slightly less than the three separate allowances. Search and Rescue technicians are the highest paid Non-Commissioned trade in the Canadian military.

As stated earlier, the Canadian military spends far too much money on wages and not enough on equipment and surprisingly this is coming from someone who earned his living as a military member. Instead of continually raising the wages to retain military members, the Government of Canada should consider allowing the members of the military and the RCMP self-direct their Employment Insurance (EI) contributions into an RRSP or a similar savings vehicle. This should be done because members of the Canadian Armed Forces and the RCMP must, like all other taxpayers, contribute to the EI program but they never get to collect on it.

When a member retires after a full career, his pension annuity is considered to be an income and is therefore subject to income tax. However, in most cases - especially if the person had been in for twenty years or more - the pension income is greater than the threshold at which Employment Insurance would pay out. In other words, if the threshold was $24,000 and the member's pension income is greater than this, he would receive nothing from EI. If the member's annuity was $22,000 the EI program would make up the other $2,000 but only for a certain length of time. Now, as most military and RCMP retirees will probably receive more than the threshold amount on retirement, they will never collect on the Employment Insurance program that they paid into for the length of their career. It would be of greater financial benefit to service members if they were allowed to place their EI monies in a registered savings plan because they could at least collect on what they paid into.

The Canadian Armed Forces is always shorthanded, especially when it comes to the combat arms trades. Hell, we barely have enough people to fully man the three infantry regiments that we do have, and I dare say the armoured corps are probably short-staffed as well. Another issue is educating the members of the military in combat arms. I hate to say it but, in my opinion, if Canada ever really had to go to war and commit all of our troops, we would be in a dire situation. We just don't have the bodies and many of those we do have are lacking in basic combat skills.

To address these two issues I have come up with a plan. To ensure that we have a ready supply of personnel for the combat arms trades I believe that **everyone** who enlists, regardless of the trade or the career path that they desire, must spend a minimum of three years in a combat arms trade of their choice (dependent upon availability). In other words, an individual will begin his or her career with the standard ten-week basic training course and then continue onto Battle School after which they will be assigned to a field unit. At the end of three years the member, who now has a solid foundation in combat arms skills, will be promoted to corporal (or, if their career path is with the officer corps, to second-lieutenant) and this individual **must** be allowed to continue on with the trade of his or her choice. This last point is imperative and it must be strictly monitored because the army has a very nasty habit of making life difficult for those individuals who would rather do anything but play soldier.

Corporal Aiden Downey was just such an individual. When Aiden first enlisted he was with an infantry unit. He rose through the ranks where he ultimately reached the rank of sergeant commanding an ADATS unit.[102] But, Aiden wasn't a happy camper. He had been soldiering for so long that he had grown tired of it. Tired of the mud, tired of digging slit trenches, tired of sleeping out in the field and now he wanted to do something different. Aiden wanted something more challenging and his plan was to remuster to the Air Force as an aero-engine technician. So, Sgt Downey went through his unit's Administration Section to request a Land Operations Reassignment Plan or LOTRP.[103] But the army does not give up its children all that easily. Once Aiden's Company Commander got wind of his planned defection, all manner of obstacles were thrown in his path. His LOTRP paperwork was "lost" several times and messages were not delivered or answered in a timely manner. Despite all of the flack

---

[102] ADATS was an Air Defence Anti-Tank system is a dual purpose short range missile system mounted on a M113 armoured personnel carrier.
[103] LOTRP, pronounced "Lot Rep".

Aiden would not give up his goal. At one point he was asked to report to his Company Commander's office.

"Sgt Downey, I would really like to know why you continue to pursue this crazy idea of joining the Air Force?"

"Well Sir, I am not happy with what I am doing and I would really like to do something different."

"If you want something different Sergeant why didn't you simply come to me? I can have you transferred to the Mortar Platoon or to the Recce Company, if you want? There may even be a promotion to warrant officer in it if you decide to stay."

"If I decide to stay will I still have to go to the field, Sir?"

"What?"

"If I decide to stay would l I have to dig trenches and sleep in the field, Sir?"

"Yes of course, Sgt Downey! This is an army unit goddam it!"

"In that case Captain Bloggins, I wish to continue with my remuster."

When push comes to shove, the army hates to lose and will often exact its pound of flesh. Sgt Downey's remuster was finally approved after eighteen long months, when it should have taken no more than six. He was finally going to leave the army and would soon be starting his aero-engine course at CFSAOE in CFB Borden. But not so fast! In the week leading up to the start of his new career, Aiden would have to return all of his issued army equipment to the Quartermaster, have his furniture and effects packed for storage, clean out his military housing and have it inspected before driving the 1500 kilometers from Gagetown, New Brunswick to Borden, Ontario. However, the army had its own plans for Sgt Downey. Starting on Monday morning and continuing until noon on Thursday Aiden and the rest of his platoon were deployed on a field exercise. Everyone in the unit knew that this was the CO's revenge and so when they returned to Base Thursday afternoon his troops took care of cleaning the equipment and the vehicle maintenance. The supply technician at the Quartermaster Stores took pity on Aiden and tore up his clothing documents so nothing had to be returned. The furniture packers had arrived Thursday afternoon and on Friday they loaded Aiden's belongings to be put into storage. That left him Friday afternoon to clean the 1½ story home and get started on the road trip. I am happy to say that despite all of the road blocks the army had placed in his path Aiden Downey was able to report on time for the start of his course.

    The ratio of officers to non-commissioned members in the Canadian Armed Forces is extremely top heavy. A Canadian Community Health Survey of Canadian Forces personnel (including civilians) carried out in 2002 was used as a basis for a Statistics Canada perspective entitled "A Profile of the Canadian Forces."[104] The survey revealed that 60% of CF personnel are ranked as Juniors - Private, Corporal or Master Corporal. The next cohort was referred to as Seniors – Sergeant through to Chief

---

[104] A Profile of the Canadian Forces, Perspectives July 2008.

Warrant – and comprised 20% of the personnel. All of the officer ranks from Second Lieutenant through to General make up the final 20%. With only 64,000 people in uniform the officer corps would be comprised of 12,800 individuals. That's a 1 in 4 ratio of officers to all non-commissioned members and a 1 in 3 ratio of officers to junior non-commissioned members. There are only 86,000 military members (both regular and reserves) and of that 40% or 34,400 members are supervisors (Juniors and Seniors combined). Another way to look at this is - 1 supervisor for every 2 ½ worker bees.

And where are all of these "supervisors" located? They certainly are not in the trenches with the troops or out on some frozen flight line trying to balance the fuel load on a Herc or helping to haul in soaking wet hawsers onto a ship's deck. According to the National Defence website the Canadian Forces Support Unit (Ottawa) "provides administrative support to approximately 10,000 military personnel employed in the NCR" (National Capital Region).[105]

Ten thousand personnel! That's 1/8th of our total military strength including reservists. It should be noted that there are no army or air force bases in the NCR. CFB Petawawa, one of the largest military bases in Canada, is two or more hours down the road so it isn't included in the NCR. The JTF2 - aka the Boys in the Black Pajamas - at Dwyer Hill are included in the NCR.[106]

---

[105] Canadian Forces Support Unit (Ottawa), www.forces.gc.ca/en, January 2018.
[106] The Joint Task Force 2 is Canada's premier special operations unit.

Although the details on the exact number and composition of its members in the JTF2 is rated Secret Squirrel, I doubt very much that it is much more than a two and a half companies, which is about three hundred able bodies. Again, ten thousand people! If they are not part of the front line troops what are they? They are administrators! They are the herd of sheep that ride the OC Transpo buses on their daily commute to and from the surrounding suburbs to downtown Ottawa. Sergeants and captains are as numerous as bugs on a bumper. Warrant officers and majors are also commuting in copious quantities. And on and on up the Chain of Command, the pyramid thinning as it goes, until it reaches the Chief of Defence Staff, who occupies a solitary position.

Do we need 10,000 people to oversee the entire armed forces? Probably not. But, again it's the whole empire-building paper pushing Chain of Command thing. Each general will have a couple of full colonels under him each of which will have an assortment of lieutenant-colonels that will command a couple of majors and a plethora of captains. Each of these positions will have the same number of corresponding non-commissioned members squared or even cubed with all of them diligently slaving away in their offices or their cubicles like so many gophers in their burrows. By the way, these 10,000 personnel are just the individuals in the NCR. There are a great many more overseers squirrelled away in the other command headquarters including: Maritime Command on the east and west coast, the RCAF, the Canadian Army, Canadian Forces Intelligence Command, Special

Operations Forces Command and Military Personnel Command. The last one is currently headed up by a Lieutenant General, a Major General and a Brigadier General each of which will their own empire.

How can this problem be solved? I truly do not know because I have yet to see a headquarters staff be reduced in size while hard core front line positions are being replaced with civilians as a means to cut costs. The CH-149 Cormorant helicopter is completely serviced and maintained by the civilian IMP Group. When the new Fixed Wing Search and Rescue aircraft comes on line in a couple of years, it too will be maintained by a civilian company as will the new CH-148 Cyclone naval helicopter. Even though these companies are fully accredited maintenance organizations, I strongly believe that military aircraft should be serviced and maintained by military personnel because military personnel do not go on strike. Don't get me wrong, I have no complaints against a unionized workplace. But, a union's tried and true contract negotiating tactic of work-to-rule and picket lines are in direct conflict with the military ethos of following orders.

The Canadian federal government has consistently said that it will increase the number of personnel and invest in new equipment. But these promises have been deferred repeatedly over the years to the point where any investment will be so exponentially more expensive that the government can't afford it. The only way that the status quo is going to change is if the Canadian public, namely John and Jane Q Taxpayer, begin to take an active interest in their military forces, because they are so much more than just an aid to civil power during times of natural disaster such as ice storms in southern Ontario, flooding in Manitoba and forest fires in British Columbia.

In his book *Who Killed the Canadian Military?* author J.L. Granatstein wrote the following:

"At root, the real killers of the Canadian Forces were you and I, the Canadian people. The military scarcely interested us, and we paid it no attention. We assumed that we were safe, our territory inviolable, and we believed ultimately that the Americans would protect us. So you and I elected our politicians, and we told them in opinion polls that we wanted health care, culture, better pensions, and a thousand other programs from the government. These were all good things, and we need them. But Canada is a rich country, and we could have both a strong military and the social services we want. Who killed the Canadian military? Ultimately, the Canadian people did.

By our indifference to the Canadian Forces, by our unwillingness to demand that troops dispatched overseas have everything they need to protect themselves and to operate effectively, Canadians have colluded with governments that sought cheap popularity by being the chore boy for the United States and refusing to cooperate fully with our friends. The media focused on petty military scandals rather than the gross scandal of governments failing to equip, sustain, and train our service personnel properly. As a result, we Canadians failed to demand that soldiers, sailors, and air-crew got the modern equipment they needed – to fight and win, to train realistically, to operate effectively on their own, and to cooperate with our allies."[107]

So there I was... Many years ago thinking of joining the Canadian military. I had been captured by the advertisements on television and that catchy jingle: *"There's no life like it and you won't regret the day."*

Do I regret the day that I signed up? No, I don't. Even though I never rose through the ranks like I had aspired I feel that the years of serving *our country* - yours and mine - were well spent. I was given the opportunity to travel to distant lands that I otherwise would not have seen and I met some fantastic individuals who I am very proud to have worked with. To my crew mates, the crew chiefs, the commanding officers and to all of the support personnel that I relied on over the years I want to say thank you for making my career enjoyable and for providing me with all of these wonderful memories.

---

[107] Who Killed the Canadian Military, J.L. Granatstein, pg. 202.

Glossary

Canadian Armed Forces Rank Structure circa 1982 to 2003

Non-Commissioned

Private (Basic)	- Pte (B)
Private (Trained)	- Pte (T)
Corporal	- Cpl
Master Corporal	- Mcpl
Sergeant	- Sgt
Warrant Officer	- WO
Master Warrant Officer	- MWO
Chief Warrant Officer	- CWO

Commissioned

Officer Cadet	- OCdt
2nd Lieutenant	- 2Lt
Lieutenant	- Lt
Captain	- Capt
Major	- Maj
Lieutenant Colonel	- LCol
Colonel	- Col
Brigadier General	- BGen
Major General	- MGen
Lieutenant General	- LGen
General	- Gen

26er	a twenty-six ounce (a fifth) bottle of alcohol
aka	also known as
apron	the edges of the flight line
barracks box	a foot locker
Bloggins	a non-specific service member
Bomarc	the nuclear tipped anti-aircraft missile was named after the manufacturer – Boeing Michigan Aeronautical Research Center
Canex Exchange	A military store also known as a Base (BX) or a Post Exchange (PX)
CDS	Chief of Defence Staff
CFTO	Canadian Forces Technical Orders
Dzus fastener	a cam lock type fastener that is used to secure the panel to the air frame
Empennage	the tail section of an aircraft including the vertical and horizontal stabilizers
fitter	aero-engine technician
French chalk	a very fine powder similar to talcum powder
fuel bowser	a military fuel truck used on a flight line
ICP	Instrument Check Pilot
JTF2	the Canadian Armed Forces special operations/anti-terrorism unit
Loonie	a one dollar Canadian coin
mickey	a thirteen ounce (a pint) bottle of alcohol
NADAR	a magnetic tape that recorded the aircraft's flight data for mission verification

NCO	non-commissioned officers – the term was revised in the late 1990's as NCM or non-commissioned member
NCO i/c	non-commissioned officer in command
NDHQ	National Defence Headquarters
NSN	National Stock Number
O6HA oxygen cart	a trailer for supplying gaseous high and low pressure oxygen to an aircraft. It holds six oxygen transport cylinders
Oh-Dark 30	military terminology for some un Godly time when you have to be awake
PLCC	Personal Liability and Clearance Certificate
PMC	President of the Mess Committee
rigger	airframe technician
skeleton crew	the bare minimum of qualified technicians required to launch and/or recover an aircraft including all servicing inspections
synch shaft	a drive shaft that synchronizes the rotation of the forward and the aft rotor heads to ensure the rotor blades mesh safely
tarmac	the flight line
TD	temporary duty
two-four	a box of beer with twenty-four bottles
wheels in the well	the landing gear has been retracted

Appendix

1. Aircraft 101007 Occurrence Report 32467
2. Liberal's New Rescue Aircraft, David Pugliese, Ottawa Citizen

OCCURRENCE REPORT: 32467

Flight Safety incident reports are produced under the authority of the Minister of National Defence (MND) pursuant to Section 4.2 of the Aeronautics Act (AA), and in accordance with A-GA-135-001/AA-001, Flight Safety for the Canadian Forces. They are prepared solely for the purpose of accident prevention and shall not be used for legal, administrative or disciplinary action.

FSOMS 32467   22 JUN 1984   AIR ACCIDENT   A CATEGORY

Status: supplemental sent
State: Closed
Safety of Flight Compromise Level:
145   FSQQ 09 22/JUN/1984 21:00

Unclassified

1. Injury Level: Green - Minor

2. Aircraft/Operated By: CF101007

3. Aircraft Ownership: 409 SQN / 6468 / 4 WG /

4. a. Location: - 49 DEG NORTH, 124 DEG WEST –
            Latitude: N49-46
            Longitude: W124-36

4. b. Date/Time: 221700Z JUN 1984

4. c. Stage of Operations: IN-FLIGHT - CLIMB OUT

5. Damage Level: Destroyed / missing

6. Personnel Injured: Pilot, AIRCREW, Green - Minor
              ACSO, AIRCREW, Green - Minor

7. Mission Type: Proficiency

8. Description: AIRCRAFT CRASH - EJECTION: ON CLIMB OUT PASSING THROUGH   APPROX 12000 FEET, 380 KIAS, A LOUD BANG WAS HEARD AND FELT, AND AIRCRAFT VIOLENTLY   YAWED RIGHT.

13. Flight/Ground Conditions: VISUAL FLIGHT (ON TOP OR BETWEEN LAYERS)   VFR/VMC

14. Light/Weather Conditions: BRIGHT DAY, GOOD VFR

16. Aircrew Information: Pilot ; Time on Duty Last 48 Hrs: hrs, Time on Duty Last 24 Hrs: hrs; Flying Hours Last 48 hrs: hrs; Past 30 Days: hrs; Total on Type: hrs; Grand total: hrs.
           ACSO CAPTAIN (NOT INSTRUCTING); Time on Duty Last 48 Hrs: 15 hrs, Time on Duty Last 24 Hrs: 2 hrs; Flying Hours Last 48 hrs: hrs; Past 30 Days: hrs; Total on Type: hrs; Grand total: hrs.

18. Aircraft Maint Data: TSN Aircraft: CF101/007, 0 hrs, TSI: 103 hrs, TSO: hrs, CF349: , CF543: , Civilian Journey Log: , Inspection: PERIODIC

20. Component Information: ENGINE WUC: SER NUM: 632158 NSN: TSN: TSO: TSI: 117 PERIODIC TSII: , Part List: ENGINE WUC: SER NUM: 630488 NSN: TSN: TSO: TSI: 117 PERIODIC TSII: , Part List:

22. A. Investigation: CONTROL STICK PUSHED FORWARD BUT NO APPARENT EFFECT. PILOT   OBSERVED FLAMES FROM RIGHT SIDE OF AIRCRAFT AND ORDERED EJECTION. BOTH   AIRCREW LANDED IN HEAVILY WOODED AREA.

23. Cause Factors: MATERIEL ENGINE UNDETECTED PROGRESSIVE BREAKDOWN

*** FINDINGS ***

LEFT ENGINE FAILED INTERNALLY DUE TO A RUPTURE OF THE SIXTEENTH STAGE COMPRESSOR DISC.

24. Preventive Measures: 1 - (SEE DETAILED DESCRIPTION)
*** PREVENTIVE MEASURES ***
A THOROUGH INSPECTION OF ALL CF101 QUICK DISCONNECT BLOCK HOLDERS WILL BE CARRIED OUT. ALL CF101 NEGATIVE "G" STRAPS WILL BE MODIFIED WITH A SMALLER RING.

PM Decision: Accepted
Completed Date: 01 JAN 1986

Liberals' new rescue aircraft could take two days to reach North Pole in disaster operation: documents

DAVID PUGLIESE, OTTAWA CITIZEN | May 8, 2017 1:57 PM ET

Canada's new search and rescue aircraft could take up to two days to reach survivors of a disaster at the North Pole but the Canadian military doesn't have a problem with that, according to recently filed court documents.

A legal battle is now underway in the Federal Court in Ottawa over the Liberal government's $4.7-billion fixed-wing search-and-rescue aircraft program.

The Italian aerospace firm, Leonardo, is angry that its C-27J aircraft, which it contends could reach the North Pole in a single flight from a military base in Winnipeg, was rejected by the federal government.

The winning aircraft, the Airbus C-295, is slower and would take two days to reach a disaster site at the North Pole or similar Arctic locations, Leonardo's representatives argue.

The company is asking the court to overturn the contract to Airbus and instead award the lucrative deal to Leonardo and its Canadian partners.

In its affidavit, Leonardo alleges the Airbus aircraft fails to meet the government's basic criteria since it can't conduct a mission to the outer regions of the military's allotted rescue area within 13 flying hours.

But that isn't a problem, according to the latest response to the court from the federal government. In fact, there are no time constraints as long as the aircraft is capable of flying to that location and staying at the scene for an hour and then returning to an airfield, the government argues.

If someone needs help, the last thing you want to do is have an eight- or 10-hour delay

References

Air Defence Anti-Tank, Wikipedia, https://en.wikipedia.org/wiki/Air_Defense_Anti-Tank_System#Missile, 11 January, 2018.

Associated Press, Forest Fires in Manitoba Force Evacuation of 18,000, July 24,1989, www.apnewsarchive.com, 20 September 2016.

Avro Arrow: The Story of the Avro Arrow from its Evolution to its Extinction, The Arrowheads, Boston Mills Press, Erin, Ontario, 1980.

Bell CH-146 Griffon, https://en.wikipedia.org/wiki/Bell_CH-146_Griffon, 14 March 2017.

Brewster, Murray, Liberals take bids for long-delayed military search planes in 2016, The Globe and Mail, 15 December 2015, https://www.theglobeandmail.com/, 08 December 2016.

Brewster, Murray, Airbus chosen to build Canada's new search planes, CBC, 07 December 2016, http://www.cbc.ca/news/politics/fixed-wing-search-planes-1.3885653, 16 December 2016.

Boeing 707, https://en.wikipedia.org/wiki/Boeing_707#Military, 06 March 2017.

Boeing CH-47 Chinook, https://en.wikipedia.org/wiki/Boeing_CH-47_Chinook, 14 March 2017.

Boeing Vertol CH-113 Labrador, Canadian Aviation and Space Museum, http://casmuseum.techno-science.ca, 14 April, 2016.

Botswana Defence Force Air Wing, https://en.wikipedia.org/wiki/Botswana_Defence_Force_Air_Wing, 22 August 2017.

Buoyancy in Salt Water vs Fresh Water for Scuba Diving, http://scuba.about.com, 06 March 2016.

C-27J Spartan, Wikipedia, https://en.wikipedia.org/wiki/Alenia_C-27J_Spartan, 15 June 2017.

Canada, Encyclopedia of Nations, www.nationsencyclopedia.com/economies/Americas/Canada, 06 June 2016

Canadian Air Search And Rescue Association, Wikipedia, https://en.wikipedia.org/wiki/Civil_Air_Search_and_Rescue_Association, 02 December, 2016

Canadian Armed Forces CH-147 Chinook Detailed List, Canadian Military Aircraft Serial Numbers, http://www.rwrwalker.ca/CF_CH147.html, 06 April 2017.

Canadian Army Advanced Warfare Center, Royal Canadian Air Force, www.rcaf-arc.forces.gc.ca/en/8-wing/canadian-army-advanced-warfare-centre.page, 12 December, 2016.

Canadian Beacon Registry, National Defence, www.cbr-rcb.ca/cbr/presentation/other_autre/faq.php, 04 December, 2016.

Canadian Broadcasting Corporation, Kristen Everson, 08 February 2016, Top General and Defence Bureaucrat were at odds over whether to buy French Warships,

Canadian Forces School of Aerospace Technology and Engineering (CFSATE), Royal Canadian Air Force, www.rcaf-arc.forces.gc.ca/en/16-wing/cf-school-aerospace-technology_engineering.page, 16 November 2016.

Canadian Forces Support Unit (Ottawa), www.forces.gc.ca/en/caf-community-bases-wings-cfsu-ottawa/index.page, 04 January 2017.

Canadian NORAD Region Forward Operating Locations, https://en.wikipedia.org/wiki/Canadian_NORAD_Region_Forward_Operating_Locations, 11 March 2017

Casa Cargolifters: C-212, C-235 & C-295, Air Vectors, http://www.airvectors.net/avc212.html, 15 June 2017.

CBC News, Boeing Super Hornet jet purchase likely to become 1st casualty in possible trade war, Murray Brewster, 27 September 2017, www.cbc.ca/news/politics, 21 October 2017.

CBC News, F-35's French rival pitches 'Canadianized' fighter jet, Terry Milewski, 18 March 2014, www.cbc.ca/news/politics, 08 November 2017.

CC-115 Buffalo, Royal Canadian Air Force, Government of Canada, www.rcaf-arc.forces.gc.ca/en/aircraft-current/cc-115.page, 08 February 2016.

Chamberlin, David T, CMSgt, USAF ANG Crew Chief 1980-2018,19 October 2017.

Common "European" Starling, Orkin Canada, www.orkincanada.ca/pests/birds/european-starling/, 20 December 2016.

Dassault Rafale, Wikipedia, https://en.wikipedia.org/wiki/Dassault_Rafale, 10 November 2017.

Defence Research and Development Canada, http://en.wikipedia.org/wiki/DRDC_Toronto, 05 June 2015

De Havilland Canada DHC-5 Buffalo, Wikipedia, https://en.wikipedia.org/wiki/De_Havilland_Canada_DHC-5_Buffalo, 20 February 2016.

Emergency Locator Changes, Australian Government, Civil Aviation Safety Authority, www.casa.gov.au/operations/standard-page/emergency-locator-transmitter-elt-changes, 04 December 2016.

Eurofighter Typhoon, Wikipedia, https://en.wikipedia.org/wiki/Eurofighter_Typhoon#Specifications, 07 November 2017.

F-101 Voodoo, McDonnell, http://fighter-planes.com/info/f101_voodoo.htm, 24 April 2015.

Flight Comment No. 4-1987, NDHQ Directorate of Flight Safety, http://d2k.ca/flightcomment2016/portfolio_category/1987/, 22 November 2016.

Flight Comment No. 2-1988, NDHQ Directorate of Flight Safety, http://d2k.ca/flightcomment2016/portfolio_category/1988/, 22 November 2016.

Globe and Mail, Liberals need to end farce over fighter jets, Richard Shimooka and David McDonough, 17 September 2017, www.globeandmail.com/opinion, 21 October 2017.

Granatstein, J.L., Who Killed the Canadian Military?, HarperCollins Publishers Ltd, Toronto Ontario, 2004.

Haida Gwaii, Wikipedia, https://en.wikipedia.org/wiki/Haida_Gwaii, 11 April 2016.

Helicopter Magazine, 29 May 2007, There's No Lift Like It, Ken Pole, www.helicoptermagazine.com, 08 April 2017.

Herring Spawn and Catch Records of British Columbia, Fisheries and Oceans Canada, www.pac.dfo-mpo.gc.ca, 21 February 2016.

HMCS Bonaventure (CVL 22), Wikipedia, https://en.wikipedia.org/wiki/HMCS_Bonaventure_(CVL_22), 25 February 2017.

HMCS Sackville, Canada's Naval Memorial, https://hmcssackville.ca/history/battles-and-conicts/cold-warcuba-2/, 26 February 2017.

In Retreat: The Canadian Forces in the Trudeau Years, Gerald Porter, Deneau and Greenburg Publishers Ltd., 1978.

Korean Air Lines Flight 007 Transcripts, https://en.wikisource.org/wiki/Korean_Air_Lines_Flight_007_transcripts, 02 July 2016.

Liquid oxygen, Air Products, http://www.airproducts.com/~/media/Files/PDF/company/safetygram-6.pdf, Safety Gram 6, 04 May 2015

Lott, Lawrence, Colonel (retired), Courtenay, British Columbia, September 2016.

Maclean's (30 June 2016), How do you find the centre of Canada?, www.macleans.ca, 17 July 2016.

McDonnell CF-101 Voodoo, Wikipedia, http://en.wikipedia.org.wiki/McDonnell_CF-101_VooDoo, 12 May 2015.

McDonnell Douglas CF-18 Hornet, Wikipedia, https://en.wikipedia.org/wiki/McDonnell_Douglas_CF-18_Hornet, 09 Mar 2017.

National Defence and the Canadian Armed Forces Pay Rates, http://www.forces.gc.ca/en/caf-community-pay/pay-rates.page, 12 December 2017

National Post, Canada's Interim Supply Ship, David Pugiliese Ottawa Citizen, 24 June 2016, http://news.nationalpost.com/news/canada, 05 April 2017.

Newcomer's Welcome Package, Thule Airbase Greenland, http://download.militaryonesource.mil/12038/Plan%20My%20Move/Thule%20Information.pdf, 08 January 2017.

NORAD and the Soviet Nuclear Threat: Canada's Secret Electronic Air War, Wilson, Gordon A.A., Dundurn Press, 2011.

Operation Calumet, Canadian Armed Forces, http://www.forces.gc.ca/en/operations-abroad-current/op-calumet.page, 26 January 2017.

Ottawa Citizen, 16 April 2014, Why the Eurofighter Typhoon Is the Best Fighter for Canada, David Pugliese, http://ottawacitizen.com/news/national/defence-watch/, 07 November 2017.

Ottawa Citizen, 10 December 2017, Canadian Chinook helicopters now at museums, two others sold to Boeing, David Pugliese, http://ottawacitizen.com/news/national/defence-watch/canadian-chinook-helicopters-now-at-museums-two-others-sold-to-boeing, 09 April 2017.

Pacific Herring, Wikipedia, http://en.wikipedia.org/wiki/Pacific_herring, 21 February 2016.

Parachutes General, Canadian Forces Technical Orders, C-22-010-013/MF-000, 04 January 2017.

Perspectives, July 2008 (Statistics Canada Catalogue no. 75-001-X), A Profile of the Canadian Forces, Jungwee Park, www.statcan.gc.ca/pub/75-001-x/2008107/pdf/10657-eng.pdf, 03 January 2018.

Reuters Business News, Dassault CEO not yet considering alternative engine suppliers, Allison Lampert, www.reuters.com/article/us-dassaultavi-falcon/, 11 October 2017, 12 November 2017.

Royal Canadian Air Force, Operation Boxtop supplies remote Canadian station, 23 October 2014, www.rcaf-arc.forces.gc.ca, 09 January 2017.

Royal Canadian Navy, Joint Support Ships, http://www.navy-marine.forces.gc.ca/en/fleet-units/jss-home.page, 21 April 2017.

Saab JAS 39 Gripen, Wikipedia, https://en.wikipedia.org/wiki/Saab_JAS_39_Gripen, 07 November 2017.

Searchmaster Course, Department of National Defence, www.forces.gc.ca/en/training-establishments/international-training-programs-courses/searchmaster-course.page 16 November 2015.

Smart Defence: A Plan for Rebuilding Canada's Military, Canadian Centre for Policy Alternatives, Michael Byers, June 2015, https://www.policyalternatives.ca/publications/reports/smart-defence, 05 February 2017.

Survival Radio, Wikipedia, http://en.wikipedia.org/wiki/Survival_radio, 02 June 2015

Tarnished Brass: Crime and Corruption in the Canadian Military, Scott Taylor and Brian Nolan, Lester Publishing Ltd., Toronto, Canada, 1996.

The History of Para Rescue and Search & Rescue Technicians, Webmaster@PARARESCUE.ca, www.pararescue.ca/Para_Rescue/History.html. 21 November 2015.

The Maple Leaf, June 2012, Vol 15 No. 6, ADM(P)/DGPASP, www.forces.gc.ca, 30 July 2016.

The Prince George Citizen (19 March 1984), King, PM together for skiing, http://pgplweb02.lib.pg.bc.ca, 22 January 2017

The Physics Hypertextbook, http://physics.info/bouyancy/summary.shtml, 03 March 2016.

The RCAF's (other) Whirlybirds (Part 2), http://natoassociation.ca/the-rcafs-other-whirlybirds-part-2/, 20 March 2017.

The Ultimate F-16 Site, Cancelled Orders, http://www.f-16.net/f-16_users_article28.html, 17 April 2017.

The Washington Post, May 11 1993, Echoes of Miniseries Murders, Swardson, Anne, www.washingtonpost.com/archive/, 10 January 2017

Thule Airforce Base in Thule Greenland, www.militarybases.com, 13 December 2016.

Toronto Sun, 30 October 2017, Canada's military among the highest paid in the world, Blanchet, Jean-Nicolas, http://torontosun.com/2014/10/30, 12 December 2017.

Valour Canada, Military History Library, Cuban Missile Crisis: Diefenbaker, Harkness and Kennedy, http://valourcanada.ca/military-history-library/cuban-missile-crisis-diefenbaker-harkness-and-kennedy/, 24 September, 2018.

Vass, Major John D.V., Retention in the Canadian Forces, Royal Military College, Kingston Ontario, 1994, www.dtic.mil/cgi-bin, 08 October, 2016.

Warbird Alley, www.warbirdalley.com/tutor.htm, 03 November 2017.

Warbird Depot, CWHM's Douglas DC-3 "Canucks Unlimited", http://www.warbirddepot.com/aircraft_transports_dc3-cwhm.asp, 16 September 2016

Winnipeg Free Press, https://answers.yahoo.com, 10 January 2017.

About the author

Blaine McMillan was born in Saskatoon, Saskatchewan and moved to British Columbia in 1972. After from graduating high school he pursued a career in the Canadian Armed Forces where he served for 22 years in the regular force. After recruit training Blaine went on to the Canadian Forces School of Aerospace Ordnance and Engineering to study Aviation Life Support Equipment. Over the course of his career Blaine was posted to CFB Comox, MFO El Gorah Egypt and CFB Winnipeg. He was qualified to carry out inspections on many Canadian Armed Forces aircraft but his favourites were the CF-101 Voodoo, the CC-115 Buffalo and CC-130 Hercules. On his retirement from the regular forces Blaine, along with his wife Irene and their two sons, returned to CFB Comox where he served more five years as a reservist. Blaine states that his most notable military accomplishments included being on the first rotation to El Gorah (1986), participating in three SAREX competitions and completing the cryogenic liquids maintenance course. He has volunteered as a Cub Scout leader and has earned his BA in criminology.

Other titles by this author

Wood Knocks and Tossed Rocks: Searching for Sasquatch with the Bigfoot Field Researchers Organization
ISBN - 978-0-9916825-0-8

Manufactured by Amazon.ca
Bolton, ON

39688725R00192